THE SOURCES OF HAMLET

Portion of page from Codex Regius 2367 (Copenhagen), containing
Snæbjörn's lines, with reference to "Amlóði" (*i.e.* Hamlet).

THE SOURCES OF
Hamlet

WITH AN ESSAY ON THE LEGEND

SIR ISRAEL GOLLANCZ

1967

OCTAGON BOOKS, INC.

New York

Published by
FRANK CASS AND COMPANY LIMITED
67 Great Russell Street, London WC1
by arrangement with Oxford University Press.

Published in the United States of America
1967 by Octagon Books, Inc.

First edition   1926
New impression   1967

Library of Congress Catalog Card No. 67-20207

Printed in Great Britain

TO

MY FRIEND AND HELPER

IN MANY GOOD CAUSES,

SIR CHARLES WAKEFIELD, Bart.,

LORD MAYOR OF LONDON IN THE YEAR OF THE

SHAKESPEARE TERCENTENARY, 1916,

WHOSE ZEAL FOR SHAKESPEARE IS BUT ONE ASPECT

OF HIS MANY-SIDED ACTIVITIES IN FURTHERING

ALL THAT IS TO THE WELFARE AND HONOUR

OF SHAKESPEARE'S ENGLAND ;

I. G.

" London, thou art the Flower of Cities all.
   Thy famous Mayor. . .
   Principal Patron, . .
   Above all Mayors, as Master most worthy !"

PREFACE

In 1898 I published a volume of strange lore, printed for the first time, entitled "Hamlet in Iceland"—the sequelæ, as it were, of the *Morbus Hamleticus* from which few young scholars are able to escape. In an introductory essay I attempted to throw new light upon the development of the Hamlet legend. The reception of the book, here and abroad, compensated for long years of labour and research, and valuable discussion ensued on certain debatable points affecting the genesis of the barbaric tale, which, though wondrously transformed by the genius of Shakespeare, is, nevertheless, the very fibre of the play. During the past quarter of a century much has been written on the subject, from many different points of view, and I have given long and careful consideration to opinions opposed to my own. Absolute agreement is hardly to be expected on such questions as the origin of the name Hamlet, and the development of the story as given by Saxo Grammaticus. Notwithstanding high authority, I am convinced it will ultimately be conceded that the story developed (as I attempted to show) under Celtic influences, and that the very name of the hero may thus be accounted for as a transformation of the common Scandinavian Aleifr, the equivalent of Olaf. I see no reason for withdrawing from this position.

I am frequently asked by students and others to reprint *Hamlet in Iceland* in a cheap and accessible form ; but it has seemed to me more advisable to revise the Introductory Essay, and, in lieu of the Icelandic texts, to add thereto the main sources of Shakespeare's play, from Saxo Grammaticus, Belleforest, and *The Hystorie of Hamblet*. It is remarkable that the 1582 text of Belleforest's version of the tragical story—the most interesting for the purposes of Shakespearian study—has not hitherto been reprinted.

By the kindness of Professor Oliver Elton I am enabled to give his translation of Saxo's Latin, opposite the original ; and I desire to express my grateful acknowledgment of his readiness in granting my request.

In preparing this volume for press I have had the valued help of my colleague, Dr. Mabel Day, and I wish again to record my best thanks for her unfailing assistance and good offices.

I. G.

King's College, London,
1 *October*, 1925.

CONTENTS

THE LEGEND OF HAMLET

I

Sem Snæbjörn kvað:

"**Hvatt kveða hræra Grótta**
hergrimmastan skerja
út fyr jarðar skauti
eylúðrs níu brúðir;
þær es, lungs, fyr löngu
líðmeldr, skipa hlíðar
baugskerðir rístr barði
ból, Amlóða mólu."
  —*Hér er kallat hafit Amlóða kvern.*

[*quote from Prose Edda*]

"'Tis said," sang Snæbjörn, "that far out, beyond the skirts of the earth, the Nine Maidens of the Island Mill stir amain the host-cruel Skerry-quern—they who in ages past ground Hamlet's meal. The good Chieftain furrows the hull's lair with his ship's beaked prow." [1]

[*waves*] [*Aegir, God of the sea.*] [*Hamlet's mill is the storm*] [*the sand.*]

To Snorri Sturlason, the glory of Icelandic historiography, we are indebted for the preservation of these lines,

---

[1] *i.e.* " Kveða níu brúðir eylúðrs hræra hvatt hergrimmastan skerja grótta út fyr jarðar skauti, þær er fyr löngu mólu Amlóða líð-meldr; baugskerðir rístr skipa hlíðar ból lungs barði."

containing the earliest known reference to the legendary hero destined to play so important a part in later literary history. The strange verse occurs in Snorri's *Skaldskapar-mál*, or Gradus to the Northern Parnassus, the second section of his famous hand-book of the Art of Poetry, known as *The Prose Edda*, composed about the year 1230. The illustrative extracts (some two hundred and fifty from sixty-five named poets, besides anonymous lays) are in many instances the only remains of the poems quoted. The work is in catechetical form, and in answer to the question, " Hvernig skal sæ kenna ? " *i.e.* " What are the names for the Sea ? " a long list of synonyms and epithets is given, together with descriptive passages from various poets, some of them clearly sailor-poets ; among these is the extract from Snæbjörn. The lines, though laboured, are evidently from some poem of adventure in Northern waters, " hatched in the storms of the ocean, and feathered in the surges of many perilous seas." The passage presents many difficulties, and various interpretations have been advanced, but the underlying reference is certainly to the great World-Mill deep down in the sea, the great cosmic force, which the ancient Northerners and other races conceived as the cause of storms and showers, and of all the disintegrating changes wrought on mountains, rocks, and shores. The fierce whirl-pools and currents of the Arctic Ocean may easily explain this great idea of a gigantic World-Machine, its terrific funnel ever ready to gorge, its cruel mill-stones, huge as

islands, ever ready to grind whatsoever the mighty swirl
has seized. This great World-Mill must be distinguished
from what is called "the Lesser Mill," which the two
captured giant-maidens, the Valkyries Menja and Fenja,
were forced to grind for greedy King Frothi, singing awhile
their "Grotta-söngr," or Mill-song. First they ground
for him peace and gold :—"May he sit on riches ; may he
sleep on down ; may his waking be happy ! It were well
ground then !" But the king's greed would not let them
rest, and in anger they prophesied evils to come :—"'The
tokens of war are waking, the beacons are kindled. On a
sudden a host shall come hither, and burn the hall over the
king's head.' . . . The maids ground on, putting forth
all their strength, the young maids were in giant fury. The
huge props flew off the bin,—the iron rivets burst. . . .
The shaft-tree shivered, the bin shot down, the massy mill-
stone rent in twain. But the Mountain-giant's bride spake
this word :—'We have ground, O Frothi, to our mind's
liking. We have stood full long at the mill.'" The maidens
tell the story of themselves and of their mill :—"Never
had this mill come out of the grit mount, nor the massy
mill-stone out of the earth, nor were the Mountain-giants'
maids thus grinding here, if thou, O king, knewest our
kindred ! We two playmates were brought up under the
earth for nine winters. We busied ourselves with mighty
feats ; we hurled the cleft rocks out of their places ; we
rolled the boulders over the giant's court, so that the earth

shook withal. We hurled the stones so fast that the massy rocks were split in twain."[1] This "Grotta-söngr" would have been lost had not Snorri inserted it in his Gradus, where he explains why gold was called "Frothi's meal." There is a prose introduction to the poem not altogether clear, for it confuses the story of Frothi with the familiar tale, "How the Sea Became Salt."

And now to return to Snæbjörn's verse. It is clear from the Prose Edda that "the Nine Maidens of the Island-Mill" are the nine daughters of Ægir, the Ocean-god. These Nereids are thus enumerated by Snorri :— "Himinglæfa, Dúfa, Blóðughadda, Hefríng, Uðr, Hrönn, Bylgja, Bára, Kólga." One of these, at least, to judge by her name, "the Dove," must have had kinship with the gentle daughter of Ægir's Celtic brother-monarch, the much-harassed Lear. The compound, "ey-lúðr," translated "Island-Mill," may be regarded as a synonym for the father of the Nine Maids. "Lúðr" is strictly "the square case within which the lower and upper quernstones rest," hence the mill itself, or quern ; "ey-lúðr" is "the island quern," *i.e.* "the grinder at islands," the Ocean-Mill, the Sea, the Sea-god, and, finally, Ægir.

"Ægir's daughters" are the surging waves of Ocean ; they work Grotti, "grinder," the great Ocean-Mill (here called "Skerja-Grotti," the grinder of skerries, the lonely rocks in the sea) "beyond the skirts of the earth," perhaps

[1] Cp. *Corpus Poeticum Boreale,* vol. i. pp. 184–188.

equivalent to "off yonder promontory." The latter force of the words (" út fyr iarðar skauti ") would perhaps suit the passage best, if Snæbjörn was pointing to some special whirlpool. Indeed, one cannot help thinking of a possible reference to the marvellous Maelström, the greatest of all whirlpools, one of the wonders of the world,—" *umbilicus maris,*" according to the old geographers,—" *gurges mirabilis Norvegiæ omnium totius orbis terrarum celeberrimus et maximus,*" as Athanasius Kircher describes it in his fascinating folio *Mundus Subterraneus.* And one recalls, too, Poe's thrilling ing narrative of the old man's descent into the Maelström, or the Moskoe-ström, as the Norwegians call it, " from the island of Moskoe in the midway." " Just opposite the promontory upon whose apex we were placed," wrote Poe, as though commenting on the Eddaic passage under discussion, " and at a distance of some five or six miles out at sea, there was visible a small, bleak-looking island ; or, more properly, its position was discernible through the wilderness of surge in which it was enveloped. About two miles nearer the land arose another of smaller size, hideously craggy and barren, and encompassed at various intervals by a cluster of dark rocks." [1] The whole story should be re-read in this connection.

[1] According to Kircher, it was supposed that every whirlpool formed round a central rock : a great cavern opened beneath ; down this cavern the water rushed ; the whirling was produced as in a basin emptying through a central hole. Kircher gives a curious picture illustrative of this theory, with special reference to the Maelström.

The real difficulty in Snorri's extract from Snæbjörn is, however, in its last lines. The arrangement of the words is confusing, the interpretation of the most important of the phrases extremely doubtful. " Liδ-meldr " in particular has given much trouble to the commentators. " Meldr," at present obsolete in Icelandic, signifies " *flour* or *corn in the mill.*" " Liδ " (or liδ) may be the neuter noun, meaning " a host, folk, people," or " ship ; " or the masculine " liδr," " a joint of the body." The editors [1] construe " liδmeldr " as equivalent to " meldr-liδ " or " meldr-liδ," and render the word " meal-vessel ; " they translate the passage, " they have for ages past been grinding at Amloδi's meal-bin (= the ocean) ; " but " mala," to grind, can hardly be synonymous with " hræra," to move, in the earlier lines, and there would be no point in the waves grinding the ocean. There seems, therefore, no reason why " meldr-liδ " should be preferred to " liδ-meldr," which might well stand for " ship-meal " (? " sea-meal," to be compared with the Eddaic phrase " græδis meldr," *i.e.* sea-flour, a poetical periphrasis for the sand of the shore). Rydberg,[2] bearing in mind the connection of the myth concerning the cosmic Grotti-Mill with the myth concerning the fate of Ýmir and other primeval giants, more especially of Ýmir's descendant Bergelmer, who, accoiding to an ingenious interpretation of a verse in *Vafpruδnis-*

---

[1] *Corp. Poet. Bor.* II., 54.   [2] *Teutonic Mythology*, pp. 388–392.

mál,[1] " was laid under the mill-stone," advanced the theory that " liǒ-meldr " means " limb-grist." According to this view, it is the limbs and joints of the primeval giants, which on Amloǒi's mill are transformed into meal. Allowing, for the nonce, that there is something to be said for " liǒ-meldr " in the sense of " limb-grist," one finds it difficult to get Rydberg's interpretation out of the words as they stand in the text. The Nine Maidens of the OceanMill grinding Amloǒi's limb-grist, *i.e.* his bones, might be plausible enough, suggestive of some story of a brave prince who sailed too near their dread abode, and received less kindly treatment than did young Macphail of Colonsay at the hands of the maiden of Corrivrekin. Snorri does not help us. The note following Snæbjörn's verse merely adds that " Here the Sea is called ' Amloǒi's quern.' "[2] No explicit explanation is to be found in early Northern poetry or saga.

---

[1] In the poem found in the *Elder Edda,* the giant tells Odin that, countless ages ere the earth was shapen, Bergelmer was born: " the first thing I remember is when he *á var lúdr um lagiǒr.*" The meaning, according to Rydberg, was not clear even to Snorri, who in the Gylfaginning interprets the verse with reference to the drowning of the frost-giants in Ýmir's blood :—" One escaped with his household : him the giants call Bergelmer. He with his wife betook himself upon his *ludr* and remained there, and from them the races of giants are descended "—a sort of giant Noah. The Resenian edition of the younger *Edda* (Copenhagen, 1665) actually reads " *fór á bát sinn* " (went on to his boat) instead of "fór upp á lúǒr sinn. *Corp. P.B.* translates the passage in the poem, " when this wise giant was laid in the Ark."

[2] Björn of Skarǒsá. in A.M. 742, writes : " Her er hafid kallad Amlöǒa melldur," *i.e.* " Here the sea is called Amloǒi's meal."

"Hamlet's mill" may mean almost anything; if, as the editors of the *Corpus Poeticum Boreale* state, Hamlet is here an Ocean Giant, his mill seems to be identical with the great World-Mill, unless the Ocean Giant was himself ground by the Nine Maidens. All this seems unlikely; indeed, though at first sight it looks as though some ancient sea-hero is alluded to in Snæbjörn's phrase, yet the later Icelandic poets were capable of such fatal ingenuity in the matter of poetical periphrases, that even so much consistency need not be expected of them. All that can be said at this point in the investigation is that the verse quoted in the *Prose Edda* gives us a reference to some old legend concerning "Amloði," whose name is identical with that of the hero known to us as Hamlet.

It is worthy of note that a few more lines of Snæbjörn's verse have been preserved; they may well all be fragments of the same poem.[1]

---

[1] The fragments are (1) four short lines, or two long lines, found in Snorri's *Edda*, edit. 1848, p. 460; and (2) four short lines in A.M. 742, 4to (not A.M. 738, as Edd. *Corp. P.B.* state, ii. p. 54; *cp.* Bugge, *Arkiv for Nordisk Filologe,* iii. pp. 335-338); the lines are there attributed to Þorðr Sjareksson, and not to Snæbjörn, by the writer of the MS., viz., Björn of Skarðsá. Þorðr lived in the first half of the eleventh century. Björn was probably mistaken in ascribing the lines to him. They certainly closely resemble Snæbjörn's, and Bugge agrees with the Edd. *Corp. P.B.* in assigning them to him, and not to the later poet: he reads the lines as follows:—

> "Sváð ór fitjar fjötre,
> flóðs ásynju blóðe
> (röst byrjask römm) systra,
> rýtr, eymylver snýter. '

From the passages preserved it is evident that Snæbjörn was a sailor-poet, and the lost poem must have been descriptive of some voyage in the Arctic seas. In *Landnáma Bók*, *i.e.* "The Book of Iceland Settlements," there is a vivid picture of a tenth-century Arctic adventurer, Snæbjörn the Boar, who went on a perilous expedition to find the unknown land, "Gunnbjörn's Reef," after having wrought vengeance, as became a chivalrous gentleman of the period, on the murderer of a fair kinswoman. It may be assumed as highly probable that this Snæbjörn is identical with the poet Snæbjörn.

His family history is not without interest. His great-grandfather, Eywind the Easterling, so called because he had come to the Hebrides from Sweden, married the daughter of Cearbhall, Lord of Ossory, who ruled as King of Dublin from 882 to 888, "one of the principal sovereigns of Europe at the time when Iceland was peopled by the noblemen and others who fled from the tyranny of Harold Harfagr."[1] Cearbhall was descended from Connla, the grandson of Crimhthann Cosgach, the victorious King of

---

i.e. "the island-mill pours out the blood of the flood goddess's sisters, (*i.e.* waves of the sea), so that (it) bursts from the feller of the land : *whirlpool begins strong*." In no other *dróttkvætt* verse does "eymylver" occur : *cp.* "eylúðr," above.

[1] Cp. *Landnáma Bók*, § 1 ; J. H. Todd's *War of the Gaedhil with the Gaill*, pp. 297–302 : the history of Cearbhall and his many descendants (he had four sons and four daughters) illustrates the close connection between Ireland and Iceland. For Cearbhall's pedigree, *cp.* Donovan's *Tribes and Territories of Ancient Ossory.*

Ireland, who is said to have flourished about a century before the Christian era. Lann or Flann, the half-sister of Cearbhall, was married to Malachy I., King of Ireland, whose daughter Cearbhall had married. Flann was the mother of King Sionna and of the Lady Gormflaith. Snæbjörn could certainly boast of a noble pedigree. His family sagas must have had much to tell of the ancient glories of the race : he may often have heard the sad story of the poetess Gormflaith, whom a cruel fate pursued : a king's daughter, the wife of three kings, forced at last to beg for bread from door to door. We have more to tell of her later on. Before letting the *Landnáma Bók* tell its story of this Snæbjörn, it may be mentioned that, about the date of his Arctic expedition (*circa* 980), his cousin, Ari Marson, is said to have landed on "White Man's Land," or "Great Ireland"—that part of the coast of North America which extends from Chesapeake Bay, including North and South Carolina, Georgia, and Florida— and became famous as one of the earliest discoverers of the New World.

Here follows the tragic story of Snæbjörn the Boar :—

" Snæbjörn, son of Eyvind the Easterling, the brother of Helgi the Lean, took land between Mjovafjord (Narrow Firth) and Langadals-á (Langdale River) ; he had his dwelling at Vatnsfjord (Waterford). His son was Holm-stein, the father of Snæbjörn Galti (the Boar) ; the mother of Snæbjörn was Kjalvör ; he and Tungu-Odd were sons of

sisters. Snæbjörn was fostered in the house of Thorodd at Thingness (but at times he was with Tungu-Odd or his mother). Hallbjörn, the son of Odd of Kiðjaberg, the son of Hallkel, the brother of Ketilbjörn the Old, took to wife Hallgerð, daughter of Tungu-Odd. The couple were with Odd during the first winter after their marriage; Snæbjörn Galti was there at the same time. Now there was no love lost between the newly wedded folk, and Hallbjörn gat him ready to depart in the spring-time, about the flitting season. While he was making his preparations, Odd went from home to the baths at Reykjaholt, where he had his sheep-folds. He had no wish to be present at Hallbjörn's departure, for he doubted whether Hallgerð would be willing to accompany her husband. Odd had previously done his best to improve matters between them.

"Hallbjörn, having saddled the horses, went to the room where the women kept. Hallgerð was sitting on the high-seat, combing her hair; the hair fell all about her to the very floor. She had the best hair of all women in Iceland, save only that Hallgerð whom folk named 'Twisted Tartan.' Hallbjörn bade his wife get up and come with him; but she sat silent. He then clutched at her; she moved not from her place. Thrice he seized her, but she moved not. Hallbjörn stood still, and said thus:—

'Here stand I as a laughing-stock
  Before her flowing tresses;
The linen goddess dares to mock,
  While grief my bosom presses.

O brewer of the sparkling ale,
No good for me thou brewest;
My heart is sore with bitter bale.
O bride, this thing thou ruest.'

Thereupon he wound her hair around his arm, and would have pulled her from her seat, but she sat and flinched not. He then drew his sword, and struck the head from off her; and so went out and rode away. His comrades were two in number, and they had with them two packhorses.

"Now there were but few men at the house when this thing befell, yet the news thereof was forthwith sent to Odd. Snæbjörn was then at Kjalvararstaðir; Odd sent a messenger to him, and bade him look to the pursuit; he himself would not go.

"Snæbjörn went in pursuit of Hallbjörn, eleven men with him; and when Hallbjörn was aware that he was approaching, his comrades bade him hurry on, but he would not yield to them. Anon Snæbjörn and his men caught them up near the hills now called Hallbjörn's Cairns. Hallbjörn and his two comrades betook themselves to the hill-top to defend themselves, and there for a time they held out. Three of Snæbjörn's men fell there, and both the companions of Hallbjörn. As for Hallbjörn, Snæbjörn struck off his foot at the ankle, and he was forced to hobble along to another hill; there he slew two more of Snæbjörn's men, but he himself was slain. Wherefore there are three cairns on that hill, and five on the other. Then Snæbjörn went home.

"Snæbjörn had a ship at the mouth of the river Grims-á ; Hrolf of Redsand bought half-rights in the vessel ; the crew were twelve on each side. Snæbjörn had Thorkel and Sumarliði, the sons of Thorgeir the Red, who was the son of Einar of Stafholt. He took with him also Thorodd of Thingness, his foster-father, and his wife. Hrolf took with him Styrbjörn, who made this ditty after a dream he had :—

> 'I see the bane
> Of both us twain,
> North out at sea
> All piteously :
> Horrors untold,
> Dire frost and cold :
> From these I gain
> Our Snæbjorn slain.'

"They went in search of Gunnbjörn's Reef; they found land; but Snæbjörn would not let them explore at night. Styrbjörn went ashore, and found there a treasure-trove in a cairn; he concealed it about his person. Snæbjörn struck him with his axe, and the treasure fell to the ground. Thereafter his men made a hut, but it was soon buried deep in the snow. One day, however, Thorkel, the son of Rauð, found that water was running along the pole which projected from the hut; they knew that spring was near, and they dug themselves out of the snow. While Snæbjörn repaired his ship, Thorodd and his wife stayed in the hut on his behalf; Styrbjörn and his comrades stayed on behalf of Hrolf. The rest of the party had gone out

hunting. Styrbjörn then up and slew Thorodd, and then turned, and, with the help of Hrolf, slew Snæbjörn. The sons of Rauð and all Snæbjörn's men were put under oath, and were allowed their lives. Thereafter they landed at Halogaland, and thence went to Iceland, and came to Vaðil. Thorkel the Muffler guessed what had befallen the sons of Rauð. Hrolf set up defences to protect himself at Strandheath. Thorkel sent Sveinung to bring him Hrolf's head. Sveinung first went to Hermund, who dwelt at Myri ; then he went to Olaf at Drangar ; and finally came to Gest at Hagi : Gest sent him to his friend, Hrolf. Sveinung slew both Hrolf and Styrbjörn, and then returned to Hagi. Gest exchanged with him sword and axe, and gave him two horses black of mane, and he ordered a man to ride round Vaðil all the way to Kollafirth, and asked Thorbjörn the Strong to claim the horses for him from Sveinung. But Thorbjörn slew Sveinung at Sveinungseyri ; Sveinung's sword had broken at the hilt. Wherefore Thorkel often bragged to Gest, when their wits were matched, that he had so got round Gest that he had sent his man to bring him the head of his friend." [1]

[1] *Hamlet in Iceland*, cp. Appendix IX. Concerning " Gunnbjörn's Reef," cp. " *Gröndlands Historiske Mindesmærker*," vol. i.

II

SOME two hundred years after the events recorded in the foregoing story, Saxo Grammaticus, the learned Dane, emulous of the great Roman historians, took upon himself, at the bidding of Absalon, " Chief Pontiff of the Danes," the task of compiling into a chronicle the history of his country. The labour was a heavy one—too heavy for his weak faculty, as he modestly puts it—for the materials to hand must have been very slight : his Danish predecessors had hitherto done but little " to vaunt the glory of their nation's achievements." His materials, apart from the influence exercised upon him by the Latin classical writers, were mainly drawn from Latin historical writers (such as Bede, Adam of Bremen, and Dudo, " *rerum aquitanicarum scriptor* "), from Danish traditions, and from Icelandic sagas and poems. As regards his indebtedness to Iceland, we know that he had at least one Icelandic friend, Arnoldus Tylensis, Arnold of Thule, a skilful narrator, learned in ancient lore. In his Preface Saxo makes handsome acknowledgment of his obligations to Arnold's countrymen.[1]

[1] " Nec Tylensium industria silentio obliteranda, qui cum ob nativam soli sterilitatem luxuriæ nutrimentis carentes, officia continuæ sobrietatis exerceant, omniaque vitæ momenta ad excolendam alienorum operum notitiam conferre soleant, inopiam ingenio pensant. Cunctarum

"Nor may the pains of the men of Thule be blotted in oblivion; for though they lack all that can foster luxury (so naturally barren is the soil), yet they make up for their neediness by their wit, by keeping continually every observance of soberness, and by devoting every instant of their lives to perfecting our knowledge of the deeds of foreigners. Indeed, they account it a delight to learn and to consign to remembrance the history of all nations, deeming it as great a glory to set forth the excellences of others as to display their own. Their stores, which are stocked with attestations of historical events, I have examined somewhat closely, and have woven together no small portion of the present work by following their narrative, not despising the judgment of men whom I know to be so well versed in the knowledge of antiquity."[1] Even more explicit in this respect was Saxo's Norwegian contemporary, Theoderic the Monk, according to whom the men of Thule, the Icelanders, were the only Northerners who had preserved the ancient history of their race; their writings were the only available sources for Northern his-

---

quippe nationum res gestas cognosse memoriæque mandare voluptatis loco reputant, non minoris gloriæ judicantes alienas virtutes disserere quam proprias exhibere. Quorum thesauros historicarum rerum pignoribus refertos curiosius consulens, haud parvam præsentis operis partem ex eorum relationis imitatione contexui; nec arbitros habere contempsi quos tanta vetustatis peritia callere cognovi."—*Saxo*, Ed. Müller and Velschow, pp. 7–8.

[1] Elton's *First Nine Books of the Danish History of Saxo Grammaticus.*

torians.[1]   There can be little doubt, however, that among
the Norwegians and Danes, popular legend, a mass of mythic
and traditional lore, still preserved, however obscurely, the
memory of the ancient gods and heroes.   In the matter of
Northern mythology, the first nine books of Saxo's History
are of supreme interest ; and it has been well said, that " the
gratitude due to the Welshman of the twelfth century,
whose garnered hoard has enriched so many poets and
romancers from his day to now, is no less due to the
twelfth-century Dane, whose faithful and eloquent enthu-
siasm has swept much dust from antique time." [2] Geoffrey's
priceless gift of Arthurian romance has not proved richer
than Saxo's wild barbaric tale of Hamlet's fate.   " Had
fortune been as kind to him as nature," so wrote the
historian, " he would have equalled the gods in glory."

[1] *Cp.* Langebek's *Script. Rer. Dan.*, vol. v.   The passages in question
are fully discussed in "Safn til Sögu I'slands og I'slenzkra Bókmenta
að fornu og nýju gefið út af hinu íslenzka bókmentafélagi," vol. i. pp.
143–148.   Theoderic repeatedly refers to his debt to the Icelanders ;
e.g. "Operæ pretium duxi, vir illustrissime, pauca hæc de antiquitate
regum Norvagiensium annotare, et prout sagaciter perquirere potuimus
ab eis, penes quos horum memoria præcipue vigere creditur, quos nos
Islendingos vocamus, qui hæc in suis antiquis carminibus percelebrata
recolunt . . . Veritatis vero sinceritas in hac nostra narratione ad illos
omni modo referenda est, quorum relatione hæc annotavimus, quia nos
non visa sed audita conscripsimus." In another passage Theodoric writes
of Norway as "illa terra, ubi nullus antiquitatum unquam scriptor
fuerit."

[2] *Cp.* Professor York Powell's Introduction to Elton's translation
of Saxo's Nine Books.   The Introduction gives a valuable summary of
the sources, together with an excellent analysis of Saxo's folk-lore, etc.

Fortune had even greater glory in store for Hamlet than his panegyrist could have hoped for.

The story of Amlethus, or Hamlet, as told by Saxo, divides clearly into two periods—the first dealing with his early career and the consummation of his vengeance, the second with his accession to power and the subsequent events of his life. The former is to be found at the end of Book III., the latter at the beginning of Book IV. The division is noteworthy. Divested of Saxo's eloquence, the story may be thus epitomized. Horwendil and Feng succeed their father, Gerwendil, as governors of Jutland. Horwendil's valour gains the favour of King Rorick, who gives him his daughter Gerutha to wife. They have a son who is named Amleth. Feng is jealous of his brother's good fortune, murders him, and takes his wife, alleging that Horwendil had treated her badly. Amleth, fearing lest too shrewd a behaviour may make his uncle suspect him, chooses to feign dullness, and pretends an utter lack of wits. He is altogether listless, and unclean in his habits, and seems to be a very freak of nature. At times he sits over the fire and fashions wooden crooks, shaping at their tips certain barbs. He says he is preparing sharp javelins to avenge his father. The courtiers grow suspicious, and try various tests; more especially they make use of his foster-sister for the purpose. A foster-brother warns him of the trap, and he baffles them. He gives cunning answers to all their questions; " he mingles craft and candour in such

wise that, though his words do not lack truth,[1] yet there is
nothing to betoken the truth and betray how far his
keenness goes." Thus, as he passes along the beach, his
companions find the rudder of a ship, and say they have
discovered a huge knife. "This," says he, "is the right
knife to carve such a huge ham;" by which he means the
sea. *Also, as they pass the sandhills they bid him look at the meal,
meaning the sand; he replies that it has been ground small by the
hoary tempests of the ocean.*[2] A friend of Feng suggests that
Amleth be spied upon while closeted with his mother.
But Amleth has his antidote for the treachery. Afraid of
being overheard by some eavesdropper, he at first resorts to
his usual imbecile ways, and crows like a noisy cock, beating his arms together to mimic the flapping of wings.
Then he mounts the straw and begins to swing his body
and jump again and again, wishing to try if aught lurks
there in hiding. Feeling a lump beneath his feet, he drives
his sword into the spot, and impales him who lies hid.
He drags him from his concealment and slays him. He
cuts the body into morsels, seethes it in boiling water, and
flings it through the mouth of an open sewer for the swine
to eat, bestrewing the mire with the hapless limbs. He

---

[1] By a printer's error Professor Elton's translation is "though his
words did lack truth;" *cp.* the original (p. 106) :—"ita astutiam veriloquio permiscebat, *ut nec dictis veracitas deesset,* nec acuminis modus
verorum indicio [Madvig, *emended from* iudicio] proderetur."

[2] " Arenarum quoque præteritis clivis, sabulum perinde ac farra aspicere jussus, eadem albicantibus maris procellis permolita esse respondit."

then returns, upbraids his mother, and explains to her his passion for vengeance. Feng cannot find his friend the spy. Jestingly, folk ask Amleth whether he knows aught ; he answers that maybe the man has fallen through the sewer, and, stifled by the filth, has been devoured by swine. His uncle at last determines to send Amleth to the King of Britain with a message that he should slay him. Before his departure Amleth gives secret orders to his mother to hang the hall with knitted tapestry, and to perform pretended obsequies for him a year hence.

Two retainers of Feng accompany him to Britain, bearing a letter graven on wood—" a kind of writing material frequent in old times ; " this letter enjoins the king to put to death the youth who is sent to him. Amleth obtains the letter, and substitutes an order for the death of his companions, adding an entreaty that the king grant his daughter in marriage to the wise youth whom he sends to him. The king receives the guests and treats them all hospitably and kindly. Amleth disdains the rich food placed before him, much to the king's annoyance. A man is sent into the sleeping-room to take note of Amleth's talk. He reports how Amleth told his companions that the bread was flecked with blood and tainted, and further, that the king had the eyes of a slave, and that the queen had in three ways shown the behaviour of a bond-maid. All this, on special investigation, turns out to be

true, and the king adores the wisdom of Amleth as though it were inspired, and gives him his daughter to wife. Moreover, in order to fulfil the bidding of his friend, he hangs Amleth's two companions. Amleth, feigning offence, treats this piece of kindness as a grievance, and receives from the king, as compensation, some gold, which he afterwards melts in the fire, and secretly causes to be poured into some hollowed sticks. After a year he returns to his own land, carrying away of all his wealth only the sticks containing the gold. He then again puts on a grotesque demeanour, and, covered with filth, enters the banquet-room where his own obsequies are being held. The guests jeer at one another, and are right merry. They ask him concerning his comrades; he points to the sticks, saying, "Here is both the one and the other." Then he plies the company with drink, and to prevent his loose dress hampering his walk, he girds his sword upon his side, and purposely drawing it several times, pricks his fingers with its point. The bystanders accordingly have both the sword and scabbard riveted across with an iron nail. The lords drink so heavily that they fall asleep within the palace. Anon, Amleth takes out of his bosom the stakes he has long ago prepared, and goes into the room where the ground is covered with the bodies of the sleeping lords. Cutting away its supports, he brings down the hanging his mother has knitted, which covers the inner as well as the outer wall of the hall; this he flings upon the sleepers, and then

applying the crooked stakes, he knots and binds them up in such insoluble intricacy that not one of the men beneath, however hard he may struggle, can manage to escape. After this he sets fire to the palace, which is soon enveloped in flames. He hurries to his uncle's chamber, and awakening him, tells him that Amleth is come, armed with his old crooks, to help him. Seizing his uncle's sword, and placing his own in its stead, he easily exacts the vengeance, long overdue, for his father's murder.

This is the story told in Book III. In Book IV. it is related how Amleth eloquently harangues the assembled Jutlanders, who appoint him Feng's successor by prompt and general acclaim ; how he returns to Britain in magnificent array, with a wondrous shield whereon all his exploits are depicted ; how his father-in-law discovers that it is his bounden duty to avenge Feng's death on his own son-in-law, and hopes to spare himself the task by deputing him to go and woo for him a fierce unwedded queen reigning in Scotland, whose suitors have invariably paid for their insolence with their lives ; how the queen, becoming enamoured of the young prince, plays on him the very trick he had himself erewhile used, changing the purport of the letter so that it reads as a commission from the king that she should wed the bearer ; how he yields to her pressing solicitations that he should transfer his wooing, and make over to her his marriage vows, and learn to prefer birth to beauty. It is further told how he returns

to Britain with a strong band of Scots, and is met by his much-injured wife, who, in spite of her wrongs, reveals to him her father's plot to entrap him. An under-shirt of mail saves him from the king's cunning blow. He is, however, anxious to exonerate himself from the guilt of treachery towards his father-in-law, and wishes to make the whole blame recoil on his Scotch queen, Hermutrude ; but the king pursues him, and so reduces his forces that he resorts to a device in order to increase the apparent number of his men. He puts stakes under some of the dead bodies of his comrades to prop them up, sets others on horseback like living men, and ties others to neighbouring stones. The plan succeeds, and the Britons, terrified at the spectacle, flee without fighting ; the king is killed, and Amleth, having seized the spoils of Britain, goes back with his wives to his own land.

Meanwhile Rorick has died, and his successor Wiglek, regarding Amleth as a usurper, has cruelly harassed Amleth's mother. This evil treatment Amleth takes at first with much forbearance, and even gives Wiglek the richest of his spoils ; but soon he seizes a chance of taking vengeance, attacks him, subdues him, and becomes his open foe. Fialler, the governor of Skaane, he drives into exile ; and the tale is, that " *Fialler retired to a spot called Undensakre which is unknown to our peoples.*" [1] Wiglek, recruited with

1 " Quem ad locum, cui Undensakre nomen est, nostris ignotum populis, concessisse est fama."

the forces of Skaane and Zealand, sends envoys to challenge Amleth to a war. Amleth foresees that the war will prove fatal, but he is more anxious about the future widowhood of Hermutrude, so greatly does he love her, than about his own death. She protests : the woman who would dread to be united with her lord in death was abominable. But ill she keeps her boast ; for when Amleth is slain by Wiglek in battle in Jutland, she yields herself to be the conqueror's spoil and bride.

This, then, is the story of Amleth as told by Saxo towards the end of the twelfth century. Whence did he obtain it ? His closing words, that " a plain in Jutland is to be found famous for Amleth's name and burial-place," seem to indicate that the local traditions were somewhat limited, and in all probability Saxo's debt to Jutland sources was but slight.[1] It is certainly interesting that a Jutland folk-tale, *De Kloge Studenter*, " The Clever Students," has much in common with Hamlet's wisdom in disdaining the King of Britain's banquet, and in discovering the secret of

[1] Müller points out that two places in Jutland are still called Ammelhede. Olrik, in *Sakses Oldhistorie Norröne sagaer og Danske Sagn*, refers to *Jyske Folkeminder*, viii. No. 152. The story told is that two petty kings lived by Virring, half-a-mile from here (Ammel and Krog) ; they quarrelled and slew each other. One, hight Ammel, lived by Ammelhede ; he is buried in a little mound right east of it. "Ammelhede " may perhaps = Amlæðæ-heðæ (Amlæðæ, according to Olrik, would be the West Danish form of the name Amlóði ; hence Saxo's Amlethus), but when once the legend had become localized in Jutland, the identification would soon follow.

his mother's low origin.[1]   This very episode must have
been one of the most popular of the legends fathered on to
Hamlet, for Saxo tells us distinctly that "others relate" a
slightly different version of the incident, but it is certainly
no intrinsic part of the Hamlet story.

As far as Iceland is concerned, we have no trace of the
Hamlet story in the sagas and poems belonging to the two
centuries intervening between Snæbjörn's verse and Saxo's
History; but it seems probable that some account of
"Amloði" was given in the lost *Skiöldunga Saga*, that
part of it which contained the Lives of the Kings of
Denmark from the earliest times.[2]   Internal evidence does
not conclusively connect Saxo's story with an Icelandic
source, but one statement seems to point to some original
document containing a reference to Northern heathendom,
such as would have been easily understood by a twelfth-
century Icelander; the force of the expression has seemingly
been missed by Saxo.   "Fialler," he writes, "retired to a
spot called *Undensakre*, which is unknown to our people."

---

[1] Cp. *Jyske Folkeminder*, vii.–viii. p. 156 ; and Olrik, p. 165.
[2] Cp. *Prolegomena, Sturlunga Saga*, p. lxxxix : "Among others we
have here to mourn the loss of the Icelandic Saga of Hamlet (Amloði),
Hagbard and Signy, King Frodi, etc., which we take all to have been
included in the mythical part.   The Skioldunga is mentioned as late as
1462 in the inventory of the church of Modrvalla."   Professor York
Powell, *Saxo Grammaticus*, p. 411, is of opinion that a brief chapter on
Amloði may have formed an episode in the early part of Skioldunga ;
there may even have been a scrap or two of verse of an old Amloði's
lay in this chapter.

Surely this represents Saxo's rationalizing of a poetical peri-phrasis for Fialler's departure from the world. "Ódáinsakr," the Land of the Undying, the Northern Elysium, was familiar enough to the Icelanders of the twelfth century ; the Danes had evidently forgotten their pagan Paradise.[1]

It may be fair to assume that Saxo's source for this passage was some Icelandic lay ; similarly, Hamlet's riddling answers to the courtiers, more especially his poetical metaphor concerning the sand of the shore, "ground small by the hoary tempests of the ocean," may well have been derived from some Icelandic original in prose or verse ; at all events, the latter passage gives us the twelfth-century explanation of Snæbjörn's reference to "Hamlet's meal," [2] whatever may have been Snæbjörn's

[1] Vedel, in his Danish translation of Saxo, places Undensakre in Skaane, the south-west province of Sweden. I cannot follow Olrik in his suggestion that Undensakre = Undornsakrar (i.e. the south-eastern fields), cp. *Sakses Oldhistorie*, p. 159. Rydberg ingeniously identifies Fialr with Falr, i.e. Balder, "the single person who by an enemy was transferred to *Ódáinsakr*." Cp. sections 44–53, 93 : the former sections give a valuable analysis of the Saga of Eric Vidforle (who, one Christmas Eve, made a vow to seek out Odainsaker), where the older pagan myth has become Christianized. E. Mogk, *Grundriss der Germanischen Mythologie*, gives a careful summary of "Life after Death" as conceived by the Northerners (vol. i. pp. 1115–16).

[2] I do not deny that the sand-downs on the west coast of Jutland, to which Olrik refers, seem to be closely associated with Hamlet's famous answer, and may well have helped the localizing of the legend ; the Icelandic words *mjöl*, meal or flour, *melr*, a sandhill, *meldr*, flour, to-gether with the old myth of the Grotti-mill, are more than enough to explain the not very remarkable simile. Olrik holds a brief for

own interpretation. The solution of the problem found in Saxo is certainly a disappointment. It surely required no dissimulating Solomon, " *stulti sapiens imitator*," to discover for folks accustomed to the conception of the Ocean-quern the analogy between the sands of the sea and the grist of the mill. Here, too, the passage in Saxo's History gives the impression of representing some more subtle myth rationalized.

But whatever Northern elements may be detected in Saxo's Hamlet story, there can be no doubt that some important incidents have been borrowed from legendary Roman history. The merest outline of the plot cannot fail to show the striking likeness between the tales of Hamlet and Lucius Junius Brutus. Apart from general resemblances (the usurping uncle ; the persecuted nephew, who escapes by feigning madness ; the journey ; the oracular utterances ; the outwitting of the comrades ; the well-matured plans for vengeance), there are certain points in the former story which must have been borrowed directly from the latter. This is especially true of Hamlet's device of putting the gold in the sticks. This could not be due to mere coincidence ; and moreover,

---

Denmark in his excellent study of Saxo; some of his alleged Danish characteristics seem doubtful ; but his comment on Hamlet's resting upon "the hoof of a beast of burden, upon a cockscomb, and also upon a ceiling," is distinctly ingenious, if one of these proves to be a plant-name peculiarly Danish, not found in Icelandic. *Cp.* O. F. Hjaltalín, *Grasafrodi*, pp. 223–224, 230.

the evidence seems to show that Saxo himself borrowed this incident from the account of Brutus in Valerius Maximus ; one phrase at least from the passage in the *Memorabilia* was transferred from Brutus to Hamlet.[1] Saxo must have also read the Brutus story as told by Livy, and by later historians whose versions were ultimately based on Dionysius of Halicarnassus, Dio Cassius, etc. ; he may have seen some such epitome of Roman history as that of his contemporary Zonaras, who has preserved a compendium of the early part of Dio's lost Roman history. One must dwell on this point, for while Livy, Valerius, and others make mention of Tarquin's murder of the elder brother of Brutus, Zonaras, as well as Dionysius of Halicarnassus, gives the important additional statement that the father of Brutus had also, from motives of jealousy, been put to death by his brother-in-law, Tarquinius Superbus.[2]   In order that the reader may be enabled

[1] Stephanius first called attention to Saxo's borrowing of the phrase *obtusi cordis esse*.   Valerius Maximus gives the following version of the story : " Quo in genere acuminis [vafritiæ] in|primis Junius Brutus referendus est, nam cum a rege Tarquinio, avunculo suo, omnem nobilitatis indolem excerpi, interque ceteros etiam fratrem suum, quod vegetioris ingenii esset, interfectum animadvertet, *obtunsi se cordis* esse simulavit eaque fallacia maximas suas virtutes texit, profectus etiam Delphos cum Tarquinii filiis, quos is ad Apollinem Pythium muneribus et sacrificiis honorandum miserat, aurum deo nomine doni clam cavato baculo inclusum tulit, quia timebat ne sibi cæleste numen aperta liberalitate venerari tutum non esset.

[2] Cp. *The Credibility of Early Roman History*, by Sir G. C. Lewis, vol. i. p. 518.

to place in juxtaposition the twin-brothers Hamlet and Brutus, the earlier portion of the tale of Brutus as told by Livy is here added ; the subsequent events connected with the rape of Lucrece are too well known to need recapitulating.[1]

" While Tarquin was thus employed (on certain defensive measures), a dreadful prodigy appeared to him : a snake, sliding out of a wooden pillar, terrified the beholders, and made them fly into the palace ; and not only struck the king himself with sudden terror, but filled his breast with anxious apprehensions : so that, whereas in the case of public prodigies the Etrurian soothsayers only were applied to, being thoroughly frightened at this domestic apparition, as it were, he resolved to send to Delphi, the most celebrated oracle in the world ; and judging it unsafe to entrust the answers of the oracle to any other person, he sent his two sons into Greece, through lands unknown at that time, and seas still more unknown. Titus and Aruns set out, and, as a companion, was sent with them Lucius Junius Brutus, son to Tarquinia, the king's sister, a young man of a capacity widely different from the assumed appearance he had put on. Having heard that the principal men in the state, and, among the rest, his brother, had been put to death by his uncle, he resolved that the king should find nothing in his capacity which he need dread, nor in his fortune which he need covet ;

[1] Livy, Book I. chap. lvi.

and he determined to find security in contempt, since in justice there was no protection. He took care, therefore, to fashion his behaviour to the resemblance of foolishness, and submitted himself and his fortune to the king's rapacity. Nor did he show any dislike to the surname of Brutus, content that, under the cover of that appellation, the genius which was to be the deliverer of the Roman people should lie concealed, and wait the proper season for exertion.

" He was, at this time, carried to Delphi by the Tarquinii, rather as a subject of sport than as a companion ; and is said to have brought, as an offering to Apollo, *a golden wand inclosed in a staff of cornel wood, hollowed for the purpose,* an emblem figurative of the state of his own capacity. When they arrived there, and executed their father's commission, the young men felt a wish to inquire to which of them the kingdom of Rome was to come ; and we are told that these words were uttered from the bottom of the cave :—' Young men, whichever of you shall first kiss your mother, he shall possess the sovereign power at Rome.' . . . Brutus judged that the expression of Apollo had another meaning, and as if he had accidentally stumbled and fallen, he touched the earth with his lips, considering that she was the common mother of all mankind." [1]

It is clear from this, that however much the Hamlet story may have already resembled the Brutus story before

[1] George Baker's translation, 1797.

its appearance in the Danish History, Saxo must have recognized the kinship of the two stories, and added to their common traits. These points of contact, however, belong only to the earlier career of Hamlet, as narrated in Saxo's Third Book. An ingenious theorist[1] has even gone so far as to maintain that the Hamlet story is nothing more than a Northern transformation of the Roman Brutus saga. He deepens the likeness between the two tales by suggesting that Tarquinia, the mother of Brutus and sister of Tarquin, was regarded as the wife of Tarquinius, and became identified with the wicked Tullia; after the murder of her husband, Tarquin's brother, who might easily have been identified with the father of Brutus, she became Tarquin's wife, aiding and abetting him as an accomplice in all his wickedness. According to this view, the name "Amloði" was merely a translation of the Latin "Brutus," i.e. "The Dullard."[2] Even as it has been suggested that the story of Brutus' pretended idiocy was invented to explain the fact of so wise a man being called by such a name, so, according to this view, the name "Amloði" was originally a common noun, meaning "simpleton," or "fool," which became the descriptive nickname of the hero. It is strange, however, that the original worker of the story should have chosen, as the Northern equivalent

[1] Dr. Detter, *Zeitschrift für Deutsches Alterthum u. Deutsche Litteratur*, vol. xxxvi. 1892.

[2] *Cp.* Dion. Hal. iv. 67 :—" εἴη δ᾽ ἂν ἐξερμηνευόμενος ὁ βροῦτος εἰς τὴν Ἑλληνικὴν διάλεκτον, ἠλίθιος."

of the Latin "*brutus*," so strange a word as "*amloði*," which is not found in the oldest Scandinavian ; its modern and mediæval uses in the Icelandic, Swedish, and Danish dialects are all suggestive of the name of the hero of some popular legend ; the etymology proposed does not carry any more conviction than the other suggestions put forward by Northern scholars." [1]

Livy's influence on Saxo is unmistakable, even in the very arrangement of the materials. Thus the story of Brutus fills the last chapters of Book I. and the earlier chapters of Book II., the former ending with Brutus' election to the consulship, the latter beginning with the consul's address to the excited people ; similarly Saxo's Hamlet story, as regards its division between Books III. and IV., seems modelled after Livy's pattern. There is, however,

[1] Dr. Detter proposes "*aml* +*óði*" : the first component (which is not found in old Icelandic, but according to Erik Jonsson is used in modern Icelandic) is said to mean "labour, or toil, without much progress" (*cp.* Icelandic *amstr*, toil ; *ama*, to annoy, vex) ; the compound is rendered "verdruss-wütend, *i.e.* "annoyingly mad." Other compounds in -*óði* are compared, *e.g. málóði*, mad in speech ; *handóðr*, mad with one's hands ; *steinóði*, stone-mad (*cp.* stone-deaf) : all these latter compounds are easily explained ; *amlóði* stands by itself, isolated. The explanation seems to me an excellent folk-etymology ; in all probability the ending of the word (*óði* = mad) helped to fix the popular usage of the name "*Amlóði*." Similarly, Carl Säve (*Aftryck ur Nord. Univ. Tidsk.* 10 *Årg.* 4 *Häft*) suggested an untenable derivation of the name from *and-blauðr*" = "*hinn and-blauði*," *i.e.* "the crack-brained, crazy person."

Dr. Vigfusson rightly withdrew his suggestion that "*amlóði*" might be connected with the Anglo-Saxon word "*homola*," one whose head has been mutilated or shaved ; adding in his "Corrigenda" : "No one knows the origin of this name."

this great difference between the matter distributed over the two books of the Danish history : the earlier incidents of Hamlet's life, found in Book III., have their analogues in Livy, while the later events, described in Book IV. (viz. the chapter of Hamlet's adventures in England, the story of Hermutrude), find no parallels in the Latin story. It seems clear that even were Dr. Detter's contentions altogether acceptable, his theory would only apply to the Hamlet of Saxo's Third Book, though even here a number of elements would have to be accounted for.

It must indeed be admitted that Saxo's Hamlet-tale has but few links connecting it definitely with Northern mythology. The reference to " Ódáinsakr " at the end of the whole story has already been considered. A more important link is to be found in the name of <u>Hamlet's father,</u> Horwendillus, the Scandinavian " Örvandill," the German " Orendel," the English " Éarendel," whose myth was Christianized by Germanic Europe, and whose star was glorified as " the true Light, which lighteth every man that cometh into the world." So the old English poet sang, in almost Miltonic strain :—

> " Eala, earendel, engla beorhtast,
> Ofer middan-geard monnum sended,
> And soð-fæsta sunnan leoma,
> Torht ofer tunglas, þu tida gehwane
> Of sylfum þe symble inlihtes ; " [1]

---

[1] *Cp.* Cynewulf's *Crist*, ed. Gollancz, pp. 10, 159.
In the *Prose Edda* it is told how Thor carried Orwendel from Jotunheim in a basket on his back ; Orwendel's toe stuck out of the

> " Hail, heavenly Light, brightest of angels thou,
> sent unto men upon this middle-earth !
> Thou art the true refulgence of the sun !
> radiant above the stars, and from thyself
> illuminest for ever all the tides of time."

basket, and got frozen ; Thor broke it off, and flung it at the sky, and made a star of it, which is called *Orvandels-tá.* In Anglo-Saxon glosses " earendel " (*cp.* Epinal gloss.), or " oerendil " (*cp.* Erfurt gloss.), is interpreted *jubar,* but " dawn " or " morning-star " would probably be a better rendering, as in the only other passage known in old English literature, viz. *The Blickling Homilies,* p. 163, l. 30 : " Nu seo Cristes gebyrd at his æriste, se niwa eorendel Sanctus Johannes ; and nu nu se leoma þære soþan sunnan God selfa cuman wille ;" *i.e.* " And now the birth of Christ (was) at its beginning, and the new day-spring (or dawn) was John the Baptist.   And now the gleam of the true Sun, God himself, shall come."   Örvandill, Éarendel, etc., are probably rightly compared with Sanskrit *usrâ,* the morning-red ; Latin, *aurora ;* Greek, ἠώς.   It is interesting to note that the old Germanic spring-goddess " Austrô " (whose existence has been evolved from Bede's " Eostre," *i.e.* West Saxon " Eastre " ; cp. *De Temporum Ratione,* c. xv.) must have been identical with *usrâ, aurora,* etc.; as Kluge points out (*v. Etymologisches Wörterbuch, sub* Ostern), the old Indo-Germanic *Aurora* became among the Germans a spring-goddess in place of a dawn-goddess : the Christian festival commemorating Christ's resurrection coincided with the pagan festival of Easter, which was celebrated at the vernal equinox, whence the transference of the pagan name to Christian purposes. " Earendel " and " Easter " have evidently the same root, and both illustrate the same interesting compromise between Old and New (*cp.* Mogk ; Paul's *Grundriss,* vol. iii. p. 374).   On the other hand, Symons (Paul's *Grundriss,* vol. iii. p. 733) supports the older view of Müllenhoff, and rejects the theory that *Orwendel* = dawn-god, and points to its oldest form *Auriuuandalus* (gen. *Auriuuandali,* found in Lombardic, anno 720) as connected with old Norse, *aurr,* moisture ; Anglo-Saxon *éar,* sea ; he holds that the hero's name = the wanderer on the sea, the seafarer ; a sort of Germanic Ulysses.   It is certainly difficult from this standpoint to explain the Anglo-Saxon use of " earendel," and recent Northern philologists (*e.g.* Noreen, cp. *Abriss aer Urgermanischen Lautlehre,* p. 89) equate *ear-* with the root signifying " to burn " in Greek εὔω, Latin *uro, Ves-*uvius, etc.

In the stories of Orwendel found in the Eddas, there is nothing strongly suggestive of Saxo's Hamlet story, though Rydberg attempted, without success, to identify Hamlet with Orwendel's famous son Svipdagr, whose adventures in giant-land to win the giant-guarded maiden are told so dramatically in the fine Eddaic *Lay of Swipday and Menglad*. If, however, in spite of the absence of evidence to support the view, it be maintained that the Hamlet-tale was originally connected with the Orwendel myth, those who favour nature-myths have here an excellent opportunity for the display of their ingenuity. "The first hero ever born," as Orwendel is described in the preface to the old German *Spielmanns Gedicht*, was certainly, as his name implies, a radiant god of dawn or of spring ; and does not Saxo make him battle with and ultimately slay King Collerus, *i.e.* King Cold ? He kills him in "a spring-tide wood," and in due course is himself slain by his own brother, and avenged by his own son. The hapless Gerutha, the giant-mother "Groa" of the *Edda*, is Mother Earth, who in the forced embraces of cruel Winter longs for the return of her beloved Spring. Some forty years ago Zinzow,[1] in an elaborate treatise, advanced some such interpretation of the Hamlet story as a nature-myth ; and more recently, the distinguished mythologist Mogk adduced the above theory in dealing with Orwendel's share

[1] *Die Hamletsage : an u. mit verwandten Sagen erläutert : ein Beitrag zum Verständniss nordisch-deutsche Sagendichtung. Von* Dr. A. Zinzow. Halle, 1877.

in Saxo's story ; while Dr. Symons maintained that Saxo's Danish legend is associated only in name, and not essentially, with the Orwendel myth. Even so, the Hamlet story may very well have borrowed certain elements from the ancient Northern myth of the struggle between Spring and Winter. From this point of view, the most difficult element of the whole story—the part played by the hero's mother—becomes illumined.

Summing up, in Saxo's "Hamlet" we have a general framework probably derived from Northern mythology (or rather from Northern mythology which had passed through the various stages of heroic-myth and pseudo-history) ; in Book III. the story presents remarkable analogues to the Brutus story, and is indebted to it for many of its most striking details ; in Book IV. the series of incidents seems to belong to an entirely different stratum of legendary lore. The consideration of this latter portion of the narrative throws light on the date, place, and origin of Saxo's materials.

III

OTHER mediæval legends suggest contact with the legendary history of early Rome. One instance must be considered side by side with the Brutus element in *Hamlet*. While Hamlet may be regarded as a sort of Northern counterpart of the Roman Brutus, another Danish prince, whom the elder Grundtvig aptly styled "Hamlet's mythical half-brother," [1] recalls the most striking element in the legend of Servius Tullius. Prince Havelok, degraded to the servile condition of scullion and buffoon, reveals his high lineage, during sleep, by the flame-breath issuing from his mouth. "*Caput arsisse Servio Tullio dormienti, quæ historia non prodidit?*" as Cicero puts it in "*De Divinatione.*" There are other parallel incidents in the careers of Servius and Havelok, more especially the rôle played by their respective wives in firing their ambition. The influence of Latin legend on both *Hamlet* and *Havelok* suggests at least the possibility of finding other links in the two stories, and some evidence as to the time and place of their origin.

In dealing with the Anglo-Danish romance of *Havelok*, three versions must be differentiated :—(i.) Gaimar's

---

[1] Cp. *Nordens Mythologi*, 1832.

37

version, found at the beginning of *Lestorie des Engles*; probably originally inserted between the lost *Lestorie des Bretons* and the extant history; (ii.) an Anglo-Norman *Lai de Havelok* found at the end of a copy of *Lestorie* in the College of Arms, Gaimar's version being omitted; (iii.) *Havelok the Dane*, an English poem belonging to the thirteenth century, probably based on popular legends, and more especially on the local legends accounting for the origin of Grimsby; the Grimsby seal, which may go back to the date of the poem, epitomizes the story. This English romance is independent of the French versions, though the author was evidently acquainted with the Anglo-Norman poem. It is of least importance for the present investigation. As regards the *Lai*, it is almost certainly derived from Gaimar's terser version,[1] which may safely be assigned to the first half of the twelfth century. Its source is unknown; it was possibly in one of the manuscripts borrowed for Gaimar by his patron's friend, Walter Espec, the noble founder of the Abbeys of Kirkham, Rievaulx, and Wardon, from Robert, Earl of Gloucester. Gildas is vaguely referred to immediately

---

[1] *Cp.* Ward's *Catalogue of MS. Romances*, vol. i. pp. 437–439, and the whole section, where the whole evidence concerning *Havelok* is dealt with; also, *Lestorie des Engles* (Hardy and Martin), (ed. Rolls Series), 1889; Madden's *Havelok the Dane* (Roxburghe Club); Skeat, *Havelok* (E.E.T.S. Extra Series IV.); Michel, *Le Lai d'Havelok le Danois*; Köster, *Sagnet om Havelok Danske*; G. Storm, *Christiania Videnskabsselskabs Forhandlinger*, 1879; *The Lay of Havelok*, ed. Skeat and Sisam, 1915.

efore the account of Havelok, but Gaimar certainly did not find any account of the Dane in any lost work of the sixth-century historian. Gaimar tells how, in the days of Constantine, Arthur's successor, King Albrict, a Dane, rules in Norfolk, while Edelsi, a Briton, rules in Lindsey ; the kings are brothers-in-law ; Edelsi's sister, Orwain, has been married to the Dane. Albrict and Orwain die, leaving Argentille, an only child, to the care of her uncle, who proves to be the proverbially cruel uncle of popular story. Hear what this felon king does ! For the inheritance which he covets, he mismarries his niece. He gives her to a lad named Cuheran, to abase her.

> *This Cuheran though a scullion*
> *was a comely lad to see,*
> *of beauteous face, and beauteous hands,*
> *of graceful form and mien ;*
> *of cheery mood, whate'er befell ;*
> *good legs, good feet, were his ;*
> *and brave he was, and theretobold,*
> *and willingly he fought ;*
> *and oft it chanced that some vile groom*
> *would play with him in sport,*
> *would hustle him, yet soon he sprawled*
> *with legs high in the air,*
> *but if the groom grew wroth thereat,*
> *he tied him with his belt,*
> *and if no other folk were nigh,*
> *would beat him with a rod :*
> *and yet withal he was so frank,*
> *he soon released his foe,*
> *if he the word of promise gave*
> *to bear him no ill grudge,*
> *and when they had embraced again,*
> *then Cuheran was glad.*

He is the most popular among all the king's servants
and Edelsi, who knows him but as "quistrun," *i.e.* a
scullion, has made him his fool (" *de lui son jugleur feseit* ").
Argentille sorely feels her disgrace, until one night she
sees a marvellous flame coming from Cuheran's mouth.
She questions him concerning his birth, and he tells her
all he knows, namely, that he is the son of poor fisher-
folk at Grimsby. They hasten thither. His "father,"
Grim, is dead ; but Grim's daughter is still living. She
knows the whole secret of his birth, though at first she
is reluctant to confide it to him, lest harm should befall
him therefrom, owing to his "folly" (*par son folage*). At
length, however, she reveals that he is the son of Gunther,
king of Denmark, who had been killed when King Arthur
conquered the land.

> *The queen in sore dismay of the fight*
> *fled thence with the rightful heir ;*
> *and you are he, Dan Havelok,*
> *King Gunther's son and heir.*
> *My father had a right good ship ;*
> *he took the queen away ;*
> *toward this land he steered his course ;*
> *but God willed otherwise.*
> *Fierce outlaws met us on the seas,*
> *they pillaged and plundered all ;*
> *the knights and all our folk they slew,*
> *nor e'en the queen they spared ;*
> *no man but father mine was spared,*
> *no woman but my mother,*
> *for friendship's sake they spared them both,*
> *them, and the children eke,*

> *both me and you, my brothers too,*
> *e'en as my father begged.*
> *And when at length we landed here,*
> *we cut our ship in twain ;*
> *shattered and battered were sides and stern,*
> *in that fight when the queen was killed :*
> *of our stout ship we made our home,*
> *by a boat we got our bread.*

So Kelloc, Grim's daughter, describes the early history of the hero, who subsequently behaves with anything but " folage." He and his wife visit Denmark, where various adventures befall them. He is ultimately discovered by his father's seneschal, who soon, by various tests, recognizes him as the true heir to the throne. The usurper King Edulf is defeated ; Havelok is acclaimed as king. Anon he calls together all his ships, and defies King Edelsi. He fights a drawn battle, but Argentille teaches him a trick by which he wins the second day. All night they fix stakes in the earth ; they fix thereon the dead men in two squadrons. The next morning, when Edelsi's men see that the host of the enemy is so great, all their flesh shudders, they lose courage, and make the king surrender :—

> *To fight is now of no avail,*
> *yield thou the lady's right,*
> *make peace, lest things fare worse.*

Argentille thus gains her heritage ; and soon after, on Edelsi's death, Havelok, king of Denmark, succeeds to Lindsey as well as Norfolk. Twenty years was he king.

The briefest summary of the romance suffices to show

that we have here a story of the Hamlet type, though the characters of the two heroes stand apart in many important respects. "They may fairly be called foster-brothers," writes Dr. Ward, in an excellent and summary analysis of the two stories ; [1] "they both grow up at the court of a 'usurping uncle,' and are both famous for their quaint sayings. But there the first resemblance ends. In the case of Havelok, the usurper is not the uncle of Havelok himself, but of Argentille. Havelok's simplicity is real. He is quite content with playing pranks before the court at Lincoln, where the king treats him as a sort of jester. He is aware of the marvellous flame-breath, but it never makes him dream of being the heir of kings, or of having any wrongs to avenge ; [2] indeed, he is ashamed of it until Argentille becomes his Valkyria (even the crowning war trick is her device, for it is done *par conseil de la reine*, l. 773) ; and she informs his splendid body with the spirit of a hero. Hamlet, on the other hand, schemes for revenge ; and his sayings are in character with his assumed madness. But the course of the two stories often brings the same incidents to the front. Thus each of the heroes is

[1] Cp. *English Historical Review*, 1895.

[2] On the other hand, as Dr. Ward points out elsewhere (*Catalogue*, p. 441), in the English poem of Havelok "the hero is never unconscious of his real position. His character is light and thoughtless before his marriage, but then it changes ; he withdraws Goldeburgh from Lincoln to Grimsby of his own accord ; he has dreams of ambition, remembers his wrongs, and prays for revenge. This brings Havelok in some respects a little closer to Hamlet."

a disinherited Danish prince ; each marries an English princess, and regains his power in Denmark ; each returns to Britain, and marches against an English king ; each is accompanied by his own Valkyria (the English Argentille and the Scottish Hermuthruda) ; each of them half loses the first day's battle, and each wins the second day by staking up the dead men in squadrons. These are marks of the same workshop, at the very least."

But the workshop in which Havelok was wrought is unmistakable ; the mark is graven on the workmanship. The researches of Köster, Storm, and Ward make it certain that "Havelok Cuheran" [1] is identical with the name of the famous Viking, perhaps the greatest warrior of the house of Ivar, Anlaf Curan, the vanquished hero of Brunanburgh and Tara.

Anlaf Curan, or Olaf o' the Sandal, was the son of Sihtric Gale, or Caoch, a Viking chief of the house of Ivar, who first came to Dublin in 888, and who subsequently gained and lost the kingship of Dublin, and died as king of Northumbria in 925 ; a year before his death he had married the sister of King Athelstan. Sihtric's son Anlaf was the child of another wife, but the Wessex king stood very much in the

---

[1] The English romance does not mention the name Cuheran at all ; the author of *Lai de Havelok* has perhaps misunderstood Gaimar, and explains "*Cuheran*" as equivalent to "*quistron*" (*i.e.* scullion) ; "*car ceo tenoient li Breton en sur language quistron ;*" Gaimar merely states that "*Cuheran estait quistrun.*" *Cuheran*, *Kvaran* = Irish, *cuarán*, a sock ; Welsh *cvran* (*cp.* W. Stokes, *Revue Celtique*, iii. p. 189).

relationship of uncle towards his sister's stepson. It was, however, the policy of Alfred's ambitious grandson to make himself king of all England, and Northumbria was to be added to his rule. He drove thence Godfrey, Sihtric's brother, Godfrey's son Anlaf, and his nephew Anlaf; the latter was destined, as Anlaf Curan, to cause much trouble to the English. Expelled from Northumbria, Anlaf took refuge at the court of Constantine III., king of Scotland, whose daughter he eventually married. Athelstan resented Constantine's alliance with the Hiberno-Danes, and in 934 sent an expedition to waste his kingdom. In 937 a mighty coalition of British and Danish chiefs was formed against Athelstan; Constantine, together with his son-in-law Anlaf, now king of the Northmen in Ireland, were at the head of the league, which soon numbered many chiefs of the west and east; the Danes and British formed a confederacy against their common West Saxon foe. Anlaf, with his cousin Anlaf Godfreyson, came to the Humber with a fleet of 615 sail, and seized York. At Brunanburgh, probably somewhere in the north-west, the opposing forces met, and the English king gained a great and decisive victory: "never had huger slaughter of heroes hapt in this isle." The importance of the issue may be gathered from the noble war-song enshrined in the Anglo-Saxon chronicle :—

> " *Five young Kings put asleep by the sword-stroke,*
> *Seven strong Earls of the army of Anlaf*
> *Fell on the war-field, numberless numbers,*
> *Shipmen and Scotsmen.*" [1]

---

[1] Tennyson's translation of the Anglo-Saxon poem.

But though the Saxon poet was so exultant in his song, we may infer that the poets of the other camp sang a different song, lauding their leader's valour, telling of the havoc he had wrought on the foe, and refusing to recognize the decisive character of the contest. At all events, on the death of Athelstan in 940, or perhaps sooner, Anlaf came again to York, and was received as king. The Danes of Mercia and East Anglia, with Wulfstan, archbishop of York, accepted his kingship, and according to Simeon of Durham, King Edmund was forced to make terms whereby the kingdom was divided between them, the English taking the south, Anlaf the north, the boundary between them being Watling Street. At this time (943), Anlaf, who had hitherto been a pagan, received the rite of baptism. It would seem that he divided Northumbria with his cousin Anlaf Godfreyson, whose life-story is so closely interwoven with his that the old historians are constantly confusing the two. Constantine's abdication made a great difference in Anlaf's position in Northumbria, and at last, in 952, he was driven thence for the last time. His marvellous career as king of Dublin culminated in 980 in his utter defeat at the battle of Tara, which shattered the power of the Scandinavians in Ireland. After the battle Anlaf left the world of action, and became a monk of the monastery of Iona, where he died the following year. His son Sitric became king of Dublin in his stead. It is worthy of note that Sitric's mother, Gormflaith, married Malachy II., the victor of Tara ; Gormflaith must be distinguished from Anlaf's

other wife, the daughter of Constantine of Scotland ; she was the sister of Maelmordha, king of Leinster, daughter of Murchadh, and granddaughter of Finn, Lord of Offaly. She is "Kormlö̆" of *Njals saga*, which describes her as "the fairest of all women, and best gifted in everything that was not in her own power," *i.e.* in all physical and natural endowments ; but "she did all things ill over which she had any power," *i.e.* in her moral conduct. She was divorced or repudiated by Malachy, and subsequently married his dispossessor, Brian, by whom she was also put away.[1]

Many legends naturally clustered round Anlaf's heroic career. One of these has been preserved by William of Malmesbury in his *Gesta Regum* and *Gesta Pontificum*. It tells how, at the battle of Brunanburgh, Anlaf, disguised as a harper, entered Athelstan's camp, and was brought before the king to display his minstrelsy. He marked well the situation of the king's tent ; but the king, warned by a soldier, removed his tent to another part of the camp. A bishop unwittingly took possession of the vacant place, and was slain in the assault which was made that night. We are acquainted with a similar story of an English king's visit to the Danish camp. There can be no doubt that the romance of "Havelok Cuheran" is little

---

[1] J. H. Todd's *War of the Gaedhil with the Gaill* (London, 1867) is the great source for all this Hiberno-Danish history. *Cp.* also Ward, Keary, Steenstrup, Robertson, who are all indebted to Todd.

more than a romance of the life of "Anlaf Curan," or rather of the many legends fathered upon him, some belonging to ancient story, some derived from various episodes in Hiberno-Anglo-Danish history. The romance must have originally been developed among a Welsh-speaking population, for "Abloec," or "Abloyc" (cp. "Habloc," the form on the Grimsby seal), is the name given to "Anlaf" in the oldest Welsh annals. It is not to be explained, as Todd suggested, as a Welsh form of "Anlaf," but rather, as Dr. Ward has pointed out, as a native Welsh heroic name (Aballach, or Avallach, otherwise Abloyc, the sixth son of the semi-mythical Cunedda) transferred to the Northern hero, its sound being nearly identical with what would have been the Welsh form of some Scandinavian variant of Anlaf. The Welsh kingdom of Strathclyde must be thought of in connection with the Welsh origin of the romance. King Owen, who ruled there during Anlaf's life, was nephew to Constantine of Scotland, Anlaf's father-in-law, and one of his allies at Brunanburgh. The events of the romance clearly belong to Constantine's reign, though by an error Gaimar confuses this tenth-century Constantine with Constantine, "the nephew of Arthur, who had the sword Calidure."

Gaimar's "Havelok" and Saxo's "Hamlet" have many traits in common, as has already been shown. *Havelok* is but a romance of "Anlaf Curan." Is any light thrown on the legendary "Hamlet" when viewed side by side with what is known of the historical Anlaf? As regards

the earlier career of Hamlet, there is nothing much more strikingly parallel than the part played by Anlaf's usurping uncle. Unfortunately, the story of Anlaf's youth has not come down to us ; there is a blank of ten years in the annals, from the death of his father in 927. But the Hamlet of Saxo's Fourth Book, who journeys to Scotland to woo the fierce virago Hermutrude,[1] whose cruel arrogance made her always loathe her wooers, may be identified with the son-in-law of Constantine of Scotland. It has been well said that while Hermutrude resembles Anlaf's first wife in her country, she resembles his second wife, Gormflaith, in her character ; for though, according to Saxo, she had previously resisted all offers of marriage by reason of her chastity, yet at Hamlet's death "she yielded herself unasked to be the conqueror's spoil and bride."

The most remarkable parallel in the "Havelok" and "Hamlet" stories is perhaps the stratagem of setting up the dead men and so gaining the battle ; this incident seems to belong peculiarly to Anglo-Danish or Hiberno-Danish history. A similar expedient is mentioned by Saxo Grammaticus as practised by Fridlevus, king of Denmark, who invades Britain after conquering Dublin ; in the Book

---

[1] The whole subject of the Hermutrude-type of woman in mediæval literature is very fully treated of by Olrik (pp. 172–179) ; Mr. A. Nutt (*Folk-lore*, 1892, 26–48) dwells on its points of contact with Marie de France's "*Eliduc*." The name "Hermutrude" is evidently a Danish borrowing of the German "Hermintrude."

of the "Wars of the Gaedhil with the Gaill," [1] the same
sort of device is resorted to in one of the last episodes of
that long struggle. The statement in Saxo and Gaimar
must be referred to the traditional exploits of Anlaf Curan.

In the case of " Havelok," the Welsh annals come to our
aid in clinching the alleged identification of " Havelok "
with " Anlaf." Do we find any similar evidence bearing
out the alleged influence of Anlaf's story on Saxo's Hamlet-
tale ? The supposed absence of all such evidence must, I
think, be answerable for the scant attention hitherto given
to the whole subject of the " Havelok-Hamlet " problem,
so that in so recent a study as Mr. Elton's valuable
Appendix to " Saxo Grammaticus," the possibility of the
equation is not even referred to. But there does exist in
ancient annals a clue of the greatest possible importance,
strangely overlooked by previous workers. Its neglect can
easily be explained : owing to a very simple but unfortunate
blunder, the translators have obscured the value of their
document, while the historians have naturally followed the
translators. In the *Annals of Ireland by the Four Masters*,[2]
under the year 917 (= 919), a striking account is given of
the great battle of Ath-Cliath, *i.e.* Kilmashogue (near Rath-
farnham, in the county of Dublin). A mighty victory was

[1] *Cp.* Todd, p. 215.
[2] *Annals of Ireland by the Four Masters*, ed. O'Donovan ; *cp.* also
Three Fragments, copied from Ancient Sources, etc. (Irish Arch. and
Celt. Soc.), 1860.

gained by the Northerners under Imhar and Sitric Gale ; twelve Irish kings and princes were struck down in the fight. Chief among these was Niall Glundubh, son of Ædh Finn-liath, king of Ireland, "after he had been three years in the sovereignty." Concerning this battle, adds the annalist, several songs were made. *Fierce and hard was the Wednesday*, is the burden of one ; *Where is the chief of the western world?* of another. "Niall said this before the battle :— *' Whoever wishes for a speckled boss, and a sword of sore-inflicting wounds, and a green javelin for wounding wretches, let him go early in the morning to Ath-Cliath.'* Celedabhaill, son of Scannall, successor of Comghall, and confessor of Niall Glundubh, was he who had requested of Niall to come to this battle ; and it was he that gave the viaticum to Niall, after having refused to give him a horse to carry him to the battle." Then follows a strange fragment of song, which the annalist had already quoted under the year 904. This, however, is its proper place. Its author was none other than Niall Glundubh's widow, Queen Gormflaith, daughter of Flann (who must not be confused with Gormflaith, daughter of Murchadh, Anlaf's wife, already referred to). These words are quoted from her lament :—

> " Olc ormsa cumaoin andá ghall
> Marbsat Niall ⁊ Cearbhall :
> Cearbhall la hUlbh comall ngle
> Niall Glúndubh la hAmhlaidhe."

"Evil to me the compliment of the two foreigners
Who slew Niall and Cearbhall;
Cearbhall was slain by Ulf, a great deed;
Niall Glundubh by Amhlaide."

The last word, "Amhlaide," is certainly the Irish form of
"Amloði" or "Hamlet." [1] O'Donovan, the editor of the
Annals, mistook the name for "Amhlaeibh," i.e. the Irish
form of Áleifr, or Óláfr, and renders it so in his translation
of the passage. The historians, including Steenstrup, have
all followed him, and state that Niall Glundubh was slain at
the battle by one of the enemy whose name was Olaf. The
confusion of "Amlaidhe" (i.e. Amlóði) with Amlaibh
(i.e. Áleifr, Óláfr) was natural enough; the dh was taken
to be a mere variant of bh. That this is not the case is
proved by the metrical system of Gormflaith's song, which
requires that "Amhlaide" should be a trisyllabic word—
the final -e cannot be ignored. This passage in the Irish
annals yields us the earliest instance of the name "Amlóði"
or "Hamlet" to be found anywhere in literature. The
Irish Queen Gormflaith, about the year 919, introduces it
into her verse as the name of one of the Northern heroes
at the battle of Ath-Cliath. Who was this "Amlaidhe,"
the slayer of Niall Glundubh? Though "The Annals of
the Four Masters" named Imhar (i.e. Ivar) and Sitric as the
leaders of the Northmen, it is probable that Imhar is an

[1] Mr. Whitley Stokes duly gives the name in his list of Norse
loan-words in Irish Annals, Bezzenberger's Beiträge, 1892.

error for Clann Ivar, "the children of Ivar,"[1] and that Sitric, the father of Anlaf Curan, was at the head of the enterprise.[2] Under these circumstances, he was certainly the cause of Niall's death. But it would seem that he was the actual slayer of the Irish king. The Saxon Chronicle (*E.* and *F.*), Simeon of Durham, Henry of Huntingdon, Gaimar, and other authorities, all state that "Sitric slew Niel," though they made the strange mistake of calling him Sitric's brother, king of Northumberland. Hodgson Hinde (Hodgson's *Northumberland*, vol. i.) has shown that this Niel was no other than Niall Glundubh, "who never was king of Northumberland, and was no Dane, nor brother of Sitric, but a genuine Irishman of the race of the Northern Hy Neill."[3] Perhaps the chroniclers have confused this Sitric with Sitriucc (one of the sons of Ivar of Limerick) who slew his brother Sichfrith. In the *Ulster Annals*, anno 888, it is stated that "Sichfrith Mac Imair rex Nordmannorum a fratre suo per dolum occisus est." The only brother we know of is Sitriucc, Lord of Limerick.

If, then, it can be shown that Sitric, the father of Anlaf Curan, was the slayer of Niel, it follows that "Amlaidhe," the Irish form of "Hamlet," in Gormflaith's

---

[1] The Ivar were probably of Norse, and not Danish, origin. *Cp.* Steenstrup, *Normannerne*, ii. iii.

[2] *Cp.* Todd.

[3] Keary (*Catalogue of English Coins: Anglo-Saxon Series*) states definitely, in his biographical note on SIHTRIC GALE, that he "slew, in battle of Kilmashogue, 919, King Njel Glundubh, K. of Dublin."

song, must have reference to him ; yet nowhere else, so
far as is discovered at present, is Sitric referred to under
this name. Two nicknames of his are well known, viz.,
"Caoch," an Irish word meaning blind or one-eyed, and
"Gale" or "Gaile," a word which, as Todd says, if it
be Irish, may signify "the champion" or "hero"; but
it cannot well be an Irish word, and Celtic scholars tell
me "this epithet wants explanation." I would hazard the
suggestion that "gaile" is the Norse *galiðr = galinn,* "be-
witched," or, more commonly, "mad" (the past participle
of *gala,* "to enchant"). May it not be that "*amlaidhe,*"
as used by Gormflaith, was synonymous with "*gaile*"?
But if Sitric's career recalled the story of "Amlóði," how
was it that his own Northern countrymen did not apply
to him this expressive nickname? As a matter of fact,
we know nothing of Sitric's early career. The annals are
silent as to his father, and as to the circumstances under
which he first came to Dublin in 888.[1]

[1] There is a curious story told by Suhm, in his *Critisk Historie af
Danmark* ii. Bd. p. 348, about the alleged discovery of some coins bearing
the inscription, "Amleth Rex Anglorum." Suhm casts doubt on the
authenticity of the reading, derived from "Resenii Descr. Jutiæ MSS.
in Atlante." The MSS. of Resenius in the Arni-Magnæan Collection
have been summarily investigated, but no such note has been discovered. Suhm probably quoted directly from Pontoppidan's *Marmora
Danica,* vol. ii. p. 81 where the following statement is made :—

"In boreali regione paræciæ Törringensis portio terræ in Lymicum
se inserens sinum insulam efficit *Helleræ* dictam, in qva Amlethus Rex
munimentum quondam extruxisse fertur. In medio hujus collis surgit
sepulchralis, qvem annis abhinc 80 cum perfodisset Andreas qvidam

Again, so far as the legend of "Amloði" is concerned, it must be borne in mind that we find no Northern reference to the name before the time of the Icelander Snæbjörn, probably some twenty or thirty years after Gormflaith's reference to "Amlaidhe." Whatever Northern elements there may be in the story of Hamlet, it has not yet been conclusively proved that the name "Hamlet" is of Northern origin. As a Teutonic word "amloði" stands absolutely isolated, and no etymology hitherto advanced by Teutonic philologists commends itself to serious consideration. The word has not yet been connected with Celtic vocables, but future investigations on the part of Celtic scholars may perhaps confirm the suggestion that "amhlair," "amadon," and "amlaidhe" may once have been synonymous in Irish speech for that most popular character among all folk, and especially the Irish, to wit, "the fool," and that "amlaidhe" may perhaps represent the confluence of the characteristic Northern name "Áleifr" (Anlaf, Olaf), Irish "Amlaibh," and some such Celtic word as "amhaide," sour, sulky,

---

Lundius, magnam vim nummorum invenit, partim ex corio clavulis argenteis confixo, partim ex auro cum imagine Viri & inscriptione : Amleth Rex Angliæ."

Probably, as Suhm suggests, if there is any truth at all in the story, Lund found some coins of "Anlaf." Keary (p. 235) gives several specimens of his coins, one bearing inscription, "Anlaf Rex Tod" (probably = totius Britanniæ). The British Museum has at least one coin of Anlaf's father, Sihtric Gale (*cp.* p. 231).

surly (*cp.* "amaideac," silly, absurd, fantastic, foolish, idiotic).

Anyhow, it would seem that among the Irish, in the Scandinavian kingdom of Dublin, Anlaf Curan's father was known as "Amlaidhe," or "Hamlet." Later on, the father and the more famous son were no doubt blended in popular story, the confusion being perhaps helped by the likeness in sound between "Amlaibh," the Irish form of "Anlaf," [1] and "Amlaidhe." In later times the two words, following phonetic law, would become absolutely identical in form.

The story of "Hamlet" in Saxo certainly owed a great debt to this Hiberno-Danish history ; and the accretions from this source grafted upon the older mythical story, especially the late matter to be found in Saxo's Fourth Book, may now easily be accounted for. Indeed, the evidence here adduced seems to point to the Celtic West, more particularly the Scandinavian kingdom of Ireland, as the locality where the Northern tale of "Hamlet," as we know it from Saxo, was finally developed some time in the eleventh century—about the same time that the Welsh minstrels of Strathclyde were forging their tale of "Havelok." [2] The tenth-century Icelander Snæbjörn

---

[1] Many Irish forms of this name are given from the Annals in Whitley Stokes' article, Bezzenberger's *Beiträge*, xviii. 116.

[2] Dr. Ward (*Cat. MSS.*, vol. i. p. 860) calls attention to the curious fact that a word almost the same in sound as Amloði formed the name of one of the old Welsh heroes. This was Amlaudd, of whom

must have known the tale at an earlier stage of its development, before the legends of the house of Ivar had been added thereto. But it may be inferred (if the interpretation of Gormflaith's "*Amlaidhe*," as equivalent to *galinn*, *i.e.* mad, be accepted) that the hero's stupidity, assumed or otherwise, was the important element of the tale as known to him. Even this earlier and simpler form of the story may have been brought to Iceland from Ireland, whither the Vikings had originally taken the story of Orwendil's son. No Scandinavian family illustrates more strikingly than Snæbjörn's (if Snæbjörn the poet and Snæbjörn the explorer are identical) the close connection between the Northerners and the Celts from the ninth to the eleventh centuries.[1] The greatest names in Hiberno-Scan-

---

nothing is known except that he was the father of heroines, one of whom was Eigr, the mother of Arthur. Dr. Ward ingeniously makes the following observation :—" This forms, at all events, some sort of connection between him and Abloyc (or Avallach), the son of Cunedda, whose name was transferred to Anlaf Curan. We think it quite possible that both names were used for Anlaf by different romancers, and that whilst one became Havelok, the other became Hamlet." More noteworthy is the Welsh form "Avloed," Anlaf Curan, cp. *Gruffydd ap Cynan*, p. 104, ed. Arthur Jones (*Manchester University Press*, 1910).

[1] The mutual influence of the Celts and the Scandinavians has received increased attention at the hands of scholars. Vigfusson boldly recognized the non-Icelandic character of many of the Eddaic songs (cp. *Corpus Poeticum Boreale*, vol. i. p. lxii.). In the Prolegomena to " The Sturlunga Saga " occurs the following statement :—" We may therefore take the Lays to be a *parallel* development in the Western Isles to the Saga in Iceland, composed for the same purpose, popular

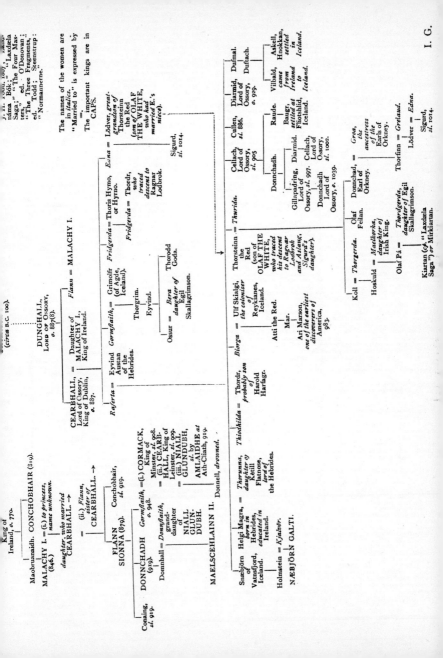

The names of the women are in *italics*. "Married to" is expressed by =. The important kings are in CAPS.

linavian history figure in his pedigree ; and the poetess
Gormflaith, whose husband, Niall Glundubh, was slain
by Amlaidhe, was among his kinsfolk ; she probably died
when he was a youth. It is indeed a curious coincidence
that the earliest instances of the name " Hamlet " should
be found in Gormflaith's Irish lament, and in Snæbjörn's
Icelandic poem of adventure in Arctic Seas.

In view of the evidence adduced tending to associate
the development of the Hamlet story with the British
Isles, it is a matter of surprise that English folk-lore and
folk-speech have not yielded any very clear traces of the
story independently of modern literary influences. It is
possible that Middle English poetry may give us some

---

entertainments, after the initiative of some great poet who arose
among the Norse emigrants somewhere in the West (Ireland, Man,
Northumberland, or Scotland, we know not which)."   Professor Bugge
is the chief exponent of the influence of Irish Christianity on Scandinavian mythology ; and as regards Northern poetry, he has recently
worked out his theory that the " Helgi" poems belong originally to
the West. In an article on " Gaelic Words and Names in the
Icelandic Sagas " (*Zeitschrift für celtische Philologie*, 1897), Professor
Craigie reasserts his contention (*Arkiv för nordisk Filologi*, x.) that
"there is abundant evidence in the Gaelic vocabulary to show that
the Celt learned much from the Scandinavian, while there is scarcely
any similar evidence to prove an Irish influence on the Norsemen."
The test of vocabulary in this case is to my mind not altogether con-
clusive. The case of Olaf Pá, who was taught Irish by his mother,
and "spoke it as well as any man" (*Laxdæla Saga*), was probably not
an isolated instance. E. Mogk's *Kelten und Nordgermanen im 9. u. 10.
Jahrhunderte*, 1892, emphasizes the Celtic influence on Northern (and
more especially Icelandic) literature.

evidence—a valuable confirmatory clue to the theory previously propounded. Alliterative poetry of the West and North-West has preserved so many fossil-remains of ancient legend, and so rich a treasury of archaic speech that the student will be prepared carefully to consider the following problem. In "The Wars of Alexander," an alliterative romance, translated for the most part from the famous "Historia de Preliis,"[1] and composed somewhere in the North of England, towards the end of the fourteenth or in the early years of the fifteenth century, we find a strange word, "amlaʒe" or "amlaugh," twice used as a term of reproach, Alexander the Great being scoffed at by Porrus of Inde as "Amlaʒe out of Grece" :—

"I, Porrus, that as principall possessid am in Ynde,
To this michare[2] out of Messedone this mandment I write
Thou Alexander, thou ape, thou Amlaʒe out of Grece,
Thou little thefe, thou losangere,[3] thou lurkare in cites . . .
Madding marred has thi mode[4] and thi mynd changid ;"

(3540–3546.)

while Darius, inquiring about Alexander's appearance, is shown by his courtiers a caricature thus graphically described :—

---

[1] Re-edited from MS. Ashmole 44, and Trinity College, Dublin, MS. D. 4. 12, by Professor Skeat, E.E.T.S., 1886 ; the former MS. was edited for the Roxburghe Club, in 1849, by Stevenson.

[2] Petty thief.   [3] Liar.   [4] Mind.

" And thai in parchement him payntid, his person him shewid,
    Ane amla3e, ane asaleny,[1] ane ape of all othire,
    A wirling,[2] a wayryngle,[3] a wawil-e3id [4] shrewe,
    The caitifeste creatour, that cried [5] was euire," (1704–1707.)

In disdain Darius sends him a ball to play with, a golden
headpiece, and a hat made of twigs, together with a letter,
bidding him abandon his folly, and bethink him that he is
but " a dwinyng, a dwa3e, and a dwer3e "—a dwarf and a
grub ; he must learn to "*feign with fairness.*" [6]

Have we in these passages some reminiscence of a
popular tale of " Hamlet " ? Or rather, is the word
" Amla3e " used much in the same sense as " Amló δ i "
in modern Icelandic ? Is it not perchance its Middle
English equivalent ? It is a curious fact that the first
editor of " The Wars of Alexander " misread the text
and printed " Amlair," evidently recalling the Irish
" amhlair," a fool. Professor Skeat, in his great edition of
the two texts, rightly prints " amla3e," " amlaugh," explain-
ing the words in the glossary as equivalent to " imbecile,

---

[1] Little ass.   [2] Dwarf.   [3] Little villain.
[4] Wall-eyed.   [5] Created.
[6] The Latin original of the two passages has been elaborately worked
up by the English poets. The letter of Porrus begins with these words :
"*Porus Indorum rex latroni Alexandro, qui latrocinando obtinet civitates,
precipiendo mandamus. Cum sis mortalis homo, quid prevales facere deo ?*"
etc. The drawing of the caricature is described in section 29 : "*Illi
vero ostenderunt ei staturam Alexandri depictam in membrana. Videns
autem illam Darius despexit eam propter parvitatem forme eius et statim
direxit ei pilam ludricam,*" etc. (Cp. *Historia de Preliis*, ed. O. Zingerle,
Breslau—1885.)

weak person," and adding without comment "Icelandic, *amlóði*." The difficulty of deriving the Middle English form from the Scandinavian is probably answerable for the omission of the word from Middle English lexicons, as well as from that great survey of English speech, the New English Dictionary. The phonological aspects of the word must first be considered. It is difficult to determine whether the letter "ʒ" (= gh) in "amlaʒe" was of any phonetic or etymological value. The poem in which the word occurs belongs to a Northern district, and was composed at so late a period that it may safely be assumed that in most cases the symbol, even when of etymological significance, was unsounded in pronunciation.[1] Still we may safely assume that in this rare word the symbol gives some clue as to origin,—no mere scribal mannerism. It may be that the final syllable of "Amlaʒe" represents a confluence with the ending -laʒe, due to the influence of the common word "out-laʒe," outlaw—an attempt to Anglicize some Gaelic vocable with an approximate sound in the

---

[1] "The Wars of Alexander" is probably half a century later than "Gawayne and the Grene Knight," "Cleanness," "Patience," and "Pearl." These latter poems (more especially the first and last, owing to their rhymes) clearly demonstrate the non-phonetic value of the symbol in such words as *might*, *light*; hence such spellings as *sorquidryʒhe*, *fayryʒe*, and such forms as ʒolʒe (= ʒolwe) by false analogy with the correct Middle English *sorʒe* (= *sorwe*).

The writer of "The Wars of Alexander" belonged, in all probability, to a more northerly district than the Gawayne-poet, whose disciple he seems to have been, if we may judge from vocabulary and characteristics of style.

second syllable. At all events, if the word should prove to be, as it seems, identical with the Scandinavian "amlóði," it can only be accounted for by derivation from the Celtic form "amlaidhe." In later Irish and Gaelic the endings -dh(e), -bh(e), -gh(e) were not sounded, though scribes continued to write them, too often erroneously. Hence it results that if the Middle English *Amlaʒe* may be traced to *Amlaidhe*, and so equate with Old Norse *amlóði*, it may similarly also equate with *Amlaibh*, *i.e.* Old Norse *Anleifr* (*Olaf*).

It would appear that the linguistic problems of "*Amlaʒe*" illustrate in an interesting manner the literary problems, already discussed, of the fusion of the legendary myth of "Amlóði" with the legendary history of Anlaf Curan. From a philological point of view, the modern Gaelic name "MacAulay" may be equivalent to "Hamlet's son," or "Olaf's son."[1]

----

[1] See footnote, *Hamlet in Iceland*, p. lx.

IV

From the investigations summarized in an earlier section of the essay, it seems at least probable that the Hamlet story, as known to the Icelander Snæbjörn, was fundamentally identical with the groundwork of the story subsequently elaborated by Saxo Grammaticus. The assumption may perhaps be hazarded that, in some form or other, the legend lived on among the myth-loving Icelanders throughout the Middle Ages independently of the more distinguished literary form impressed upon it by the genius of the Danish historian. A noteworthy passage in a later Danish history, " Series Regum Daniæ," compiled by the learned Icelander Torfæus, who flourished in the seventeenth century, may perhaps have had reference to some such " old wives' tale," containing elements derived from pre-Saxo times. "As regards Saxo's Amlethus," observes Torfæus, "as a boy at home in Iceland I frequently heard the story of *Amlode* told by wretched old crones, but I regarded it as merely an old wives' tale ; later on, however, when I came across Saxo's noble account of the hero, I abandoned my boyish notion, and thenceforth left my friends no peace, but worried them to find out for me the old story I had once heard ; yet without success. At last, a few years ago, they sent me a story of Amlode, but no

sooner had I perused it than I cast it aside, as altogether
worthless and quite modern. It actually makes Hamlet not
a Dane but a Spaniard ! It must have been composed after
the time of the Scythian Tamberlaine, for some of the details
are certainly derived from his history." [1]

The book sent to Torfæus was clearly not the story he
had heard in his youth ; yet the worthless volume may well
have merited more serious attention on the part of the
historian. In spite of the borrowings from Tamberlaine's
history, and the general romanticizing of the Northern story,
some of the closest elements might still have been preserved
therein. The manuscript sent to Torfæus is extant among
the MSS. at Copenhagen.[2] It is substantially identical with
the "Ambales Saga" issued in the present volume.

Other antiquaries followed up the efforts of Torfæus to
discover an older Icelandic Hamlet Saga. The great name

[1] "Ad Saxonis Amlethum quod attinet, ego in patria puer a vetulis
anibusque et ejusdem furfuris homuncionibus Amlodii historiam narra-
tam audivi, inque tenerrima illa aetate pro fabula tantum aestimavi.
Verum postquam adultior, suada Saxonis expositam amplificatamque
conspexi, conceptam prius persuasionem ut puerilem antiquavi. Exinde
amicorum quosvis sollicitare non destiti ut illam historiam ubique
quaererent, qui se nihil profecisse scriptis, ad me literis crebro questi
sunt. Tandem ante aliquot annos eam nactus, lectione omnino indig-
nam deprehendi, anilem quippe nec tressis fabulam, nuperque confictam ; *quae Amlodium istum non Danum sed Hispanum fuisse suggerit.*
Fabulam post Tamerlanis seu Tamercutli tempora confictam esse ex eo
liquet, quod ex ejus gestis aliquid ibi assutum compareat" (*Series Regum
Daniæ*, lib. III. cap. vii) ; Torfæus was born in 1636.

[2] Cp. *Hamlet in Iceland*; Summary of Manuscripts, Appendix XV. 14.

of Arni Magnusson must be mentioned in this connection. He commissioned one Jón Thorlaksson (known as "the Saga spoiler") to send him any such saga he might come across. Demand called forth supply ; and Arni, some time in 1705, received a copy of a professedly ancient story of Amlode; he was not, however, deceived by Jón's professions. The manuscript in question is preserved among Arni's collections, enriched with the following note : " *Me, nimirum decipere voluit vir bonus, et persuadere se rem vetustatam mihi mittere. Sed non ego credulus illi.* "[1]

By this time Arni had got together several manuscripts of the more interesting Saga, a version of which Torfæus had previously received from his friends in Iceland ; his collection included, too, a long ballad-cycle on the same theme, a rhyming version of the fictitious saga.

During the last two hundred years the " Ambales Saga " has excited the curiosity of many students of the Hamlet story, and it has seemed desirable that it should at length be rendered accessible.[2]

[1] Cp. *ibid.* 16 ; *Hamlet in Iceland*, Appendix VII. Vedel's Danish translation of Saxo's History (1575) had clearly been used by the ancient sagaman !

[2] Dr. Ward (*Cat. MS. Romances*, Brit. Mus. 1883) was, I think, the first of modern scholars to summarize the contents of the Saga. Soon after, the present writer began collecting information on the Saga and Rimur. A short account of his results was read before the New Shakespeare Society in 1889 (*vide Transactions N. Shak. Soc.*). Meanwhile a small printed chap-book *Sagan af Ambalis Kongi*, appeared at Reykjavik (" hjá Einari Þorðarsyni," 1886), evidently a normalized text of a poor modern manuscript. Recently Dr. Detter (*Zeitschrift für*

There can be no question that in its present form the Saga is a modern production, belonging to the sixteenth or perhaps early seventeenth century. The value of the text depends mainly on the possibility that, more especially in the earlier chapters, there may still be found elements belonging to the pre-Saxo Hamlet legend. That the bulk of the Saga is drawn from the Danish history, remodelled under the influence of popular folk-tales, Charlemagne and Arthurian romances, and the stories of Tamberlaine, cannot for a moment be doubted. The name "Ambales," evidently evolved from "Amblethus," a late variant of "Amlethus," points to some such epitome of Saxo as that attributed to the monk Gheysmer. This epitome, probably composed about the middle of the fourteenth century,[1] was soon translated into Low German, and in this form appeared in print as early as 1485, a quarter of a century before the same honour was accorded to Saxo's Latin original. This Low German version may well have been in the hands of the Icelandic writer of *Ambales*. The book is now so scarce that

---

Deutsches Alterthum, 1892), gave an account of the Saga, based on Dr. Otto Jiriczek's researches, which were subsequently (1896) published in the *Weinhold Festschrift* of the *Germanistische Abhandlungen* (Breslau)— a valuable summary of the contents of the Arni-Magnæan MSS., with references to the more important differences. It is strange that both Dr. Detter and Dr. Jiriczek were unaware of the published articles of English scholars on the subject.

[1] *Cp.* Velschow's Saxo Grammaticus : *notæ uberiores.* Gheysmer was the scribe, and not the author, according to this view.

probably no copy is to be found in England ; and Schmeller, the bibliographer of Low German literature, makes the same statement with reference to the libraries of Germany. A careful transcript of the illustrative chapters from one of the Copenhagen copies of the book, will be found among the Appendices, accompanied by the Latin of Gheysmer's epitome.

Of the *Ambales Saga* there are many manuscripts, though the oldest cannot be assigned to an earlier date than the seventeenth century. In all probability none of the extant copies represent the original form of the Saga. The versions may be broadly divided into two classes, according to their nearness to the Arni-Magnæan MSS. 521*a* and 521*c* respectively. There are minute and unimportant differences in style, vocabulary, names, incidents, divisions of the chapters. The second of the two classes seems to preserve the better version. The Saga in *Hamlet in Iceland*, printed without normalization from a more modern manuscript, belongs substantially to this class.[1]

[1] Cp. *Hamlet in Iceland*, Appendices VI. and XV. The specimens in Appendix VI. illustrate the sort of differences to be found in the MSS. I have not deemed it necessary to give lists of various readings. The following may be noted :—Page 1, line 11, "Selina, etc.," so *c* (*i.e.* A.M. 521*c*), not in *a* (*i.e.* A.M. 521*a*); Holmsetuland (1, 14), *a* Smaland ; Sigurdur (4, 45), *a* Sigvarŏr ; *a* Artabani (14, 22), *c* Arthibanis ; Mordia (18, 40), *a* Mandia, *c* Mondia ; Victor (22, 24), *c* Vygþor ; Roso (26, 54), *a c* Rasi ; Anga (54, 2), *a* Angany ; Dyla (56, 5), *c* Tyla ; Vallanus (56, 9), *a c* Valianus ; Fyris (64, 7), *a c* Tyrus ; [(?) *read* Leta] Ceta (72, 3), *a c* Leta ; Batellus (84, 68), *a* Batthas. *c* Batar ; Karon (86, 86), *a c* Garon ; Actamund (86, 87), *a c* Artamund ; Silla

It is hardly necessary to calculate the many divergences in the *Ambales Saga* as compared with Saxo's Amlethus story. The main question is this : Is there any incident in the Saga which may be referred to the older independent version of the story current in Iceland ? One such incident is certainly noteworthy. The most striking divergence from Saxo's account is the statement that Ambales had an elder brother who was killed by the slayer of his father because he showed unfeigned resentment, while Ambales saved his life by concealing his feelings under the guise of heartless folly. Saxo says nothing of an elder brother. Now, this

---

(102, 2), *a c* Salla ; Barastatis edur Bastianus (148, 8), *a* Bastianus, *c* Bajasetes eður Bastianus ; Tambis (158, 3), *c* Cambis, Cambris.

Perhaps the most important difference between the two recensions is the verse p. 110, 38–40, which is not found in *a ; c* reads as follows :—

> "mann sá-eg stunginn mitt undir kerru
> mann eg það ekki,
> sá hjélt svínum við sælkjöri
> sá-eg þá hrekki."

i.e. "I saw a man stuck under a car ; I remember it not. Swine did he tend with dainty morsels ; I saw the trick." This is a better version than the corrupt text of the lines in my own MS.: "hét" is evidently an error for "hé[l]t."

As regards Ambales' nickname of "Amloði," there is, I think, good reason for inferring that this passage was not in the earliest form of the Saga, but was added later to account for the likeness of "Ambales" to the proverbial "Amloði" ; *a*, while substantially agreeing with the statement on p. 12, ll. 98–103, adds the following words: "lá jafnan í eldaskála við öskudyngju ok kom sier allilla, var hans nafni umbreytt ok var Amloði kallaðr," *i.e.* "he always kept in the firestead among the ash-heaps, and was surly ; so they changed his name from Ambales to Amloði."

very point differentiates the various versions of the Brutus story. According to some historians, Tarquin had put to death the father of Brutus as well as his elder brother; other historians (notably Livy) refer only to the brother's murder. "Amlethus" has but to avenge his father's death; the early history of "Ambales" more closely resembles that of Brutus, in that he narrowly escapes an elder brother's fate. The resemblance can hardly be accidental; furthermore, this detail must needs be independent of Saxo's version. It does not, however, necessarily follow that we have here an element derived from a version of the Hamlet story earlier than Saxo's. Comparative mythologists existed before the nineteenth century, and it would not be surprising to find that scholars of the sixteenth century had recognized the debt Saxo's Danish Amlethus owed to the Roman Brutus. Indeed, I have recently found proof of this in certain pseudo-annals of Iceland preserved in manuscripts at the British Museum and in Denmark. The annalist gives, under "anno mundi 3430," a somewhat full account of Tarquinius Superbus, together with the story of Lucrece. The next entry is a brief reference to Odin's reign in Denmark; a short note on Cincinnatus follows; then it is stated that Orvendil was king of Denmark; Plato's fame is recorded in a couple of lines; and then follows an epitome of the story of Hamlet, unmistakably drawn from Saxo. One can see at a glance that the four brief entries dividing the paragraphs dealing with Tar-

quinius Superbus and Hamlet are but annalistic padding, and that Hamlet has stepped into the place of Brutus; the Icelandic annalist recognized the identity of the two stories, and naturally preferred the Northern to the Roman hero.[1]

This evidence that scholars two or three hundred years ago definitely regarded Hamlet and Brutus as twin-brothers, does not absolutely negative the possibility that the author of the *Ambales Saga* engrafted upon his romanticizing of Saxo certain elements of a current folk-tale of Amlode derived in far-off pre-Saxo days from Roman legend. The Icelandic form of Hamlet's name, "Amloði," is perhaps the best evidence we possess that some story of the hero was once on the lips of the people, though by the sixteenth century, if not sooner, the name had degenerated into a mere nickname for "an imbecile weak person, one of weak bodily frame, wanting in strength or briskness, unable to do his work, not up to the mark."[2]   According to the

---

[1] Cp. *Hamlet in Iceland*, App. XII. and XV*d*. Finn Magnusson must have known the fictitious character of these Annals. The Odda Annals are older than 1580, but yet of the sixteenth century. Torfæus (*Series*, p. 121) quotes Björn of Skarðsa about these Annals, but he never saw them. All the Icelandic Annals seem to go back 'o a common source, perhaps Annals of the thirteenth century. Sœmund the Wise may have written or copied annals. See *Annales regii*, A.D. 1047: "Svá segir Sœmundr prestr hinn fródi." (*Cp.* Gustav Storm, *Islandske Annales.*)

[2] *Cp.* Cleasby-Vigfusson, *sub voce*; amlóðaligr, *imbecile*; amlóða-skapr, *imbecility*; amlóðast, *to behave as an amloði*. Torfæus (*Series Reg. Dan.* p. 302) quotes from an old Swedish rhyme " *rett som han vore en amblode,*" *i.e.* "he behaved as if he were a Hamlet." *Cp.* Norwegian *amlod*, subs.; *amloda, amloa*, verb.

Saga, Ambales is called "Amlode," because of his strange
unlikeness to ordinary beings. One wonders whether many
of the old hearers or readers of his story recognized the
identity of the two names, and understood the evolution
of the name of Amlode's mother, "Amba." "Call him
after thy name, for he shall resemble thee and his mother's
kin," bade the Norn before she departed ; and the queen
names him "Ambales." "But the king and the courtiers
call him 'Amlode.' " It would indeed be remarkable if,
together with the nickname, the traditional associations of
the word, handed down from distant ages, did not find a
place in the *Ambales Saga*, and so, in spite of its fictitious
character, the Saga may well preserve some noteworthy traits
of the ancient story, lost in Saxo's more stately history.

The Icelandic folk-tale of *Brjám*, though first written
down from oral tradition in 1705, is certainly nothing but
a levelling down of the story of "Hamlet," cleverly blended
with another folk-tale of the "Clever Hans" type. The
interest attaching to *Brjám* is mainly due to the fact
that it substantially agrees with the *Ambales Saga* where
the Saga diverges from Saxo. So clearly is this the case,
that one must conclude that the folk-tale has been evolved
from the Saga, or it must be taken as evidence that the
Sagaman availed himself of some popular tale of Amlode
for certain striking elements of his romantic transformation
of Saxo's story, and furthermore, that this popular tale is
preserved in the story of *Brjám*. There are no definite

criteria to determine the point, but the impression given
by the romance of *Ambales*, and general considerations
of literary methods, tend to support that view that the
old heroic myth of " Amloði " had been reduced to the
humbler condition of a folk-tale before the composition
of the *Ambales Saga*. It is easy, moreover, to understand
why the hero of the folk-tale, as we have it, is not named
" Amlode," but " Brjám." " Amlode " had already ceased
to be used as a mere personal name ; the story is therefore
told of an " amlode " whose name was Brjám.[1] Possibly
the latter name is not without significance in connection
with previous observations tending to associate the development of the Hamlet story with the critical period of the
Norsemen's occupation of Ireland. " Brjám " is the Icelandic form of the Irish " Brian " ; and the very occurrence
of the name in Iceland is evidence of the close relationship
of Norsemen and Irish in early times. In view of what
has been said concerning " Hamlet " and *The Wars of
the Gaedhil with the Gaill*, it is at least a strange chance
(if not something more) that the name of the hero in the
folk-tale should be identical with that of the mighty hero
of the decisive battle of Clontarf (1014), the closing scene
in the long struggle between the Irish and Norsemen. The
noble history of Ireland's King Alfred, the famous Brian

[1] Maurer and Detter call attention to the modern Icelandic "brjáni,"
an idiot ; Detter, ingeniously but not convincingly, suggests that perhaps
this was the original name of the hero of the tale, and that only later
was the Irish name assigned to him. *Cp.* Cleasby, subs. *brjá*, etc.

Borumha,[1] inspired alike Irish chronicler and Icelandic sagaman. In dealing with the events of his reign, it must be borne in mind that the hostile Norsemen were intimately connected with their Irish foes ; the wife of Sitric, Anlaf Curan's son, was Brian's daughter ; Brian's wife was Sitric's mother, the notorious Queen " Gormflaith of the Three Leaps." Oral tradition certainly confused at times the achievements of the two sides. An interesting instance has already been referred to ; in the story of Havelok Curan, as well as in that portion of Saxo's account of " Hamlet " seemingly derived from the legendary history of Curan, it is told how the wounded men tied to stakes retrieved the fortunes of their party. This device, according to Irish annals, was the crowning act of heroism on the part of Brian's brave Dalcassian soldiers. Of this deed sang Moore in his famous war-song :—

> " Remember the glories of Brian the brave,
> Though the days of the hero are o'er ;
>
> .   .   .   .   .
>
> Forget not our wounded companions, who stood
> In the day of distress by our side ;
> While the moss of the valley grew red with their blood,
> They stirr'd not, but conquer'd and died."

It is indeed a noteworthy coincidence that the name of " Brjám " should take the place of " Amlode " in the Icelandic folk-tale, which without further comment herewith follows.

---

[1] *Cp.* Joyce, *History of Ireland;* Todd, *The Wars of the Gaedhil;* etc.

THE STORY OF BRJÁM [1]

I

ONCE upon a time there lived a king and queen who ruled their realm. They were rich and wealthy, and scarcely knew the number of their precious possessions. They had one daughter ; she was brought up as most other story-children. For a time nothing befell there, in the way of tales or tidings, noisings or news, unless one were to tell a lying tale.

Now in Wall-nook dwelt an old man and his wife. They had three sons.[2] One cow supported the whole family. This cow was so good that she gave milk three times a day, and at noon she came by herself home from the pasture.

Once the king went a-hunting with his men, and passed by the herds belonging to him ; the old man's cow was

[1] There are two variant versions of the story, one found in Arnason's collection (cp. *Hamlet in Iceland*, Appendix VIII.), the other in Maurer's *Isl. Volkss. der Gegenwart*. The latter is the better version in certain important respects ; it gives "three sons" instead of "seven," and makes Brjám the youngest and not the eldest son. The translation is based on Arnason's text (cp. Magnusson and Powell's *Icelandic Legends*), modified where necessary by Maurer's epitomized version ; the chief changes are noted. I have divided the story into three divisions : the first and third show clearly their derivation from the Hamlet-tale ; the second, while it contains the riddling element suggested in the original tale, was evidently derived from a folk-tale of the "Clever Hans" type. A noteworthy feature of this section is the potency of the fool's words ; they are not only oracular but also magical.

[2] Arnason, "seven sons."

there near the herds.   The king said : " What a fine cow have I there ! "

" Nay, sir," said his men, " that cow is not yours ; it belongs to the old man in the cottage yonder."

The king answered : " It shall be mine."

And so the king rode home ; and when he had sat down to drink, he recalled the cow, and resolved to send his men to the carl asking him to exchange it for another.   The queen prayed him not to do this, as the poor folks had nothing but the cow for their support.   The king, however, would not listen, and sent three men to bargain with the carl.   He and his children were out in the fields when the messengers came.   They told him the king's message, that he wished to take his cow in exchange for another.

The carl answered : " The king's cow is not dearer to me than mine is."

They pressed him, but he would not give way, and at last the king's men killed him.   Then the children set up a wail, all but the youngest,[1] whose name was Brjám.   The messengers asked the children where they felt the greatest pain.   They struck their breasts, but Brjám slapped his buttocks and grinned.[2]   Then the king's men killed the two children who had slapped their breasts, but said there was nothing lost by letting Brjám live, for he was a witless fool.   The king's men then went home, and took with them the cow.   But Brjám went in to his mother, and told her all that had befallen, and her grief and sorrow were great.   He bade her not weep, for they gained little thereby ; he would do what he could.

---

[1] Arnason, " the eldest son."   [2] Cp. *Hamlet in Iceland*, pp. 80–81.

II

Once it so happened that the king was having a bower made for his daughter, and had given to the builder enough gold to gild it both within and without. Brjám came to the place, behaving like a fool, as was his wont.

The king's men said to him : "What good word have you for this, Brjám ?"

He answered : "Lessen measure much, my men !" and went away.

But the gold that had been given them wherewith to gild the bower shrunk so much that it was only enough for half the building. They went and told the king ; he thought they had stolen the gold, and had them all hanged.

Brjám went home and told his mother. She answered : "You should not have said it, my son."

He asked : "What should I have said, mother ?"

She replied : "You should have said, 'Grow three-thirds !'"

"I shall say it to-morrow, mother," quoth Brjám.

Next morning he met some people carrying a body to the grave. They asked him : "What good word have you for this, Brjám ?"

"Grow three-thirds, my men !" he said. Then the corpse grew so heavy that the carriers let it fall to the ground. Brjám went home and told his mother.

She said : "You should not have said that, my son."

He asked : "What should I then have said, mother ?"

"'God grant peace to thy soul, thou dead !' you should have said," replied his mother.

"I shall say it to-morrow, mother," answered he.

Next morning he went to the palace of the king and saw a barber strangling a dog.[1] He went up to him, and the barber said : "What good word have you for this, Brjám ?"

He answered : "God grant peace to thy soul, thou dead ! "

At this the barber laughed, but Brjám ran off to his mother, and told her what had happened.

She said : "You should not have said that."

"What should I then have said ?" he asked her.

She answered : "You should have said, 'Why ! is it the king's thievish cur you are handling there ?' "

"I will say it to-morrow, mother," quoth he.

He went to the palace next morning, and it so happened that the king's men were driving the queen round the city. Brjám stepped up to them. "What good word have you for this, Brjám ?" said they.

"Why ! is it the king's thievish cur you are handling there, my men ?" said he.

They cursed him. The queen bade them desist, nor do the boy any harm. He ran home to his mother and told her.

She said : "You should not have said it, my son."

"What should I then have said ?" asked he.

She answered : "You should have said, 'Is it the glorious life most precious to the king which you have charge of now, my men ?' "

"I shall say it to-morrow, my mother," answered the son.

Next morning he went toward the palace and found two

---

[1] Maurer, "hangman hanging a thief."

of the king's men flaying a mare. He walked to them and said : " Why ! is it the glorious life most precious to the king which you have charge of now, my men ? "

They hooted at him, and he ran off to his mother and told her all. She said : " Do not go thither any more ; some day or other they will kill you."

" Nay, my mother, they will not kill me," said he.

III

Once the king had ordered his men to go out a-fishing. They were getting ready to go in two large boats. Brjám came to them and asked them to let him go with them ; but they drove him away and mocked at him. They asked him, however, " What will the weather be like to-day ? " He looked now up at the sky, and now down to the ground, and said : " Wind and not windy, wind and not windy, wind and not windy ! "[1] They laughed at him. They rowed out to the fishing-bank, and loaded both boats with fish ; but when they turned to row ashore a storm arose, and both boats were lost.

Now nothing of note happened, till once on a time the king bade all his friends and favoured comrades to a grand banquet. Brjám asked his mother to give him leave to go to the palace that he might see how tbe banquet went off. When all had taken their places at the richly furnished tables, Brjám went to the smithy, and began shaping small pieces of wood with his knife. Those who saw him at work asked him what he meant thereby. He answered :

[1] Maurer, "vindi og ei vindi," *i.e.* " windy and not windy " with perhaps a play on " ei," *not*, and " æ," *aye*.

" Avenge father, not avenge father." [1]   They said : "You don't look unlike it," and so went away.   He drove sharp spits of steel into the ends of his pieces of wood, and then stole into the guest room, and nailed quietly to the floor the clothes of all who sat at table, and then walked off. When the guests attempted to get up from their seats in the evening, they found themselves fixed to the benches ; and they charged each other with having done this ; and at last it came to blows, and one killed the other, till none were left alive.

When the queen heard this she was sorely grieved, and she bade them bury the dead.   That morning Brjám came back to the palace, and offered himself as the queen's servant.   She was glad to get him, for she had but few servants left.   Brjám discharged his duty well, and at last married the king's daughter, and became king in that realm, and laid aside all his hare-brained folly.   Thus ends this story." [2]

[1] Maurer's version, " Hefna papa, hefna papa," *i.e.* " To avenge father, to avenge father."   The various versions of the *Ambales Saga* give the ambiguous version with the negative (cp. *Hamlet in Iceland*, p. 82) ; A.M. 521 *a*, *b*, " hann kvaðst til föðurhefnda ætla og ekki hafa " : A.M. 521 *c*, " en hann kvað til föðurhefnda, að hefna þá og ekki hefna þá."   The printed text reads "pa" for " þa," which corroborates a suggestion already made by Dr. Jiriczek (*Germanistische Abhandlungen*, 1896, xii. Heft).

[2] While Brjám represents a levelling down of the Hamlet-tale, a brief reference must be made to *Hrolfssaga Kraka* (Fornaldar Sögur, ed. Rafn, 1829, vol. i.) for parallels to the main elements of Saxo's Amlethus story.   Helgi and Hroar, the heroes of the saga, have many points in common with Hamlet, so far as motive for vengeance and method of vengeance are concerned.   Dr. Detter, in the article already referred to, attempts to work out the direct influence of the Hamlet

saga on the saga as represented by the late version preserved in *Fornaldar Sögur*, and by the fragmentary verses of the *Helgakviða.* Mr. Elton seems to me to have summed up the case excellently (*cp.* Appendix to *Saxo Grammaticus*) :—"The comparison only establishes that Saxo's tale of Amleth is parallel in its three chief elements to an Icelandic saga, which concerns a historical king, Hrolf Kraki, included by Saxo in his Danish list, but represented by him as living at a period long before Amleth."

Mr. Vigfusson's note on *Hrolf Kraki's Saga* (v. *Prolegomena* to *Sturlunga Saga*), runs as follows :—"Only seventeenth-century paper copies of one vellum. Whether corruption is due to transcribers or is earlier we know not. There is a part of Biarkamal paraphrased in it (with a little better treatment than Helgi's Lays received from the Volsung composer), and it contains traditions such as must have existed in the lost part of Skiöldunga, whence indeed it may have been taken. False stuffings and fictitious episodes."

As regards the ground elements of his saga, attested by the Helgi Lay, Dr. Detter ingeniously points out that Hamal's words, "you thought you had harboured a sheep (einen Hammel), but it was a grey wolf," recall Cicero's (*De Divinatione*, i. 22) citation of a fragment of Accius to the effect that Tarquin dreamed he led two rams to the altar, and while he slew one the other struck him down from behind. The augur warned him to beware of him who pretended to be as simple as a sheep (*hebetem æque ac pecus*), but who had a wise heart in his breast. The parallel is striking in view of the undoubted influence of Roman legend on the Hamlet story.

V

"Margr prísar sumarið fyrir fagran fugla-söng ;
   En eg hæli vetrinum því nóttin er löng."

*"Many love the summer, for the fair birds' song ;
   But I like the winter best, for the nights are long."* [1]

As early as the thirteenth century the great Sagas of
Iceland were already becoming " unread classics," and were
giving place in popular estimation to " Spurious Sagas "
(*Skrök Sögur*) and " Fictitious Sagas " (*Riddara Sögur*) ; the
former based, however slightly, on Icelandic tradition, the
latter founded directly on the Romances of Chivalry, or,
at all events, indebted for much of their machinery to the
mediæval Romance Cycles.   From the French Metrical
Romances the idea was probably taken of casting the Sagas,
the Old Sagas as well as the later Spurious and Fictitious
Sagas, into metrical form—*rímur*, as they were called, or
" ballad-cycles," though the varied forms of versification
employed in these rhyming romances were derived from
mediæval Latin verse of the " Golias " type, and not from
Romance metres.[2]   A " ballad-cycle " (*rímur*) represents

[1] *Prolegomena* to *Sturlunga Saga*, p. clix.
[2] On the metres of the *rímur*, *cp.* Wisén's *Riddara-rímur* ;
Brægfræði, by Helgi Sigurdson, etc.   The oldest *rímur* date probably

80

the versifying of the successive chapters of a Saga, each ballad of the cycle corresponding roughly to a chapter of the prose original, and giving an opportunity for pause to minstrel and to audience, much like a scene in a drama. Any number of ballads (*ríma*) go to the making of one cycle, and the whole work may extend to almost any length. The number of sections more commonly found is some five-and-twenty, and the average length about seven thousand lines. The long winter nights were passed in listening to the story unravelled in the successive ballads, the wandering *rímur*-chanter meanwhile being the welcome guest of the household, more especially of the women-folk, whose praise was sure to find some place in many a prelude of the *rímur*.

The diction of these romances exhibits the influence of Mediæval Court Poetry at its worst. Conventional periphrases, too often beyond the comprehension of the simple hearers, and therefore perhaps all the more welcome, constitute the chief apparelling of the verse. Yet despite these "shreds and patches," the *rímur* are of interest to the student from many standpoints. The very shreds and patches recall regal splendour long gone by. Even the most modern of *rímur* link themselves, by their phraseology, to the elaborate mythology of Northern paganism ; by their mastery of alliterative effect, to the characteristic system of

---

from about the middle of the fourteenth century, *Olafs Ríma* in the Flatey-Book being the earliest specimen preserved.

Teutonic versification ; by many of their quaint devices, to
the oldest extant remains of Northern poetry. The *rimur-*
writers of the nineteenth century play with runes much
in the same way as the eighth-century Anglo-Saxon poet,
Cynewulf. By runic signatures, acrostic-wise, they attest
their authorship ; by means of the same archaic symbols
they tell us many autobiographical facts—the name of their
patrons, their homesteads, and important data in their
life-history.

This personal note is often the main, if not the only
charm of these special versified Sagas ; it is to be heard for
the most part in that portion of the ballads which gives
the poet the chance of indulging his fancy, to wit, in the
lyrical prologue at the beginning of each *rima.*[1] To judge
from its name, *mansöngr,* this prelude was originally a love-
song, addressed to the poet's lady-love ; but although,
according to the practice of the *rimur*-poets, the *mansöngr*
often deals with the writer's love troubles, its scope is by
no means limited thereto. The theme may be as varied
as the poet's own life, or the troubles which beset the
poetic career, or the vicissitudes of life in general. The
prevailing tone is elegiac. The poet is young and crossed
in love ; or, ageing, harks back to the distant days when
he knew himself the cynosure of maidens' eyes. " The

---

[1] *Cp.* Dr. Kölbing's *Beiträge zur Vergleichenden Geschichte der
Romantischen Poesie u. Prosa des Mittelalters* ; Möbius, *Vom isländischen
Mansöngr," Ztschr. für d. phil. Ergänzungsbd.,* p. 42 ff., etc.

Ageing Poet" might be the title of many of the preludes. Again, the poet of the *mansöngr* often replies to the "aspersions" of carping critics, to his own foes, or to those who hate all poets; he gives utterance to a long-drawn wail on the low estate of poetry contrasted with its former glory. The "Tears of the Muses" might be a fitting title for a collection of these preludes. "Poetic Art" might summarize another division, where the writer tells the difficulties of his task, dwells upon the failure of poetic aspiration, and describes the toilsome ordeal of becoming a poet; he invokes to his aid all the benign powers of Eddaic song-craft. The "Biographical *Mansöngr*" gives a summary of the poet's life-song; epitomizes his literary achievements; links itself more particularly to the circumstances of the special work in hand; or deals with some fateful event in the poet's career—some weird episode calculated to call forth new interest in the personality of the writer.

There can be little doubt that these "autobiographical notes" must too often be regarded as mere conventions—the necessary items in a properly composed *rimur*; yet occasionally, though rarely, we have evidence to show that some of the most remarkable personal allusions, though seemingly conventional adjuncts, were based on actual fact, or well-authenticated family history.

These general considerations of the characteristic features of *rimur* will prepare the reader for the statement that the

Ambales Saga went through the process of being be-rhymed; no less than four ballad-cycles exist, dating from the seventeenth century, if not earlier, onward.[1]

---

[1] A detailed account of four ballad-cycles is given in *Hamlet in Iceland*, Introduction, pp. lxxix–xcvi, and pp. 195–241; also a Summary of MSS. c. 18, and Appendix II.; Páll lived from *c.* 1600–*c.* 1670. A short riddle by Páll is printed in Arnason, *Islenskar Gátur*, Copenhagen, 1887, No. 1194 (*q. v.*).

VI

Saxo's story of Amlethus reached England through the medium of Belleforest's *Histoires Tragiques*, which, in its turn, probably after the publication of the Second Quarto of *Hamlet*, was rendered into English, *The Historie of Hamblet*, preserved in the unique copy now again reprinted. It is not my purpose in this volume to discuss at length the sources of the English play, and its relationship to Saxo's story. I may, however, quote in conclusion what I have said elsewhere on this subject. In the story as in the play we have the murder of the father by a jealous uncle; the mother's incestuous marriage with the murderer; the son's feigned madness in order to execute revenge: there are the vague originals of Ophelia and Polonius; the meeting of mother and son; the voyage to England: all these familiar elements are found in the old tale. But the ghost, the play-scene, and the culmination of the play in the death of the hero as well as of the objects of his revenge, these are elements which belong essentially to the Elizabethan Drama of vengeance. It is of course unnecessary to dwell on the subtler distinction between the easily understood Amleth and the " eternal problem " of Hamlet.

Taine has said that the Elizabethan Renaissance was a

Renaissance of the Saxon genius ; from this point of view it is significant that its crowning glory should be the presentment of a typical Northern hero—an embodiment of the Northern character :

"Dark and true and tender is the North."

APPENDIX

THE AMBALES SAGA

CHAPTER I

THERE lived a king hight Donrek, and he was King of Spain, and Hispania, and Cimbria, and Cumbria, and divers other islands and realms : he was passing rich and mighty, what with his folk and a many brave retainers ; many a vassal-king and dukes and earls owed him their service and helped him nobly in his land's defence and in achieving treasure. As for him, he was the hardiest fighter, far-seeing, fierce to foes, yet kind and gentle unto friends, and wise of counsel,—great wisdom was lent him. His queen hight Selina ; they both were very aged when this saga befell. The king gat three sons by his queen ; she was daughter of Hawk, King of Holstein, after whom the king's first son was named ; the second hight Balant, after the king's father ; the third Salman, after King Donrek's foster-father. The brothers were all great warriors, and they were grown up when this saga befell.

Now when King Donrek died, the lands were parted into inheritances, and Spain fell to Hawk, Hispania to Balant, while Salman became King of Cimbria. Balant ruled Hispania till his death, and he was a hardy fighter. King Hawk held his heritage but a short while, for a heathen king slew him and usurped his realm ; he hight

Malpriant, by birth of Scythia ; the saga will tell of him
anon.   Salman was King of Cimbria, the which lieth to the
east of Valland, and was under Rome at the time ; and he
there became a fierce-tempered warrior, alike indomitable
of will as invincible in warfare, yet therewithal gentle unto
friends ; his was a righteous rule, and he was beloved of all,
the greatest and the least ; in battle he never failed of
victory.   He took to wife a noble dame, Amba by name,
daughter of the Duke of Burgundy in France.   King
Salman greatly loved his queen, and suffered her to take no
hurt, nor brooked he aught a man might do in her despite :
their wedded life was of honourable accord ; she was of
gentle mood and yielding to her lord, and therewithal of
so discerning mind that men deemed her passing wise ; all
marvelled at her and at her wisdom, and they loved her
from their hearts ; oft-times she saved the king from error.
They had not been together long when the queen bore a
man-child, fair and noble, and the child was brought afore
the king that he might give it a name ; the king let be-
sprinkle it with water in Christian baptism,—for the king
kept the faith of Christian men after the papal rite,—and
the boy was given the name of Sigurd, and therewith the
lands afore-named, save Spain, the which King Malpriant
cowed from Christianity, as has been told.

CHAPTER II

Now time passed and the queen was with child a
second time.   But there in the land of the king was a
spae-wife or wise woman, come of high descent ; she was

not of elfin-kind, but so grim withal that folk were adread
of her; and she was eke a great clerk of necromancy and of
ancient lore; she was sprung from the eastern realm
of Gardar, and had fared through northern lands, and
was held in worship of kings and noble chiefs, for she
was sought whenas queens and the wives of famous men
were a-nigh child-bearing, that she might bespeak the
children's fate and fortune, the which men deemed followed her spells mostwhiles at least; wherethrough she
grew mightily rich and very masterful.   Now when Queen
Amba bore the aforenamed son, the witch was not be-
sought to sit by her as was the wont; whereat the witch
waxed very wroth, and she enfierced her wrath by magic
spells.   And when the time was nigh the queen should
be abed, the witch betook herself to the palace of
the king, till she met the queen within her pleasaunce,
when she greeted her thus :—" Thy fortune and thy
life's delight stand now in fairest bloom, but lay this to
heart that ere long thou shalt lose all save life alone.
Thy king shall be slain in war; of his weapons none
shall strike home when he fights against his foes; thy son
too shall meet a death of shame, and so hard shall it go
with thee that death shall seem thee dearer than life;
and that son of thine thou goest with shall be of little
joy to thee, for all men shall hold him witless.   Ofttimes
have I met with honour from princes higher than ye be,
and the greatest of men and chieftains have ne'er slighted
me in anywise, much less my peers, but ye two have
done so exceedingly,—but your pride shall be brought
low."   At this foreboding of the witch the queen was
sorely troubled, and she went afore the king, and told

him of all that had passed. The king grew very wroth, called his men to him, and bade them seize the witch and let her die a wretched death, but the queen spake :— "Our bale is not thus bettered, for if the witch sees not remedy for our woes none other will avail, and more belike, if some friendliness be shown her." The king said : "Dost thou deem that from that evil sprite aught of friendship will be shown us for our son's avail ?" "I will assay it," said the queen, "and let us spread a banquet for the witch with great pomp and largess, and I would now, king, that thou go with me to her on this errand." The king made answer that the worst of sprites might to her in his stead. The queen went then from the king to seek the witch, and made her blithe of speech, though her heart was sad within. As she reached her the witch was journey-bound ; the queen said to her :—"From my want of wisdom have I done this to put dishonour on thee, and I would fain now make amends, and I offer thee our friendship, and gifts, and feasts, and all the worship we may show thee, and I would that thou bide with us here until my child be born into the world." The witch said :—"This I shall not grant, for it will be long time ere thy folly may be mended, but I shall come again when thy child-bed begins, and thou shalt then not need to seek me out." Thus they spake and the witch went her way. And when the queen knew her sickness near, the witch came again, and she was then otherwise than she was erst, in her temper to wit. The queen gave her a blithe welcoming, and the witch was wondrous tender with her, and placed her on a stately bed. The queen had a long sickness and hard, and bore at length

a man-child, the which was very big and unsightly, dark-skinned, and with bristle hair, black as coal, yet beautiful by reason of his eyes. The queen had the boy brought afore the king, but he became thereat most cross and heavy, and forthwith bade them take the child away ; he would pay the child no heed, nor give it a name, but least would he set eyes upon the witch, or have aught friendly dealing with her ; whereat the queen was sore aggrieved, and the witch was filled with grim anger ; and all men deemed the king's behaviour was unseemly herein. The witch nurtured the queen with greatest care, and brought her from her bed at the wonted time ; she tarried there thereafter for three months, and the queen bade her live there to the day of her death, or so long as she would : the witch said something else was toward. The queen sped her with rich farewell-gifts, and the witch was well content ; but the day the witch was going thence she entered the chamber where the queen abode and where the child was fostered ; the queen was holding her little son in her arms, at the breast ; the witch grew sad, for now she felt tenderly towards the queen ; fain would she bid her farewell. Said she to the queen :—
"To no one have I been angered out of all measure save to thee, and evil have I boded for thee and thine. This may not be bettered, for fate above rules, swayed by Him who is mightier than men, but 'tis meet that I should guerdon thy kindliness, and this son of thine shall profit of thy merit somewhat at least ; he shall be the honour of all his race : thou shalt name him after thine own name, for he shall favour thee and his mother's kin."
Then she kissed the queen and the boy, weeping the

while, and said :—" My mere promise will stand him in little stead." She then went her way, but the queen sat still beside the cradle of the child, rocking it to soothe the child ; she heaved a deep sigh from her troubled breast and called the boy Ambales. Now the king's sons grew up in the realm each unlike the other in all things. Sigurd was passing fair to look on, and hard-tempered so that he yielded no whit to any man, and in all skill and cunning he was most famed and foremost. Ambales was all unsightly, much bigger than his brother, would hearken unto none, nor learn aught good ; but was most stubborn with all men ; he was larger-limbed than other folk ; in all his ways he seemed to have but few his like, and the courtiers and the king called him Amlode. So time passed till the king's sons were ten and eight years old, and in these years nought befell but what is told.

HAMLET

FROM THE HISTORIA DANICA OF

SAXO GRAMMATICUS,

The Latin text from the Editio Princeps, 1514; with English
translation by PROFESSOR OLIVER ELTON, from "The First
Nine Books of the Danish History," 1894.

SAXO GRAMMATICUS

. . . HORWENDILLUS et Fengo, quorum pater Gerwendillus
Jutorum praefectus extiterat, eidem a Rorico, in Jutiae
praesidium surrogantur. At Horwendillus triennio tyran-
nide gesta, per summam rerum gloriam piraticae incubuerat:
cum Rex Norvagiae Collerus operum ejus ac famae magnitu-
dinem emulatus: decorum sibi fore existimavit si tam late
patentem Piratae fulgorem superior armis obscurare quivisset.
Cujus classem varia fretum navigatione scrutatus offendit.
Insula erat medio sita pelago quam Piratae collatis utrinque
secus navigiis obtinebant. Invitabat duces jocunda littorum
species. Hortabatur exterior locorum amoenitas interiora
nemorum verna perspicere: lustratisque saltibus secretam sylva-
rum indaginem pererrare: ubi forte Collerum Horwendil-
lumque invicem sine arbitris obvios incessus reddidit. Tunc
Horwendillus prior regem percontari nisus quo pugnae genere
decernere libeat praestantissimum affirmans quod paucissi-
morum viribus aederetur. Duellum siquidem ad capessendam

Collerus &
Horwen-
illus.

HAMLET

At this time Horwendil and Feng, whose father Gerwendil had been governor of the Jutes, were appointed in his place by Rorik to defend Jutland. But Horwendil held the monarchy for three years, and then, to win the height of glory, devoted himself to roving. Then Koll, King of Norway, in rivalry of his great deeds and renown, deemed it would be a handsome deed if by his greater strength in arms he could bedim the far-famed glory of the rover; and, cruising about the sea, he watched for Horwendil's fleet and came up with it. There was an island lying in the middle of the sea, which each of the rovers, bringing his ships up on either side, was holding. The captains were tempted by the pleasant look of the beach, and the comeliness of the shores led them to look through the interior of the spring-tide woods, to go through the glades, and roam over the sequestered forests. It was here that the advance of Koll and Horwendil brought them face to face without any witness. Then Horwendil endeavoured to address the king first, asking him in what way it was his pleasure to fight, and declaring that one best which needed the courage of

fortitudinis palmam omni certaminis genere efficacius fore:
quod propria virtute subnixum alienae manus opem excluderet.
Tam fortem juvenis sententiam ammirans Collerus: cum mihi
(inquit) pugnae delectum permiseris maxime utendum judico:
quae tumultuationis expers duorum operam capit. Sane et
audacior, et victoriae promptior aestimatur. In hoc communis
nobis sententia est: hoc ultro judicio convenimus. At
quoniam exitus in dubio manet invicem humanitati deferen-
dum est: nec adeo ingeniis indulgendum: ut extrema
negligantur officia. Odium in animis est: adsit tamen
pietas quae rigori demum opportuna succedat. Nam etsi
mentium nos discrimina separant: naturae tamen jura con-
ciliant. Horum quippe consortio jungimur, quantuscunque
animo livor dissociet. Haec itaque pietatis nobis conditio
sit: ut victum victor inferiis prosequatur. His enim suprema
humanitatis officia inesse constat: quae nemo pius obhorruit:
Utraque acies id munus rigore deposito concorditer exequa-
tur: Facessat post fatum livor, simultasque funere sopiatur.
Absit nobis tantae crudelitatis specimen: ut quanquam vivis
odium intercesserit: alter alterius cineres persequamur.
Gloriosum victori erit si victi funus magnifice duxerit.
Nam qui defuncto hosti justa persolverit superstitis sibi

as few as possible. For, said he, the duel was the surest
of all modes of combat for winning the meed of bravery,
because it relied only upon native courage, and excluded all
help from the hand of another. Koll marvelled at so
brave a judgment in a youth, and said : " Since thou hast
granted me the choice of battle, I think it is best to employ
that kind which needs only the endeavours of two, and is
free from all the tumult. Certainly it is more venturesome,
and allows of a speedier award of the victory   This thought
we share, in this opinion we agree of our own accord. But
since the issue remains doubtful, we must pay some regard
to gentle dealing, and must not give way so far to our
inclinations as to leave the last offices undone. Hatred is in
our hearts ; yet let piety be there also, which in its due time
may take the place of rigour. For the rights of nature
reconcile us, though we are parted by differences of purpose ;
they link us together, howsoever rancour estrange our spirits.
Let us, therefore, have this pious stipulation, that the conqueror shall give funeral rites to the conquered. For all
allow that these are the last duties of human kind, from
which no righteous man shrinks. Let each army lay aside
its sternness and perform this function in harmony. Let
jealousy depart at death, let the feud be buried in the tomb.
Let us not show such an example of cruelty as to persecute
one another's dust, though hatred has come between us in
our lives. It will be a boast for the victor if he has borne
his beaten foe in a lordly funeral. For the man who pays

favorem adsciscit : vivumque beneficio vincit : quisquis extincto studium humanitatis impenderit. Est et alia non minus luctuosa calamitas : quae vivos interdum damnata corporum parte contingit. Huic non segnius quam ultimae sorti succurrendum existimo. Saepe enim incolumi spiritu membrorum clades pugnantibus incidit. Quae sors omni fato tristior duci solet : quod mors omnium memoriam tollat : vivens vero proprii corporis stragem negligere nequeat. Hoc quoque malum ope excipiendum est. Conveniat igitur alterius ab altero laesionem denis auri talentis sarciri. Nam si pium est alienis calamitatibus compati : quanto magis propriis misereri ? Nemo naturae non consulit. Quam qui negligit : sui parricida est.

In haec data acceptaque fide pugnam ineunt. Neque enim eis aut metui occursus novitas, aut vernantis loci jocunditas, quo minus inter se ferro occurrerent respectui fuit. Horwendillus appetendi hostis quam muniendi corporis nimio animi calore avidior redditus, neglecta clypei cura ambas ferro manus injecerat. Nec audaciae eventus defuit. Collerum siquidem scuto crebris ictibus absumpto spoliatum desecto tandem pede exanimem occidere coegit. Quem ne

Colleri
caedes.

the rightful dues over his dead enemy wins the goodwill of
the survivor; and whoso devotes gentle dealing to him who
is no more, conquers the living by his kindness.   Also there
is another disaster, not less lamentable, which sometimes
befalls the living—the loss of some part of their body; and
I think that succour is due to this just as much as to the
worst hap that may befall.   For often those who fight keep
their lives safe, but suffer maiming; and this lot is commonly
thought more dismal than any death; for death cuts off
memory of all things, while the living cannot forget the
devastation of his own body.   Therefore this mischief also
must be helped somehow; so let it be agreed, that the injury
of either of us by the other shall be made good with ten
talents [marks] of gold.   For if it be righteous to have
compassion on the calamities of another, how much more is it
to pity one's own?   No man but obeys nature's prompting;
and he who slights it is a self-murderer."

After mutually pledging their faiths to these terms, they
began the battle.   Nor were their strangeness in meeting one
another, nor the sweetness of that spring-green spot, so heeded
as to prevent them from the fray.   Horwendil, in his too
great ardour, became keener to attack his enemy than to
defend his own body; and, heedless of his shield, had
grasped his sword with both hands; and his boldness did
not fail.   For by his rain of blows he destroyed Koll's
shield and deprived him of it, and at last hewed off his foot
and drove him lifeless to the ground.   Then, not to fail of

pacto abesset regio funere elatum magnifici operis tumulo,
ingentique exequiarum apparatu prosecutus est. Deinde
sororem ejus Selam nomine Piraticis exercitam rebus, ac
bellici peritam muneris persecutus occidit.

Horwen-
dillus rex
XIX.

Triennium fortissimis militiae operibus emensus, opima
spolia, delectamque praedam Rorico destinat, quo sibi propiorem amicitiae ejus gradum consciceret. Cujus familiaritate
fultus filiae ejus Geruthae connubium impetravit: ex qua
filium Amlethum sustulit.

Fengo XX
Fengonis
insidiae in
fratrem.

Tantae felicitatis invidia accensus Fengo: fratrem insidiis
circumvenire constituit.   Adeo ne a necessariis quidem
secura est virtus.   At ubi datus parricidio locus: cruenta
manu funestam mentis libidinem satiavit.   Trucidati quoque
fratris uxore potitus incestum parricidio adjecit.   Quisquis
enim uni se flagitio dederit: in aliud mox proclivior ruit. Ita
alterum alterius incitamentum est.   Idem atrocitatem facti
tanta calliditatis audacia texit: ut sceleris excusationem
benivolentiae simulatione componeret, parricidiumque pietatis
nomine coloraret.   Gerutham siquidem quanquam tantae man-
suetudinis esset: ut neminem vel tenui laesione commoverit:
incitatissimum tamen mariti odium expertam: salvandaeque
ejus gratia fratrem a se interfectum dicebat quod mitissimam
et sine felle foeminam gravissimum viri supercilium perpeti
indignum videretur.   Nec irrita propositi persuasio fuit.
Neque enim apud principes fides mendacio deest ubi scurris

his compact, he buried him royally, gave him a howe of lordly make and pompous obsequies. Then he pursued and slew Koll's sister Sela, who was a skilled warrior and experienced in roving.

He had now passed three years in valiant deeds of war; and, in order to win higher rank in Rorik's favour, he assigned to him the best trophies and the pick of the plunder. His friendship with Rorik enabled him to woo and win in marriage his daughter Gerutha, who bore him a son Amleth.

Such great good fortune stung Feng with jealousy, so that he resolved treacherously to waylay his brother, thus showing that goodness is not safe even from those of a man's own house. And behold, when a chance came to murder him, his bloody hand sated the deadly passion of his soul. Then he took the wife of the brother he had butchered, capping unnatural murder with incest. For whoso yields to one iniquity, speedily falls an easier victim to the next, the first being an incentive to the second. Also the man veiled the monstrosity of his deed with such hardihood of cunning, that he made up a mock pretence of goodwill to excuse his crime, and glossed over fratricide with a show of righteousness. Gerutha, said he, though so gentle that she would do no man the slightest hurt, had been visited with her husband's extremest hate; and it was all to save her that he had slain his brother; for he thought it shameful that a lady so meek and unrancorous should suffer the heavy disdain of her husband. Nor did his smooth words fail in their intent; for

interdum gratia redditur: obtrectatoribus honos. Nec dubi-
tavit Fengo: parricidales manus flagitiosis inferre complexibus: geminae impietatis noxam pari scelere prosecutus.

Amlethus
se stolidum
simulat.

Quod videns Amlethus ne prudentius agendo patruo
suspectus redderetur, stoliditatis simulationem amplexus extre-
mum mentis vitium finxit: eoque calliditatis genere, non solum
ingenium texit: verum etiam salutem defendit. Quotidie
maternum larem pleno sordium torpore complexus abjectum
humi corpus obscoeni squaloris illuvie respergebat. Turpatus
oris color: illitaque tabo facies ridiculae stoliditatis dementiam
figurabant. Quicquid voce edebat deliramentis consentaneum
erat. Quicquid opere exhibuit profundam redolebat inertiam.
Quid multa? Non virum aliquem: sed delirantis fortunae
ridendum diceres monstrum. Interdum foco assidens, favillas-
que manibus verrens: ligneos uncos creare, eosdemque igni
durare solitus erat. Quorum extrema contrariis quibusdam
hamis, quo nexuum tenaciores existerent informabat. Rogatus quid ageret: acuta se referebat in ultionem patris spicula
praeparare. Nec parvo responsum ludibrio fuit, quod ab
omnibus ridiculi operis vanitas contemneretur: quanquam ea
res proposito ejus postmodum opitulata fuerit. Quae solertia
apud altioris ingenii spectatores primam ei calliditatis sus-
pitionem injecit. Ipsa nanque exiguae artis industria,
arcanum opificis ingenium figurabat. Nec credi poterat
obtusi cordis esse: cui tam exculto manus artificio calluisset,

at courts, where fools are sometimes favoured and backbiters preferred, a lie lacks not credit. Nor did Feng keep from shameful embraces the hands that had slain a brother; pursuing with equal guilt both of his wicked and impious deeds.

Amleth beheld all this, but feared lest too shrewd a behaviour might make his uncle suspect him. So he chose to feign dulness, and pretend an utter lack of wits. This cunning course not only concealed his intelligence but ensured his safety. Every day he remained in his mother's house utterly listless and unclean, flinging himself on the ground, and bespattering his person with foul and filthy dirt. His discoloured face and visage smutched with slime devoted foolish and grotesque madness. All he said was of a piece with these follies; all he did savoured of utter lethargy. In a word, you would not have thought him a man at all, but some absurd abortion due to a mad fit of destiny. He used at times to sit over the fire, and, raking up the embers with his hands, to fashion wooden crooks, and harden them in the fire, shaping at their tips certain barbs, to make them hold more tightly to their fastenings. When asked what he was about, he said that he was preparing sharp javelins to avenge his father. This answer was not a little scoffed at, all men deriding his idle and ridiculous pursuit; but the thing helped his purpose afterwards. Now it was his craft in this matter that first awakened in the deeper observers a suspicion of his cunning. For his skill in a trifling art betokened the hidden talent of the craftsman;

denique exactissima cura praeustorum stipitum congeriem asservare solebat. Fuere ergo qui illum vegetioris ingenii asserentes sapientiam simplicitatis praetextu occulere, profundumque animi studium calliditatis commento obscurare putarent : nec aptius astum deprehendi posse quam si illi inter latebras usquam excellentis formae foemina applicaretur quae animum ejus ad amoris illecebras provocaret. Naturae siquidem tam praeceps in venerem esse ingenium : ut arte dissimulari non possit : vehementiorem quoque hunc motum fore, quam ut astu interpellari queat : ideoque si is inertiam fingeret, futurum : ut occasione suscepta voluptatis ilico viribus obtemperaret. Procurantur igitur qui juvenem in longinquas nemorum partes equo perductum eo tentamenti genere aggrederentur. Inter quos forte quidam Amlethi collacteus aderat, a cujus animo nondum sociae educationis respectus exciderat, hic praeteriti convictus memoriam praesenti imperio anteponens, Amlethum inter deputatos comites instruendi potius quam insidiandi studio prosequebatur, quod eum ultima passurum non dubitaret, si vel modicum sensati animi indicium praebuisset. Maxime vero si Veneris palam rebus uteretur. Quod ipsi quoque Amletho obscurum non fuit. Equum siquidem conscendere jussus ita se de cervice industria collocavit ut suum ipsius cervici dorsum obvertens : adversa caudam fronte spectaret. Quam frenis quoque complecti

nor could they believe the spirit dull where the hand had acquired so cunning a workmanship. Lastly, he always watched with the most punctual care over his pile of stakes that he had pointed in the fire. Some people, therefore, declared that his mind was quick enough, and fancied that he only played the simpleton in order to hide his understanding, and veiled some deep purpose under a cunning feint. His wiliness (said these) would be most readily detected, if a fair woman were put in his way in some secluded place, who should provoke his mind to the temptations of love; all men's natural temper being too blindly amorous to be artfully dissembled, and this passion being also too impetuous to be checked by cunning. Therefore, if his lethargy were feigned, he would seize the opportunity, and yield straightway to violent delights. So men were commissioned to draw the young man in his rides into a remote part of the forest, and there assail him with a temptation of this nature. Among these chanced to be a foster-brother of Amleth, who had not ceased to have regard to their common nurture; and who esteemed his present orders less than the memory of their past fellowship. He attended Amleth among his appointed train, being anxious not to entrap, but to warn him; and was persuaded that he would suffer the worst if he showed the slightest glimpse of sound reason, and above all if he did the act of love openly. This was also plain enough to Amleth himself. For when he was bidden mount his horse, he deliberately set himself in such a fashion that he turned

coepit perinde atque ea parte ruentis equi impetum modera-
turus. Qua astutiae meditatione patrui commentum illusit:
insidias expugnavit. Ridiculum satis spectaculum fuit, cum
idem habenae expers, regente caudam sessore procurreret.

Procedens Amlethus cum obvium inter arbusta lupum
habuisset: comitibus tenerioris aetatis equum occurrisse dicenti-
bus perpaucos hujusmodi in Fengonis grege militare subjunxit:
ut modesto ita faceto imprecationis genere patrui divitias
insecutus. Qui cum illo prudenti responso usum astruerent:
ipse quoque se de industria locutum asseveverabat, ne aliqua
ex parte mendacio indulgere videretur. Falsitatis enim alienus
haberi cupiens ita astutiam veriloquio permiscebat: ut nec
dictis veracitas deesset, nec acuminis modus verorum iudicio
proderetur.

Idem littus praeteriens cum comites invento periclitatae
navis gubernaculo cultrum a se eximiae granditatis repertum
dixissent: eo inquit praegrandem pernam secari convenit:
profecto mare significans, cujus immensitati gubernaculi magni-
tudo congrueret. Harenarum quoque praeteritis clivis, sabulum
perinde ac farra aspicere jussus eadem albicantibus maris

his back to the neck and faced about, fronting the tail; which he proceeded to encompass with the reins, just as if on that side he would check the horse in its furious pace. By this cunning thought he eluded the trick, and overcame the treachery of his uncle. The reinless steed galloping on, with the rider directing its tail, was ludicrous enough to behold.

Amleth went on, and a wolf crossed his path amid the thicket. When his companions told him that a young colt had met him, he retorted, that in Feng's stud there were too few of that kind fighting. This was a gentle but witty fashion of invoking a curse upon his uncle's riches. When they averred that he had given a cunning answer, he answered that he had spoken deliberately: for he was loth to be thought prone to lying about any matter, and wished to be held a stranger to falsehood; and accordingly he mingled craft and candour in such wise that, though his words did not lack truth, yet there was nothing to betoken the truth and betray how far his keenness went.

Again, as he passed along the beach, his companions found the rudder of a ship which had been wrecked, and said they had discovered a huge knife. "This," said he, "was the right thing to carve such a huge ham;" by which he really meant the sea, to whose infinitude, he thought, this enormous rudder matched. Also, as they passed the *Hamlet's Mill* sandhills, and bade him look at the meal, meaning the sand, he replied that it had been ground small by the hoary tempests

procellis permolita esse respondit. Laudato a comitibus responso : idem a se prudenter editum asseverabat. Ab hisdem, quo majorem exercendae libidinis audaciam sumeret de industria relictus, immissam a patruo foeminam perinde ac fortuitu oblatam obscuro loco obviam recepit : constuprassetque ni collactens ejus tacito consilii genere insidiarum indicium detulisset. Considerans enim quonam aptius modo occultum monitoris officium exequi, periculosamque juvenis lasciviam praecurrere posset : repertam humi paleam : oestri praetervolantis caudae submittendam curavit. Egit deinde ipsum in ea potissimum loca quibus Amlethum inesse cognovit : eoque facto maximum incauto beneficium attulit, nec callidius transmissum indicium : quam cognitum fuit. Siquidem Amlethus viso Oestro : simulque stramine quod caudae insitum gestabat : curiosius pernotato tacitum cavendae fraudis monitum intellexit. Igitur insidiarum suspitione conterritus, quo tutius voto potiretur exceptam amplexibus foeminam : ad palustre procul invium protrahit. Quam etiam peracto concubitu : ne rem cuiquam proderet : impensius obtestatus est. Pari igitur studio petitum ac promissum est silentium. Maximam enim Amletho puellae familiaritatem vetus educationis societas conciliabat : quod uterque eosdem infantiae procuratores habuerit.

Domum itaque reductus cunctis an veneri indulsisset per

of the ocean. His companions praising his answer, he said
that he had spoken it wittingly. Then they purposely left
him, that he might pluck up more courage to practise wanton-
ness. The woman whom his uncle had dispatched met him
in a dark spot, as though she had crossed him by chance ;
and he took her and would have ravished her, had not his
foster-brother, by a secret device, given him an inkling of
the trap. For this man, while pondering the fittest way to
play privily the prompter's part, and forestall the young man's
hazardous lewdness, found a straw on the ground and
fastened it underneath the tail of a gadfly that was flying
past ; which he then drove towards the particular quarter
where he knew Amleth to be : an act which served the
unwary prince exceedingly well. The token was interpreted
as shrewdly as it had been sent. For Amleth saw the gadfly,
espied with curiosity the straw which it wore embedded in its
tail, and perceived that it was a secret warning to beware of
treachery. Alarmed, scenting a trap, and fain to possess
his desire in greater safety, he caught up the woman in his
arms and dragged her off to a distant and impenetrable fen.
Moreover, when they had lain together, he conjured her
earnestly to disclose the matter to none, and the promise of
silence was accorded as heartily as it was asked. For both
of them had been under the same fostering in their childhood ;
and this early rearing in common had brought Amleth and
the girl into great intimacy.

So, when he had returned home, they all jeeringly asked

ludibrium interrogantibus : puellam a se constupratam fatetur.
Interrogatus rursum quo rem loco egerit, quove pulvino usus
fuerit : ungulae jumenti, cristaeque Galli : laquearibus quoque
tecti innixum se dixit.   Horum enim omnium particulas
vitandi mendacii gratia cum tentandus proficisceretur, con-
traxerat.   Quae vox multo circumstantium risu excepta est,
quanquam nihil rerum veritati per jocum detraxerit.   Puella
quoque ea de re interrogata : Nihil eum tale gessisse perhibuit.
Fides negationi habita est eo quidem pronius quo minus
satellites facti conscios fuisse constabat.   Tum is qui prae-
standi indicii gratia Oestrum signaverat ut salutem Amlethi
vaframenti sui beneficio constitisse monstraret nuper se
ejus unice studiosum extitisse dicebat.   Nec inepta juvenis
responsio fuit.   Ne enim indicis meritum negligere putaretur,
quiddam straminis gerulum subitis adlapsum pennis quodque
paleam posteriore corporis parte defixam gestaret sibi con-
spectum retulit.   Quod dictum est ut ceteros cachinno con-
cussit ita Amlethi fautorem prudentia delectavit.

Superatisque omnibus arcanamque juvenilis industriae seram
patefacere nequeuntibus : quidam amicorum Fengonis prae-
sumptione quam solertia abundantior fore negabat : ut inextri-
cabile calliditatis ingenium usitato insidiarum genere proderetur.
Majorem quippe ejus pervicaciam esse, quam ut levibus
experimentis attingi debeat.   Quamobrem multiplici illius

him whether he had given way to love, and he avowed that he had ravished the maid.   When he was next asked where he did it, and what had been his pillow, he said that he had rested upon the hoof of a beast of burden, upon a cockscomb, and also upon a ceiling.   For, when he was starting into temptation, he had gathered fragments of all these things, in order to avoid lying.   And though his jest did not take aught of the truth out of the story, the answer was greeted with shouts of merriment from the bystanders.   The maiden, too, when questioned on the matter, declared that he had done no such thing; and her denial was the more readily credited when it was found that the escort had not witnessed the deed.   Then he who had marked the gadfly in order to give a hint, wishing to show Amleth that to his trick he owed his salvation, observed that latterly he had been singly devoted to Amleth.   The young man's reply was apt.   Not o seem forgetful of his informant's service, he said that he nad seen a certain thing bearing a straw flit by suddenly, wearing a stalk of chaff fixed on its hinder parts.   The cleverness of this speech, which made the rest split with laughter, rejoiced the heart of Amleth's friend.

Thus all were worsted, and none could open the secret lock of the young man's wisdom.   But a friend of Feng, gifted more with assurance than judgment, declared that the unfathomable cunning of such a mind could not be detected by any vulgar plot, for the man's obstinacy was so great that it ought not to be assailed with any mild measures; there

astutiae simplicem tentationis modum afferri non oportere. Subtiliorem itaque rationis viam altiore animi sensu a se repertam dicebat: executioni non incongruam et propositae rei indagationi efficacissimam. Fengone siquidem per ingentis negotii simulationem de industria absentiam praestante solum cum matre Amlethum cubiculo claudi oportere, procurato antea viro qui ambobus insciis in obscura aedis parte consiste- ret. Quid illis colloquio foret attentius excepturus. Futurum enim ut si quid filius saperet: pud maternas aures eloqui non dubitaret, nec se genitricis fidei credere pertimesceret. Idem se explorationis ministrum cupidius offerebat, ne potius auctor consilii quam executor videretur. Delectatus sententia Fengo facta longinquae profectionis simulatione discedit. Is vero qui consilium dederat: conclave quo cum matre Amlethus recludebatur tacite petivit, submissusque stramento delituit. Nec insidiarum Amletho remedium defuit. Veritus enim ne clandestinis cujuspiam auribus exciperetur: primum ad ineptae consuetudinis ritum decurrens: obstrepentis Galli more occen- tum edidit: brachiisque pro alarum plausu concussis concenso stramento corpus crebris saltibus librare coepit: si quid illic clausum delitesceret experturus. At ubi subjectam pedibus molem persensit: ferro locum rimatus suppositum confodit, egestumque latebra trucidavit. Cujus corpus in partes con-

were many sides to his wiliness, and it ought not to be
entrapped by any one method. Accordingly, said he, his
own profounder acuteness had hit on a more delicate way,
which was well fitted to be put in practice, and would effect-
ually discover what they desired to know. Feng was
purposely to absent himself, pretending affairs of great import.
Amleth should be closeted alone with his mother in her
chamber; but a man should first be commissioned to place
himself in a concealed part of the room and listen heedfully
to what they talked about. For if the son had any wits at
all he would not hesitate to speak out in the hearing of his
mother, or fear to trust himself to the fidelity of her who
bore him. The speaker, loth to seem readier to devise than
to carry out the plot, zealously proffered himself as the agent
of the eavesdropping. Feng rejoiced at the scheme, and
departed on pretence of a long journey. Now he who had
given this counsel repaired privily to the room where Amleth
was shut up with his mother, and lay down skulking in the
straw. But Amleth had his antidote for the treachery.
Afraid of being overheard by some eavesdropper, he at first
resorted to his usual imbecile ways, and crowed like a noisy
cock, beating his arms together to mimic the flapping of wings.
Then he mounted the straw and began to swing his body and
jump again and again, wishing to try if aught lurked there in
hiding. Feeling a lump beneath his feet, he drove his sword
into the spot, and impaled him who lay hid. Then he
dragged him from his concealment and slew him. Then,

scissum, aquis ferventibus coxit, devorandumque porcis per
os cloacae patentis effudit, atque ita miseris artubus coenum
putre constravit. Taliter elusis insidiis conclave repetit.
Cunque mater magno ejulatu questa praesentis filii socordiam
deflere coepisset : quid inquit mulierum turpissima gravissimi
criminis dissimulationem falso lamenti genere expetis quae
scorti more lasciviens nefariam ac detestabilem thori con-
ditionem secuta viri tui interfectorem pleno incesti sinu
amplecteris : et ei qui prolis tuae parentem extinxerat obscoe-
nissimis blandimentorum illecebris adularis ? Ita nempe equae
conjugum suorum victoribus maritantur : brutorum natura
haec est ut in diversa passim conjugia rapiantur : hoc tibi
exemplo prioris mariti memoriam exolevisse constat. Ego
vero non ab re stolidi speciem gero cum haut dubitem quin
is qui fratrem oppresserit : in affines quoque pari crudelitate
debacchaturus sit unde stoliditatis quam industriae habitum
amplecti praestat et incolumitatis praesidium ab extrema
deliramentorum specie mutuari. In animo tamen paternae
ultionis studium perseverat : sed rerum occasiones aucupor :
temporum opportunitates opperior. Non idem omnibus locus
competit. Contra obscurum immitemque animum altioribus
ingenii modis uti convenit. Tibi vero supervacuum sit meam
lamentari desipientiam quae tuam justius ignominiam deplo-
rare debueras. Itaque non alienae, sed propriae mentis vitium
defleas : necesse est. Caetera silere memineris. Tali convitio

Amlethi
ad matrem
verba.

cutting his body into morsels, he seethed it in boiling water, and flung it through the mouth of an open sewer for the swine to eat, bestrewing the stinking mire with his hapless limbs. Having in this wise eluded the snare, he went back to the room. Then his mother set up a great wailing, and began to lament her son's folly to his face; but he said: "Most infamous of women! dost thou seek with such lying lamentations to hide thy most heavy guilt? Wantoning like a harlot, thou hast entered a wicked and abominable state of wedlock, embracing with incestuous bosom thy husband's slayer, and wheedling with filthy lures of blandishment him who had slain the father of thy son. This, forsooth, is the way that the mares couple with the vanquishers of their mates; for brute beasts are naturally incited to pair indiscriminately; and it would seem that thou, like them, hast clean forgot thy first husband. As for me, not idly do I wear the mask of folly; for I doubt not that he who destroyed his brother will riot as ruthlessly in the blood of his kindred. Therefore it is better to choose the garb of dulness than that of sense, and to borrow some protection from a show of utter frenzy. Yet the passion to avenge my father still burns in my heart; but I am watching the chances, I await the fitting hour. There is a place for all things; against so merciless and dark a spirit must be used the deeper devices of the mind. And thou, who hadst been better employed in lamenting thine own disgrace, know it is superfluity to bewail my witlessness; thou shouldst weep for the blemish in thine own mind, not

laceratam matrem ad excolendum virtutis habitum revocavit, praeteritosque ignes praesentibus illecebris praeferre docuit.

Reversus Fengo insidiosae explorationis auctorem nusquam repertum diutinae inquisitionis studio prosequebatur : nemine se eum uspiam conspexisse dicente. Amlethus quoque an ullum ipsius vestigium deprehenderit per jocum rogatus in cloacam illum ivisse retulit perque ejus ima collapsum : ac nimia coeni mole obrutum a subeuntibus passim porcis esse consumptum. Quod dictum tametsi veri confessionem exprimeret : quia specie stolidum videbatur, auditoribus ludibrio fuit.

Cunque Fengo privignum indubitatae fraudi suspectum tollere vellet : sed id tum ob avi ejus Rorici, tum ob conjugis offensam exequi non auderet : Britanniae regis officio necandum duxit, innocentiae simulationem alieno ministerio quaesiturus. Ita dum occultare saevitiam cupit, amicum inquinare, quam sibi infamiam consciscere maluit. Discedens Amlethus matri tacite jubet, textilibus aulam nodis instruat, suasque post annum inferias falso peragat : eoque tempore reditum pollicetur. Proficiscuntur cum eo bini Fengonis satellites, literas ligno insculptas (nam id celebre quondam genus chartarum erat)

for that in another's. On the rest see thou keep silence."
With such reproaches he rent the heart of his mother and
redeemed her to walk in the ways of virtue ; teaching her to
set the fires of the past above the seductions of the present.

When Feng returned, nowhere could he find the man who
had suggested the treacherous espial ; he searched for him
long and carefully, but none said they had seen him anywhere.
Amleth, among others, was asked in jest if he had come on
any trace of him, and replied that the man had gone to the
sewer, but had fallen through its bottom and been stifled by
the floods of filth, and that he had been devoured by the
swine that came up all about that place. This speech was
flouted by those who heard ; for it seemed senseless, though
really it expressly avowed the truth.

Feng now suspected that his stepson was certainly full of
guile, and desired to make away with him, but durst not do
the deed for fear of the displeasure, not only of Amleth's
grandsire Rorik, but also of his own wife. So he thought
that the King of Britain should be employed to slay him, so
that another could do the deed, and he be able to feign
innocence. Thus, desirous to hide his cruelty, he chose
rather to besmirch his friend than to bring disgrace on his
own head. Amleth, on departing, gave secret orders to his
mother to hang the hall with woven knots, and to perform
pretended obsequies for him a year thence ; promising that he
would then return. Two retainers of Feng then accompanied
him, bearing a letter graven on wood—a kind of writing

secum gestantes : quibus Britannorum regi transmissi sibi

juvenis occisio mandabatur. Quorum Amlethus quietem
capientium loculos perscrutatus literas deprehendit : quarum
perlectis mandatis, quicquid chartis illitum erat curavit abradi :
novisque figurarum apicibus substitutis, damnationem suam in
comites suos, mutato mandati tenore, convertit. Nec mortis
sibi sententiam ademisse, et in alios periculum transtulisse
contentus, preces hujusmodi falso Fengonis titulo subnotatus
adjecit : ut Britanniae rex prudentissimo ad se juveni misso
filiam in matrimonium erogaret.

At ubi in Britanniam ventum, adeunt legati regem : litera-
asque quas alienae cladis instrumentum putabant, propriae
mortis indices obtulerunt. Quo dissimulato rex hospitali
illos humanitate prosequitur. Tunc Amlethus omnem regiarum
dapum apparatum perinde ac vulgare edulium aspernatus :
summam epularum abundantiam miro abstinentiae genere
aversatus est : nec minus potioni, quam dapibus pepercit.
Admirationi omnibus erat : quod alienigenae gentis juvenis
accuratissimas regiae mensae delitias, et instructissimas luxu
epulas : tanquam agreste aliquod obsonium, fastidiret. Soluto
convivio rex quum amicos ad quietem dimitteret per quen-
dam cubiculo immissum, nocturna hospitum colloquia clan-

material frequent in old times ; this letter enjoined the king
of the Britons to put to death the youth who was sent over
to him.   While they were reposing, Amleth searched sheir
coffers, found the letter, and read the instructions therein.
Whereupon he erased all the writing on the surface, substituted
fresh characters, and so, changing the purport of the instructions, shifted his own doom upon his companions.   Nor was
he satisfied with removing from himself the sentence of death
and passing the peril on to others, but added an entreaty that
the King of Britain would grant his daughter in marriage to a
youth of great judgment whom he was sending to him.   Under
this was falsely marked the signature of Feng.

Now when they had reached Britain, the envoys went to
the king, and proffered him the letter which they supposed
was an implement of destruction to another, but which really
betokened death to themselves.   The king dissembled the
truth, and entreated them hospitably and kindly.   Then
Amleth scouted all the splendour of the royal banquet like
vulgar viands, and abstaining very strangely, rejected that
plenteous feast, refraining from the drink even as from the
banquet.   All marvelled that a youth and a foreigner should
disdain the carefully-cooked dainties of the royal board and
the luxurious banquet provided, as if it were some peasant's
relish.   So, when the revel broke up, and the king was
dismissing his friends to rest, he had a man sent into the
sleeping-room to listen secretly, in order that he might hear
the midnight conversation of his guests.   Now, when

destino explorationis genere cognoscenda curavit. Interrogatus igitur a sociis Amlethus : quid igitur ita hesternis epulis
perinde ac venenis abstinuisset ? panem cruoris contagio resper-
sum : potioni ferri saporem inesse : carneas dapes humana
cadaveris oliditate perfusas : ac veluti quadam funebris nidoris
affinitate corruptas dicebat. Addidit quoque regem servilibus
oculis esse : reginam tria ancillaris ritus officia prae se tulisse :
non tam coenam, quam ejus auctores plenis opprobrii convitiis
insecutus. Cui mox socii pristinum mentis vitium exprobrantes,
variis petulantiae ludibriis insultare coeperunt : quod probanda
culparet : causaretur idonea : quod insignem regem, excultam-
que moribus foeminam parum honesto sermone lacesseret :
laudemque meritos extremi dedecoris opprobrio respersisset.

Quibus rex ex satellite cognitis, talium auctorem supra
mortalem habitum, aut sapere, aut desipere testatus est : tam
paucis verbis perfectissimam industriae altitudinem complec-
tendo. Accersitum deinde villicum unde panem adsciverat
percontatur. Qui quum eum domestici pistoris opera con-
fectum assereret, sciscitatur item ubi materiae ejus seges
crevisset : et an ullum illic humanae stragis indicium extaret.
Qui respondit haud procul abesse campum vetustis interfec-
torum ossibus obsitum : et adhuc manifesta antiquae stragis
vestigia prae se ferentem : quem a se perinde ac caeteris

Amleth's companions asked him why he had refrained from the feast of yestereve, as if it were poison, he answered that the bread was flecked with blood and tainted; that there was a tang of iron in the liquor; while the meats of the feast reeked of the stench of a human carcase, and were infected by a kind of smack of the odour of the charnel. He further said that the king had the eyes of a slave, and that the queen had in three ways shown the behaviour of a bondmaid. Thus he reviled with insulting invective not so much the feast as its givers. And presently his companions, taunting him with his old defect of wits, began to flout him with many saucy jeers, because he blamed and cavilled at seemly and worthy things, and because he attacked thus ignobly an illustrious king and a lady of so refined a behaviour, bespattering with the shamefullest abuse those who merited all praise.

All this the king heard from his retainer; and declared that he who could say such things had either more than mortal wisdom or more than mortal folly; in these few words fathoming the full depth of Amleth's penetration. Then he summoned his steward and asked him whence he had procured the bread. The steward declared that it had been made by the king's own baker. The king asked where the corn had grown of which it was made, and whether any sign was to be found there of human carnage? The other answered, that not far off was a field, covered with the ancient bones of slaughtered men, and still bearing plainly all the signs of ancient carnage; and that he had himself planted

feraciorem opimae ubertatis spe, verna fruge consertum dicebat.
Itaque se nescire an panis hoc tabo vitiosi quicquam saporis
contraxerit. Quo audito rex Amlethum vera dixisse
conjectans: unde lardum quoque allatum fuisset cognoscere
curae habuit. Ille sues suos per incuriam custodia elapsos
putri latronis cadavere pastos asseverabat. Ideoque forte eorum
carnibus corruptioni affinem incessisse saporem. Quum rex
in hoc quoque veracem Amlethi sententiam comperisset:
quonam liquore potionem miscuisset inquirit. Ut farre, et
aqua temperatam cognovit, demonstratum sibi scaturiginis
locum in altum fodere aggressus, complures gladios rubigine
adesos repperit, ex quorum odore lymphas vitium traxisse
existimatum est. Alii ideo potionem notatam referunt: quod
in ejus haustu apes abdomine mortui alitas deprehenderit:
vitiumque referri gustu, quod olim favis inditum extitisset
A quo rex culpati saporis causas competenter aeditas videns,
quum ab eodem exprobratam sibi oculorum ignominiam, ad
generis foeditatem pertinere cognosceret, clam conventa matre,
quis sibi pater extitisset inquirit. Qua neminem se praeter
regem passam dicente, rem quaestione ex ea cognoscendam
minatus, quod servo ortus esset accepit notatae originis

this field with grain in springtide, thinking it more fruitful than the rest, and hoping for plenteous abundance ; and so, for aught he knew, the bread had caught some evil savour from this bloodshed. The king, on hearing this, surmised that Amleth had spoken truly, and took the pains to learn also what had been the source of the lard. The other declared that his hogs had, through negligence, strayed from keeping, and battened on the rotten carcase of a robber, and that perchance their pork had thus come to have something of a corrupt smack. The king, finding that Amleth's judgment was right in this thing also, asked of what liquor the steward had mixed the drink ? Hearing that it had been brewed of water and meal, he had the spot of the spring pointed out to him, and set to digging deep down; and there he found, rusted away, several swords, the tang whereof it was thought had tainted the waters. Others relate that Amleth blamed the drink because, while quaffing it, he had detected some bees that had fed in the paunch of a dead man ; and that the taint, which had formerly been imparted to the combs, had reappeared in the taste. The king, seeing that Amleth had rightly given the causes of the taste he had found so faulty, and learning that the ignoble eyes wherewith Amleth had reproached him concerned some stain upon his birth, had a secret interview with his mother, and asked her who his father had really been. She said she had submitted to no man but the king. But when he threatened that he would have the truth out of her by a trial, he was told that

ambiguitatem extorto confessionis indicio perscrutatus. Igitur ut conditionis suae rubore contusus : ita juvenis prudentia delectatus : eundem cur reginam servilium morum exprobratione maculasset, interrogat. Sed dum conjugis comitatem nocturno hospitis sermone lacessitam doluit, eandem ancilla matre creatam didicit. Siquidem ille tria se circa eam servilis ritus vitia denotasse dicebat. Unum quod ancillae more pallio caput obduxerit. Alterum, quod vestem ad gressum succinxerit. Tertium quod ciborum reliquias dentium angustiis inhaerentes stipite eruerit, erutasque commanducaverit. Matrem quoque ejus in servitutem captivitate redactam memorabat : ne potius servili more, quam genere esse videretur.

Cujus industriam rex perinde ac divinum aliquod ingenium veneratus, filiam ei in matrimonium dedit. Affirmationem quoque ejus tanquam coeleste quoddam testimonium amplexatus est. Caeterum comites ipsius ut amici mandatis satisfaceret, proxima die suspendio consumpsit. Quod beneficium Amlethus tanquam injuriam simulata animi molestia prosecutus, aurum a rege compositionis nomine recepit : quod postmodum igni liquatum clam cavatis baculis infundendum curavit.

he was the offspring of a slave. By the evidence of the avowal thus extorted he understood the whole mystery of the reproach upon his origin. Abashed as he was with shame for his low estate, he was so ravished with the young man's cleverness, that he asked him why he had aspersed the queen with the reproach that she had demeaned herself like a slave ? But while resenting that the courtliness of his wife had been accused in the midnight gossip of a guest, he found that her mother had been a bondmaid. For Amleth said he had noted in her three blemishes showing the demeanour of a slave ; first, she had muffled her head in her mantle as bond-maids do; next, that she had gathered up her gown for walking ; and thirdly, that she had first picked out with a splinter, and then chewed up, the remnant of food that stuck in the crevices between her teeth. Further, he mentioned that the king's mother had been brought into slavery from captivity, lest she should seem servile only in her habits, yet not in her birth.

Then the king adored the wisdom of Amleth as though it were inspired, and gave him his daughter to wife ; accepting his bare word as though it were a witness from the skies. Moreover, in order to fulfil the bidding of his friend, he hanged Amleth's companions on the morrow. Amleth, feigning offence, treated this piece of kindness as a grievance, and received from the king, as compensation, some gold, which he afterwards melted in the fire, and secretly caused to be poured into some hollowed sticks.

Apud quem annum emensus impetrata profectionis licentia
patriam repetit: nihil secum ex omni regiarum opum apparatu
praeter gerulos auri bacillos deportans. Ut Jutiam attigit,
praesentem cultum pristinis permutavit moribus : quibus ad
honestatem usus fuerat in ridiculae consuetudinis speciem de-
industria conversis. Cumque triclinium in quo suae duce-
bantur exequiae squalore obsitus intrasset, maximum omnibus
stuporem injecit: quod obitum ejus falso fama vulgaverat.
Ad ultimum horror in risum concessit exprobrantibus sibi
mutuo per ludibrium convivis vivum affore : quem ipsi perinde
ac defunctum inferiis prosequerentur. Idem super comitibus
interrogatus : ostensis quos gestabat baculis, hic inquit et
unus et alius est. Quod utrum verius, an jocosius protulerit
nescias. Siquidem ea vox quanquam a plerisque vana
existimata fuerit, a veri tamen habitu non descivit : quae
peremptorum loco pensationis eorum pretium demonstrabat.
Pincernis deinde quo majorem convivis hilaritatem afferret
conjunctus, curiosiore propinandi officio fungebatur. Et ne
gressum laxior vestis offenderet latus gladio cinxit: quem
plerumque de industria distringens, supremo digitos acumine
vulnerabat. Quamobrem a circumstantibus curatum : ut
gladius cum vagina ferreo clavo trajiceretur. Idem quo
tutiorem insidiis aditum strueret, petitam poculis nobilitatem
crebris potionibus oneravit : adeoque cunctos mero obruit : ut

When he had passed a whole year with the king he obtained leave to make a journey, and returned to his own land, carrying away of all his princely wealth and state only the sticks which held the gold. On reaching Jutland, he exchanged his present attire for his ancient demeanour, which he had adopted for righteous ends, purposely assuming an aspect of absurdity. Covered with filth, he entered the banquet-room where his own obsequies were being held, and struck all men utterly aghast, rumour having falsely noised abroad his death. At last terror melted into mirth, and the guests jeered and taunted one another, that he whose last rites they were celebrating as though he were dead, should appear in the flesh. When he was asked concerning his comrades, he pointed to the sticks he was carrying, and said, "Here is both the one and the other." This he observed with equal truth and pleasantry ; for his speech, though most thought it idle, yet departed not from the truth ; for it pointed at the weregild of the slain as though it were themselves. Thereon, wishing to bring the company into a gayer mood, he joined the cupbearers, and diligently did the office of plying the drink. Then, to prevent his loose dress hampering his walk, he girded his sword upon his side, and purposely drawing it several times, pricked his fingers with its point. The bystanders accordingly had both sword and scabbard riveted across with an iron nail. Then, to smooth the way more safely to his plot, he went to the lords and plied them heavily with draught upon draught, and drenched them all so

debilitatis temulentia pedibus intra regiam quieti se traderent, eundemque convivii et lecti locum haberent. Quos quum insidiis opportunos animadverteret: oblatam propositi facultatem existimans, praeparatos olim stipites sinu excipit: ac deinde aedem in qua proceres passim fusis humi corporibus permixtam somno crapulam ructabantur, ingressus, compactam a matre cortinam, quae etiam interiores aulae parietes obducebat, rescissis tenaculis decidere coegit. Quam stertentibus super-jectam, adhibitis stipitum curvaminibus adeo inextricabili nodorum artificio colligavit: ut nemo subjectorum tametsi validius adniteretur consurgendi effectum assequi posset. Post haec tectis ignem injicit: qui crebrescentibus flammis late incendium spargens totos involvit penates: regiam con-sumpsit, omnesque aut profundum carpentes somnum, aut frustra assurgere conantes, cremavit. Inde petito Fengonis cubiculo: qui prius a comitibus in tabernaculum perductus fuerat, gladium forte lectulo cohaerentem arripuit, suumque ejus loco defixit. Excitato deinde patruo, proceres ejus igne perire retulit: adesse Amlethum veterum uncorum suorum ope succinctum: et jam debita paternae cladis supplicia exigere avidum. Ad hanc vocem Fengo lectulo desiliens dum proprio defectus gladio nequicquam alienum distringere

Fengonis caedes.

deep in wine, that their feet were made feeble with drunkenness, and they turned to rest within the palace, making their bed where they had revelled. Then he saw they were in a fit state for his plots, and thought that here was a chance offered to do his purpose. So he took out of his bosom the stakes he had long ago prepared, and went into the building, where the ground lay covered with the bodies of the nobles wheezing off their sleep and their debauch. Then, cutting away its supports, he brought down the hanging his mother had knitted, which covered the inner as well as the outer walls of the hall. This he flung upon the snorers, and then applying the crooked stakes, he knotted and bound them up in such insoluble intricacy, that not one of the men beneath, however hard he might struggle, could contrive to rise. After this he set fire to the palace. The flames spread, scattering the conflagration far and wide. It enveloped the whole dwelling, destroyed the palace, and burnt them all while they were either buried in deep sleep or vainly striving to arise. Then he went to the chamber of Feng, who had before this been conducted by his train into his pavilion; plucked up a sword that chanced to be hanging to the bed, and planted his own in its place. Then, awakening his uncle, he told him that his nobles were perishing in the flames, and that Amleth was here, armed with his old crooks to help him, and thirsting to exact the vengeance, now long overdue, for his father's murder. Feng, on hearing this, leapt from his couch, but was cut down while, deprived of his own

conatur opprimitur. Fortem virum, aeternoque nomine
dignum: qui stultitiae commento prudenter instructus,
augustiorem mortali ingenio sapientiam admirabili ineptiarum
simulatione suppressit: nec solum propriae salutis obtentum ab
astutia mutuatus, ad paternae quoque ultionis copiam eadem
ductum praebente pervenit. Itaque et se solerter tutatus: et
parentem strenue ultus: fortior, an sapientior existimari
debeat, incertum reliquit.

Explicitus est liber Tertius : Incipit Quartus

Peracta vitrici strage Amlethus facinus suum incerto
populariam judicio offerre veritus, latebris utendum existimavit:
donec quorsum inconditae plebis vulgus procurreret didicisset.
Igitur vicinia quae noctu incendium speculata fuerat, mane
causam conspecti ignis nosse cupiens, collapsam in cineres
regiam animadvertit: ruinasque ejus adhuc tepidas perscrutata
nihil praeter informes combustorum corporum reliquias repperit.
Adeo autem vorax flamma omnia perederat: ut ne index
quidem extaret: ex quo tantae cladis causa accipi posset.
Corpus quoque Fengonis ferro confossum inter cruentas
spectabatur exuvias. Aliis indignatio patens: aliis moeror:
quibusdam gaudium occultum incesserat. Hi ducis lament-
abantur interitum: hi sopitam parricidae tyrannidem gratu-

sword, he strove in vain to draw the strange one. O valiant Amleth, and worthy of immortal fame, who being shrewdly armed with a feint of folly, covered a wisdom too high for human wit under a marvellous disguise of silliness! and not only found in his subtlety means to protect his own safety, but also by its guidance found opportunity to avenge his father. By this skilful defence of himself, and strenuous revenge for his parent, he has left it doubtful whether we are to think more of his wit or his bravery. *End of Book Three.*

Amleth, when he had accomplished the slaughter of his stepfather, feared to expose his deed to the fickle judgment of his countrymen, and thought it well to lie in hiding till he had learnt what way the mob of the uncouth populace was tending. So the whole neighbourhood, who had watched the blaze during the night, and in the morning desired to know the cause of the fire they had seen, perceived the royal palace fallen in ashes ; and, on searching through its ruins, which were yet warm, found only some shapeless remains of burnt corpses. For the devouring flame had consumed everything so utterly, that not a single token was left to inform them of the cause of such a disaster. Also they saw the body of Feng lying pierced by the sword, amid his blood-stained raiment. Some were seized with open anger, others with grief, and some with secret delight. One party bewailed the death of their leader, the other gave thanks that the tyranny of the fratricide was now laid at

labantur. Ita regiae necis eventus dividua spectatorum sententia excipiebatur.

Ea vulgi tranquillitate Amlethus relinquendarum latebrarum fidutiam adeptus, accersitis quibus arctiorem patris memoriam inhaerere cognoverat, concionem petit: in qua orationem hujusmodi habuit. Non vos moveat proceres praesens calamitatis facies: si quos miserabilis Horwendilli exitus movet non vos inquam moveat: quibus in regem fides: in parentem pietas servata est. Parricidae, non regis intueamini funus. Luctuosior siquidem illa facies erat, quum ipsi regem nostrum ab iniquissimo parricida (ne dicam fratre) flebiliter jugulatum vidistis. Ipsi laceros Horwendilli artus: ipsi corpus crebris vulneribus absumptum plenis miserationis oculis aspexistis. Quem ab atrocissimo carnifice spiritu spoliatum, ut patria libertate exueretur: quis dubitet? una manus ei fatum, et vobis servitutem injecit. Quis igitur tam amens: ut Fengonis crudelitatem Horwendillianae praeferat pietati? Mementote qua vos Horwendillus benevolentia foverit: justitia coluerit: humanitate dilexerit. Memineritis ademptum vobis mitissimum regem: justissimum patrem: subrogatum tyrannum: suffectum parricidam: erepta jura: contaminata omnia: pollutam flagitiis patriam: impositum cervicibus jugum: ereptum libertatis arbitrium. Et nunc his finis:

Amlethi oratio.

rest. Thus the occurrence of the king's slaughter was greeted by the beholders with diverse minds.

Amleth, finding the people so quiet, made bold to leave his hiding. Summoning those in whom he knew the memory of his father to be fast-rooted, he went to the assembly and there made a speech after this manner:

"Nobles! Let not any who are troubled by the piteous end of Horwendil be troubled by the sight of this disaster before you: be not ye, I say, troubled, who have remained loyal to your king and duteous to your father. Behold the corpse, not of a prince, but of a fratricide. Indeed, it was a sorrier sight when ye saw our prince lying lamentably butchered by a most infamous fratricide—brother, let me not call him. With your own compassionating eyes ye have beheld the mangled limbs of Horwendil; they have seen his body done to death with many wounds. Surely that most abominable butcher only deprived his king of life that he might despoil his country of freedom! The hand that slew him made you slaves. Who then so mad as to choose Feng the cruel before Horwendil the righteous? Remember how benignantly Horwendil fostered you, how justly he dealt with you, how kindly he loved you. Remember how you lost the mildest of princes and the justest of fathers, while in his place was put a tyrant and an assassin set up; how your rights were confiscated; how everything was plague-stricken; how the country was stained with infamies; how the yoke was planted on your necks, and how your free will

quum suis auctorem criminibus obrutum suorum poenas
scelerum parricidam pependisse cernatis. Quis mediocriter
prudens spectator beneficium injuriae loco duxerit? Quis
mentis compos proprium in auctorem scelus recidisse
condoleat? Quis cruentissimi lictoris cladem defleat:
aut crudelissimi tyranni justum lamentetur interitum?
Praesto est auctor rei, quem cernitis. Ego quidem et
parentem et patriam ultione prosequutum me fateor. Opus:
quod vestris pariter manibus debebatur, exercui. Quod vos
mecum communiter condecebat, solus implevi. Adde quod
neminem tam praeclari facinoris socium habui: nec cujuspiam
mihi comes opera fuit: quanquam haud ignorem vos huic
manum daturos negotio: si petissem a quibus fidem regi:
benivolentiam principi servatam non dubito. Sed sine vestro
discrimine nefarios puniri placuit: Neque enim alienos
humeros oneri subjiciendos putabam: cui sustentando proprios
suffecturos credebam. Incineravi ego alios, solum Fengonis
truncum vestris manibus concremandum reliqui: in quo saltem
justae ultionis cupidinem exsatiare possitis. Concurrite
alacres: extruite rogum: exurite impium corpus: decoquite
scelestos artus: spargite noxios cineres: disjicite immites
favillas: non urna, non tumulus nefandas ossium reliquias
claudat. Nullum parricidii vestigium maneat: nullus con-

was forfeited! And now all this is over; for ye see the
criminal stifled in his own crimes, the slayer of his kin
punished for his misdoings. What man of but ordinary wit,
beholding it, would account this kindness a wrong? What
sane man could be sorry that the crime has recoiled upon the
culprit? Who could lament the killing of a most savage
executioner? or bewail the righteous death of a most cruel
despot? Ye behold the doer of the deed; he is before you.
Yea, I own that I have taken vengeance for my country and
my father. Your hands were equally bound to the task
which mine fulfilled. What it would have beseemed you to
accomplish with me, I achieved alone. Nor had I any
partner in so glorious a deed, or the service of any man to
help me. Not that I forget that you would have helped this
work, had I asked you; for doubtless you have remained
loyal to your king and loving to your prince. But I chose
that the wicked should be punished without imperilling you;
I thought that others need not set their shoulders to the
burden when I deemed mine strong enough to bear it.
Therefore I consumed all the others to ashes, and left only
the trunk of Feng for your hands to burn, so that on this at
least you may wreak all your longing for a righteous vengeance. Now haste up speedily, heap the pyre, burn up the
body of the wicked, consume away his guilty limbs, scatter
his sinful ashes, strew broadcast his ruthless dust: let no urn
or barrow enclose the abominable remnants of his bones.
Let no trace of his fratricide remain; let there be no spot

taminatis artibus intra patriam locus existat : nulla contagium
vicinia contrahat : non mare, non solum damnati cadaveris
hospitio polluatur. Caetera ego praebui : id solum vobis
pietatis officium relictum est. His exequiis prosequendus
tyrannus : hac pompa parricidae funus ducendum. Sed neque
ejus cineres qui patriam libertate nudaverit a patria tegi
convenit. Praeterea quid meas revolvam aerumnas ? calami-
tates recenseam ? retexam miserias ? quas ipsi me plenius
nostis. Ego a vitrico ad mortem quaesitus a matre con-
temptus : ab amicis consputus annos flebiliter exegi : dies
calamitose duxi : incertum vitae tempus periculis ac metu
refertum habui. Postremo omnem aetatis partem maxima
cum rerum adversitate miserabiliter emensus sum. Saepe me
tacitis intra vos questibus sensu vacuum gemebatis deesse
ultorem patri : parricidio vindicem. Quae res occultum mihi
vestrae charitati indicium attulit : in quorum animis necdum
regiae cladis memoriam exolevisse cernebam. Cujus itaque
tam asperum pectus : tam saxeus rigor : quem non passionum
mearum compassio molliat, aerumnarum miseratio non flectat ?
Miseremini alumni vestri : moveamini infortuniis meis : qui ab
Horwendilli nece immunes geritis manus. Miseremini quoque
afflictae genitricis meae et reginae quondam vestrae : extincto
congaudete dedecori : quae viri sui fratrem interfectoremque

in his own land for his tainted limbs ; let no neighbourhood suck infection from him ; let not sea nor soil be defiled by harbouring his accursed carcase. I have done the rest ; this one loyal duty is left for you. These must be the tyrant's obsequies, this the funeral procession of the fratricide. It is not seemly that he who stripped his country of her freedom should have his ashes covered by his country's earth.

" Besides, why tell again my own sorrows ? Why count over my troubles ? Why weave the thread of my miseries anew ? Ye know them more fully than I myself. I, pursued to the death by my stepfather, scorned by my mother, spat upon by friends, have passed my years in pitiable wise, and my days in adversity ; and my insecure life has teemed with fear and perils. In fine, I passed every season of my age wretchedly and in extreme calamity. Often in your secret murmurings together you have sighed over my lack of wits : there was none (you said) to avenge the father, none to punish the fratricide. And in this I found a secret testimony of your love ; for I saw that the memory of the King's murder had not yet faded from your minds.

" Whose breast is so hard that it can be softened by no fellow-feeling for what I have felt ? Who is so stiff and stony, that he is swayed by no compassion for my griefs ? Ye whose hands are clean of the blood of Horwendil, pity your fosterling, be moved by my calamities. Pity also my stricken mother, and rejoice with me that the infamy of her who was once your queen is quenched. For this weak

complexa, geminum ignominiae pondus foemineo perpeti corpore cogebatur. Quamobrem ut ultionis studium occultarem, obscurarem ingenium, adumbratum non verum inertiae habitum amplexatus sum : stoliditatis figmento usus, sapientiae commentum texui : quod nunc an efficax fuerit, utrum finis sui complementum attigerit, vestro conspectui patet : vos tantae rei arbitros habere contentus sum. Ipsi parricidales favillas pedibus proculcatis : despicamini cineres ejus, qui jugulati fratris uxorem polluit, flagitio temeravit, dominum laesit, majestatem proditionis scelere lacessivit, acerbissimam vobis tyrannidem intulit, libertatem ademit, incesto parricidium cumulavit. Me tam justae vindictae ministrum, tam piae lutionis aemulum patricio suscipite spiritu, debito prosequimini cultu, benigno refovete contuitu. Ego patriae probrum dilui, matris ignominiam extinxi, tyrannidem reppuli, parricidam oppressi, insidiosam patrui manum mutuis insidiis elusi : cujus, si superesset, in dies scelera percrebrescerent. Dolebam et patris et patriae injuriam : illum extinxi vobis atrociter : et supra quam viros decuerat, imperantem. Recognoscite beneficium : veneramini ingenium meum regnum si merui date : habetis tanti auctorem muneris, paternae potestatis haeredem, non

woman had to bear a twofold weight of ignominy, embracing
one who was her husband's brother and murderer. Therefore, to hide my purpose of revenge and to veil my wit, I
counterfeited a listless bearing; I feigned dulness; I planned
a stratagem; and now you can see with your own eyes
whether it has succeeded, whether it has achieved its purpose
to the full; I am content to leave you to judge so great a
matter. It is your turn: trample under foot the ashes of the
murderer! Disdain the dust of him who slew his brother,
and defiled his brother's queen with infamous desecration,
who outraged his sovereign and treasonably assailed his
majesty, who brought the sharpest tyranny upon you, stole
your freedom, and crowned fratricide with incest. I have
been the agent of this just vengeance; I have burned
for this righteous retribution: uphold me with a high-
born spirit; pay me the homage that you owe; warm me
with your kindly looks. It is I who have wiped off my
country's shame; I who have quenched my mother's dishonour; I who have beaten back oppression; I who have
put to death the murderer; I who have baffled the artful hand
of my uncle with retorted arts. Were he living, each new
day would have multiplied his crimes. I resented the wrong
done to father and to fatherland: I slew him who was
governing you outrageously and more hardly than it beseemed
men. Acknowledge my service, honour my wit, give me
the throne if I have earned it; for you have in me one who
has done you a mighty service, and who is no degenerate

degenerem, non parricidam : sed legitimum regni successorem
et pium noxae parricidalis ultorem. Debetis mihi recuperatum
libertatis beneficium, exclusum afflictantis imperium, ademptum
oppressoris jugum, excussum parricidae dominium, calcatum
tyrannidis sceptrum. Ego servitute vos exui, indui libertate :
restitui culmen : gloriam reparavi : tyrannum sustuli : carni-
ficem triumphavi. Praemium penes vos est : ipsi meritum
nostis : a vestra merces virtute requiritur.

Flexerat hac oratione adolescens omnium animos ; quosdam
ad miserationem, alios ad lachrymas usque perduxit. At ubi
quievit moeror, rex alacri cunctorum acclamatione censetur.

Amlethus
regnat rex
xxi
Plurimum quippe spei in ejus industria ab universis repone-
batur : qui tanti facinoris summam profundissimo astu texuerat
incredibili molitione concluserat. Mirari illum complures
videres, tanto temporis tractu subtilissimum texisse consilium.

Britanniam
repetit.
His apud Daniam gestis, ternis navigiis impensius adornatis
socerum visurus ac conjugem, Britanniam repetit. In clien-
telam quoque armis praestantem juventutem adciverat,
exquisito decoris genere cultam : ut sicut cuncta despicabili
dudum habitu gesserat : ita nunc magnificis ad omnia paratibus

heir to his father's power ; no fratricide, but the lawful
successor to the throne ; and a dutiful avenger of the crime
of murder.   You have me to thank for the recovery of the
blessings of freedom, for release from the power of him who
vexed you, for relief from the oppressor's yoke, for shaking
off the sway of the murderer, for trampling the despot's
sceptre under foot.   It is I who have stripped you of slavery,
and clothed you with freedom ; I have restored your height
of fortune, and given you your glory back ; I have deposed
the despot and triumphed over the butcher.   In your hands
is the reward : you know what I have done for you : and
from your righteousness I ask my wage."

Every heart had been moved while the young man thus
spoke ; he affected some to compassion, and some even to
tears.   When the lamentation ceased, he was appointed king
by prompt and general acclaim.   For one and all rested the
greatest hopes on his wisdom, since he had devised the whole
of such an achievement with the deepest cunning, and accomplished it with the most astonishing contrivance.   Many could
have been seen marvelling how he had concealed so subtle a
plan over so long a space of time.

After these deeds in Denmark he equipped three vessels
lavishly, and went back to Britain to see his wife and her
father.   He had also enrolled in his service the flower of
the warriors, and arrayed them very choicely, wishing to have
everything now magnificently appointed, even as of old he had
always worn contemptible gear, and to change all his old

Scuti
pictura.

uteretur : et quicquid olim paupertati tribuerat, ad luxuriae impensam converteret. In scuto quoque sibi parari jusserat omnem operum suorum contextum ab ineuntis aetatis primordiis auspicatus exquisitis picturae notis adumbrandum curavit. Quo gestamine perinde ac virtutum suarum teste usus, claritatis incrementa contraxit. Istic depingi videres Horwendilli jugulum : Fengonis cum incestu parricidium : flagitiosum patruum : fratruelem ridiculum : aduncas stipitum formas : suspicionem vitrici : dissimulationem privigni : procurata tentamentorum genera : adhibitam insidiis foeminam : hiantem lupum : inventum gubernaculum : praeteritum sabulum : initum nemus : insitam oestro paleam : instructum indiciis adolescentem : elusis comitibus rem seorsum cum virgine habitam. Cerneres itaque adumbrari regiam : adesse cum filio reginam : trucidari insidiatorem : trucidatum decoqui : cloacae coctum infundi : infusum suibus objici : coeno artus insterni : instratos belluis absumendos relinqui. Videres etiam ut Amlethus dormientium comitum secretum deprehenderit : ut obliteratis apicibus, alia figurarum elementa substituerit : ut dapem fastidierit : potionemque contempserit : ut vultum regis arguerit : ut reginam sinistri moris notaverit. Aspiceres quoque legatorum suspendium : adolescentis nuptias figurari : Daniam navigio repeti : inferias convivio celebrari : comitum loco baculos percontanti-

devotion to poverty for outlay on luxury. He also had a shield made for him, whereon the whole series of his exploits, beginning with his earliest youth, was painted in exquisite designs. This he bore as a record of his deeds of prowess, and gained great increase of fame thereby. Here were to be seen depicted the slaying of Horwendil; the fratricide and incest of Feng; the infamous uncle, the whimsical nephew; the shapes of the hooked stakes; the stepfather suspecting, the stepson dissembling; the various temptations offered, and the woman brought to beguile him; the gaping wolf; the finding of the rudder; the passing of the sand; the entering of the wood; the putting of the straw through the gadfly; the warning of the youth by the tokens; and the privy dealings with the maiden after the escort was eluded. And likewise could be seen the picture of the palace; the queen there with her son; the slaying of the eavesdropper; and how, after being killed, he was boiled down, and so dropped into the sewer, and so thrown out to the swine; how his limbs were strewn in the mud, and so left for the beasts to finish. Also it could be seen how Amleth surprised the secret of his sleeping attendants, how he erased the letters, and put new characters in their places; how he disdained the banquet and scorned the drink; how he condemned the face of the king and taxed the queen with faulty behaviour. There was also represented the hanging of the envoys, and the young man's wedding; then the voyage back to Denmark; the festive celebration of the funeral rites; Amleth, in answer to

bus ostendi : Juvenem pincernae partes exequi : districto per
industriam ferro, digitos exulcerari : gladium clavo pertundi :
convivales plausus augeri : increbrescere tripudia : aulaeam
dormientibus injici : injectam uncorum nexibus obfirmari :
pertinacius sopitos involvi : tectis torrem immitti : cremari
convivas : depastam incendio regiam labefactari : Fengonis
cubiculum adiri : gladium eripi : inutilem erepti loco constitui :
regem privigni manu proprii mucronis acumine trucidari.
Haec omnia excultissimo rerum artificio militari ejus scuto
opifex studiosus illeverat, res formis imitatus, et facta figurarum
adumbratione complexus. Sed et comites ipsius quo se
nitidius gererent, oblitis tantum auro clypeis utebantur.

Quos Britanniae rex benignissime exceptos regii apparatus
impensis prosequitur. Qui inter epulandum, an Fengo viveret,
integrisque fortunis esset cupide percontatus, cognoscit e genero
ferro periisse : de cujus frustra salut perquireret. Cunque
interfectorem ejus crebris percontationibus investigaret, eundem
cladis ejus auctorem, ac nuntium extare didicit. Quo audito
tacitum animi stuporem contraxit : quod ad se promissam
quondam Fengonis ultionem pertinere cognosceret. Ipse
equidem ac Fengo ut alter alterius ultorem ageret, mutua

questions, pointing to the sticks in place of his attendants, acting as cup-bearer, and purposely drawing his sword and pricking his fingers; the sword riveted through, the swelling cheers of the banquet, the dance growing fast and furious; the hangings flung upon the sleepers, then fastened with the interlacing crooks, and wrapped tightly round them as they slumbered; the brand set to the mansion, the burning of the guests, the royal palace consumed with fire and tottering down; the visit to the sleeping-room of Feng, the theft of his sword, the useless one set in its place; and the king slain with his own sword's point by his stepson's hand. All this was there, painted upon Amleth's battle-shield by a careful craftsman in the choicest of handiwork; he copied truth in his figures, and embodied real deeds in his outlines. Moreover, Amleth's followers, to increase the splendour of their presence, wore shields which were gilt over.

The King of Britain received them very graciously, and treated them with costly and royal pomp. During the feast he asked anxiously whether Feng was alive and prosperous. His son-in-law told him that the man of whose welfare he was vainly inquiring had perished by the sword. With a flood of questions he tried to find out who had slain Feng, and learnt that the messenger of his death was likewise its author. And when the king heard this, he was secretly aghast, because he found that an old promise to avenge Feng now devolved upon himself. For Feng and he had determined of old, by a mutual compact, that one of them should

quondam pactione decreverant. Trahebat itaque regem hinc
in filiam pietas, in generum amor : inde charitas in amicum : et
praeterea jurisjurandi firmitas, ipsa quoque mutuae obtestationis
religio : quam violare nefarium erat. Tandem cum affinitatis
contemptu juratori apraeponderavit fides : conversusque ad
ultionem animus necessitudini religionem anteposuit. Sed
quoniam hospitalitatis sacra violare nefas credebatur, aliena
manu ultionis partes exequi praeoptavit, innocentiae speciem
occulto facinore praetenturus. Igitur insidias officiis texit :
laedendique curam adumbratis benivolentiae studiis, obscuravit.
Et quia conjunx ejus nuper morbo consumpta fuerat,
Amlethum reparandarum nuptiarum legationem suscipere
jubet admodum se singulari ipsius industria delectatum
praefatus. Regnare siquidem in Scotia foeminam asserebat :
cujus vehementer connubium affectaret. Sciebat namque eam
non modo pudicitia coelibem : sed etiam insolentia atrocem
proprios semper exosam procos : amatoribus suis ultimum
irrogasse supplicium : adeo ut ne unus quidem e multis extaret
qui procationis ejus poenas capite non luisset.

Proficiscitur itaque Amlethus quanquam periculosa legatio
imperaretur, injuncti muneris obsequium non detrectans : sed
partim domesticis servis, partim regis vernaculis fretus.
Ingressusque Scottiam quum haud procul reginae penatibus

act as avenger of the other. Thus the king was drawn one
way by his love for his daughter and his affection for his son-
in-law, another way by his regard for his friend, and moreover by his strict oath and the sanctity of their mutual
declarations, which it was impious to violate. At last he
slighted the ties of kinship, and sworn faith prevailed. His
heart turned to vengeance, and he put the sanctity of his oath
before family bonds. But since it was thought sin to wrong
the holy ties of hospitality, he preferred to execute his revenge
by the hand of another, wishing to mask his secret crime with
a show of innocence. So he veiled his treachery with
attentions, and hid his intent to harm under a show of zealous
goodwill. His queen having lately died of illness, he
requested Amleth to undertake the mission of making him
a fresh match, saying that he was highly delighted with his
extraordinary shrewdness. He declared that there was a
certain queen reigning in Scotland, whom he vehemently
desired to marry. Now he knew that she was not only
unwedded by reason of her chastity, but that in the cruelty
of her arrogance she had always loathed her wooers, and had
inflicted on her lovers the uttermost punishment, so that not
one out of all the multitude was to be found who had not paid
for his insolence with his life.

Perilous as this commission was, Amleth started, never
shrinking to obey the duty imposed upon him, but trusting
partly in his own servants, and partly in the attendants of the
king. He entered Scotland, and, when quite close to the

abesset recreandorum equorum gratia junctum viae pratum
accessit: ibique loci specie delectatus quieti consuluit
jocundiore rivi strepitu somni cupidinem provocante, ordinatis
qui stationem eminus observarent. Quo audito regina denos
juvenes exterorum adventum, apparatumque speculaturos emit-
tit. Quorum unus vegetioris ingenii, elusis vigilibus pervicacius
subiens clypeum Amlethi, quem capiti forte dormiturus
affixerat tanta lenitate submovit: ut ne superjacentis quidem
quietem turbaret, aut cujuspiam ex tanto agmine somnum
perrumperet: dominam non modo nuntio, sed etiam rerum
indicio certiorem redditurus. Delegatas quoque ei literas
loculis quibus asservabantur pari calliditate subduxit. Quibus
regina ad se perlatis clypeum curiosius contemplata ex affixis
notulis totius argumenti summam elicuit: eumque affore
intellexit qui exactissimo prudentiae consilio fretus, de patruo
paternae cladis poenas acceperit. Literas quoque nuptiarum
suarum petitionem continentes intuita, totos obliteravit apices
quod senum admodum connubium abhorreret: juvenum
complexus appeteret. Inscripsit autem mandatum perinde
atque a Britanniae Rege sibi transmissum, et ejus titulo pariter
ac nomine consignatum: quo se latoris peti conjugio simularet.
Quinetiam facta quae ex ejus scuto cognoverat, scripto

abode of the queen, he went into a meadow by the wayside
to rest his horses. Pleased by the look of the spot, he
thought of resting—the pleasant prattle of the stream exciting
a desire to sleep—and posted men to keep watch some way
off. The queen on hearing of this, sent out ten warriors to
spy on the approach of the foreigners and their equipment.
One of these, being quick-witted, slipped past the sentries,
pertinaciously made his way up, and took away the shield,
which Amleth had chanced to set at his head before he slept,
so gently that he did not ruffle his slumbers, though he was
lying upon it, nor awaken one man of all that troop ; for he
wished to assure his mistress not only by report but by some
token. With equal address he filched the letter entrusted to
Amleth from the coffer in which it was kept. When these
things were brought to the queen, she scanned the shield
narrowly, and from the notes appended made out the whole
argument. Then she knew that here was the man who,
trusting in his own nicely-calculated scheme, had avenged on
his uncle the murder of his father. She also looked at the
letter containing the suit for her hand, and rubbed out all the
writing ; for wedlock with the old she utterly abhorred, and
desired the embraces of young men. But she wrote in its
place a commission purporting to be sent from the King of
Britain to herself, signed like the other with his name and
title, wherein she pretended that she was asked to marry the
bearer. Moreover, she included an account of the deeds of
which she had learnt from Amleth's shield, so that one would

complectenda curavit: ut et clypeum literarum testem, et literas clypei interpretes existimares. Deinde eos quorum exploratione usa fuerat scutum referre, literasque loco suo restituere jubet: eodem fallaciae genere Amlethum insequuta, quo eum in cavillandis comitibus usum acceperat.

Interea Amlethus clypeum capiti fraude subductum expertus, occlusis de industria oculis quietem callidius simulat: quod vero sopore amiserat, ficto recuperaturus. Alteram quippe fallendi vicem hoc pronius ab insidioso quaerendam putavit: quo solam prosperius egerit, nec eum opinio fefellit. Speculatorem quippe clandestino aditu scutum ac chartam pristino loco reponere cupientem prosiliens corripit, captumque vinclorum poena coercuit. Deinde excitatis comitibus Reginae penates accedit. Cui ex soceri persona consalutatae scriptum, ejusdemque sigillo obsignatum porrexit. Quod quum accepisset Hermvthruda perlegissetque (reginae id nomen erat) operam Amlethi industriamque verbis impensioribus prosecuta: justas Fengonem poenas pependisse dicebat: ipsum vero Amlethum rem humana aestimatione majorem incomprehensae profunditatis ingenio molitum: quod non solum paterni exitii, maternique concubitus ultionem inscrutabili sensus altitudine commentus fuisset: verum etiam regnum ejus a quo crebras insidias expertus fuerat conspicuis probitatis operibus occupasset. Quamobrem mirari se tam eruditi ingenii virum

have thought the shield confirmed the letter, while the letter explained the shield. Then she told the same spies whom she had employed before to take the shield back, and put the letter in its place again; playing the very trick on Amleth which, as she had learnt, he had himself used in outwitting his companions.

Amleth, meanwhile, who found that his shield had been filched from under his head, deliberately shut his eyes and cunningly feigned sleep, hoping to regain by pretended what he had lost by real slumbers. For he thought that the success of his one attempt would incline the spy to deceive him a second time. And he was not mistaken. For as the spy came up stealthily, and wanted to put back the shield and the writing in their old place, Amleth leapt up, seized him and detained him in bonds. Then he roused his retinue, and went to the abode of the queen. As representing his father-in-law, he greeted her, and handed her the writing, sealed with the king's seal. The queen, who was named Hermutrude, took and read it, and spoke most warmly of Amleth's diligence and shrewdness, saying, that Feng had deserved his punishment, and that the unfathomable wit of Amleth had accomplished a deed past all human estimation; seeing that not only had his impenetrable depth devised a mode of revenging his father's death and his mother's adultery, but it had further, by his notable deeds of prowess, seized the kingdom of the man whom he had found constantly plotting against him. She marvelled therefore that a man of such

uno nuptiarum errore labefactari potuisse : qui quum humanas
paene res claritate transscendat, in ignobilem, obscuramque
copulam prolapsus videatur. Quippe conjugem ejus servis
parentibus esse : quanquam eos fortuna regiis honoribus
exornasset. In expetendis siquidem conjugiis prudenti non
formae fulgorem : sed generis metiendum. Quapropter si rite
copulam appetat, prosapiam aestimet, nec specie capiatur : quae
quum illecebrarum irritamentum sit, multorum candorem
inaniter fucata detersit. Esse vero quam sibi nobilitate
parem asciscere possit. Se siquidem nec rebus tenuem nec
sanguine humilem ejus amplexibus idoneam fore : utpote
quam nec regiis opibus vincat : nec avito splendore praecellat.
Quippe reginam se esse : et nisi refragaretur sexus, regem
existimari posse : immo quod verius est : quemcunque toro suo
dignata fuerit, regem existere : regnumque se cum amplexibus
dare. Ita et nuptiis sceptrum, et sceptro nuptias respondere.
Nec parvi beneficii esse eam proprios offerre amplexus : quae
circa alios ferro repulsam exequi consueverat. Hortatur
itaque placendi studium in se transferat, in se votum nuptiale
deflectat : genusque formae praeferre discat. Haec dicens,
astrictis in eum complexibus ruit.

Ille tam comi virginis eloquio delectatus, in mutua pro-

instructed mind could have made the one slip of a mistaken marriage ; for though his renown almost rose above mortality, he seemed to have stumbled into an obscure and ignoble match. For the parents of his wife had been slaves, though good luck had graced them with the honours of royalty. Now (said she), when looking for a wife, a wise man must reckon the lustre of her birth and not of her beauty. Therefore, if he were to seek a match in a proper spirit, he should weigh the ancestry, and not be smitten by the looks ; for though looks were a lure to temptation, yet their empty bedizenment had tarnished the white simplicity of many a man. Now there was a woman, as nobly born as himself, whom he could take. She herself, whose means were not poor nor her birth lowly, was worthy his embraces, since he did not surpass her in royal wealth nor outshine her in the honour of his ancestors. Indeed she was a queen, and but that her sex gainsaid it, might be deemed a king ; nay (and this is yet truer), whomsoever she thought worthy of her bed was at once a king, and she yielded her kingdom with herself. Thus her sceptre and her hand went together. It was no mean favour for such a woman to offer her love, who in the case of other men had always followed her refusal with the sword. Therefore she pressed him to transfer his wooing, to make over to her his marriage vows, and to learn to prefer birth to beauty. So saying, she fell upon him with a close embrace.

Amleth was overjoyed at the gracious speech of the

rumpit oscula : alternos complexuum nodos conserit : sibique
quod virgini placitum protestatur. Fit deinde convivium :
accersuntur amici : corrogantur primores : nuptiae peraguntur.
Quibus expletis, quum nupta Britanniam repetit, valida Scot-
thorum manu propius subsequi jussa : cujus opera adversum
varios insidiarum objectus uteretur. Redeunti Britannici regis
filia : quam in matrimonio habebat, occurrit : quae quanquam se
superductae pellicis injuria laesam quereretur, indignum tamen
aiebat : maritali gratiae pellicatus odium anteferri neque se
adeo virum aversaturam : ut quod ei fraudulentius intentari sciat,
silentio occultare sustineat : habere enim se pignus conjugii
filium : cujus saltem respectus conjugalem matri charitatem
commendare debuerat. Ipse enim (inquit) matris suae pellicem
oderit, ego diligam : tuos in me ignes nulla calamitas sopiet :
nullus livor extinguet : quin et in te sinistre excogitata detegam,
et quas deprehenderim insidias pandam. Quamobrem
cavendum tibi socerum putes : quod ipse legationis proventum
carpseris : omnemque ejus fructum in temet, eluso mittentis
voto, pervicaci usurpatione transtuleris. Qua voce se con-
jugali, quam paternae charitati propiorem ostendit.

Haec loquente ea adest Britanniae rex : generumque arctius

maiden, fell to kissing back, and returned her close embra
protesting that the maiden's wish was his own. Then a
banquet was held, friends bidden, the chief nobles gathered,
and the marriage rites performed. When they were accomplished, he went back to Britain with his bride, a strong band
of Scots being told to follow close behind, that he might have
its help against the diverse treacheries in his path. As he
was returning, the daughter of the King of Britain, to whom
he was still married, met him. Though she complained that
she was slighted by the wrong of having a paramour put over
her, yet, she said, it would be unworthy for her to hate him
as an adulterer more than she loved him as a husband; nor
would she so far shrink from her lord as to bring herself to
hide in silence the guile which she knew was intended against
him. For she had a son as a pledge of their marriage, and
regard for him, if nothing else, must have inclined his mother
to the affection of a wife. "He," she said, "may hate the
supplanter of his mother, I will love her; no disaster shall
put out my flame for thee; no ill-will shall quench it, or
prevent me from exposing the malignant designs against thee,
or from revealing the snares I have detected. Bethink thee,
then, that thou must beware of thy father-in-law, for thou
hast thyself reaped the harvest of thy mission, foiled the
wishes of him who sent thee, and with wilful trespass seized
over all the fruit for thyself." By this speech she showed
herself more inclined to love her husband than her father.

While she thus spoke, the King of Britain came up and

quam affectuosius amplexatus, convivio excipit, liberalitatis specie fraudis propositum celaturus. Amlethus cognita fraude metum dissimulanter habuit, ducentisque equitibus in comitatum receptis, subarmalem vestem indutus obsequitur invitanti : maluitque regiae simulationi periculose parere, quam turpiter repugnare. Adeo honestatem in cunctis observandam

Amletho parantur a Britanno insidiae.

putabat. Quem comminus obequitantem rex sub ipsa bipatentium portarum testudine adortus jaculo transegisset, ni ferrum subarmalis togae durities reppulisset. Amlethus levi recepto vulnere, eo loci se contulit : ubi Scotticam juventutem expectandi officio fungi jusserat : captivo novae conjugis speculatore ad regem remisso : qui se destinatas dominae literas loculorum custodiae furtim exemisse testando, crimen in Hermutrudam refunderet : ipsumque accurato genere excusationis reatu

Stratagema novum.

proditionis absolveret. Quem rex avidius fugientem insequi non moratus, majore copiarum parte privavit : ita ut Amlethus die postero salutem praelio defensurus, desperatis admodum resistendi viribus ad augendam multitudinis speciem exanima sociorum corpora, partim subjectis stipitibus fulta, partim propinquis lapidibus affixa : alia viventum more equis imposita, nullo armorum detracto perinde ac praeliatura seriatim in

embraced his son-in-law closely, but with little love, and welcomed him with a banquet, to hide his intended guile under a show of generosity. But Amleth, having learnt the deceit, dissembled his fear, took a retinue of two hundred horsemen, put on an under-shirt [of mail], and complied with the invitation, preferring the peril of falling in with the king's deceit to the shame of hanging back. So much heed for honour did he think that he must take in all things. As he rode up close, the king attacked him just under the porch of the folding doors, and would have thrust him through with his javelin, but that the hard shirt of mail threw off the blade. Amleth received a slight wound, and went to the spot where he had bidden the Scottish warriors wait on duty. He then sent back to the king his new wife's spy, whom he had captured. This man was to bear witness that he had secretly taken from the coffer where it was kept the letter which was meant for his mistress, and thus was to make the whole blame recoil on Hermutrude, by this studied excuse absolving Amleth from the charge of treachery. The king without tarrying pursued Amleth hotly as he fled, and deprived him of most of his forces. So Amleth, on the morrow, wishing to fight for dear life, and utterly despairing of his powers of resistance, tried to increase his apparent numbers. He put stakes under some of the dead bodies of his comrades to prop them up, set others on horseback like living men, and tied others to neighbouring stones, not taking off any of their armour, and dressing them in due order of line

aciem, cuneumque digesserit.   Nec rarius mortuorum cornu
erat, quam viventium globus.   Stupenda siquidem illa facies
erat : quum extincti raperentur ad praelia : defuncti decernere
cogerentur.   Quae res auctori otiosa non fuit quum ipsa
extinctorum imagines lacessentibus solis radiis immensi
agminis speciem darent.   Ita enim inania illa defunctorum
simulacra pristinum militum numerum referebant : ut nihil ex
eorum grege hesterna strage diminutum putares.   Quo
aspectu territi Britanni pugnam praecurrere fuga, a mortuis
superati : quos vivos oppresserant.   Quae victoria nescio
callidior, an foelicior existimanda sit.   Rex dum segnius
fugam intendit, ab imminentibus perimitur Danis.   Victor
Amlethus ingenti praeda acta, convulsisque Britanniae spoliis,
patriam cum conjugibus petit.

Interea defuncto Rorico, Vigletus regnum adeptus : Amlethi
matrem omni petulantiae genere fatigatam regiis opibus
vacuefecerat : filium ejus fraudato Lethrarum rege : cui
dignitatum jura dandi tollendique jus esset, Jutiae regnum
occupasse conquestus.   Quam rem Amlethus tanta animi
moderatione excepit : ut Vigleto splendidissimis victoriae suae
manubiis donato, calumniam beneficio rependere videretur.
Quem postmodum exigendae ultionis occasione suscepta, bello
lacessitum devicit atque ex occulto hoste manifestus evasit.
Fiallerum Scaniae praefectum exilio adegit : quem ad locum

Angliae
subjugatio
tertia a
Danis.

Vigletus
xxii Rex aut
potius
tyrannus
Iutiae.

and wedge, just as if they were about to engage. The wing
composed of the dead was as thick as the troop of the living.
It was an amazing spectacle this, of dead men dragged out to
battle, and corpses mustered to fight. The plan served him
well, for the very figures of the dead men showed like a vast
array as the sunbeams struck them. For those dead and
senseless shapes restored the original number of the army so
well, that the mass might have been unthinned by the slaughter
of yesterday. The Britons, terrified at the spectacle, fled
before fighting, conquered by the dead men whom they had
overcome in life. I cannot tell whether to think more of the
cunning or of the good fortune of this victory. The Danes
came down on the king as he was tardily making off, and
killed him. Amleth, triumphant, made a great plundering,
seized the spoils of Britain, and went back with his wives to
his own land.

Meanwhile Rorik had died, and Wiglek, who had come to
the throne, had harassed Amleth's mother with all manner of
insolence and stripped her of her royal wealth, complaining
that her son had usurped the kingdom of Jutland and
defrauded the King of Leire, who had the sole privilege of
giving and taking away the rights of high offices. This
treatment Amleth took with such forbearance as apparently
to return kindness for slander, for he presented Wiglek with
the richest of his spoils. But afterwards he seized a chance
of taking vengeance, attacked him, subdued him, and from a
covert became an open foe. Fialler, the governor of Skaane,

cui Undensakre nomen est, nostris ignotum populis, concessisse est fama. Post haec quum a Vigleto Scaniae
Sialandiaeque viribus recreato per legatos ad bellum pro-
vocaretur, mirifica animi industria duas circa se res : quarum
alteri probrum : alteri periculum inesset, fluctuari pervidit.
Sciebat quippe sibi si provocationem sequeretur imminere
vitae periculum : si refugeret, instare militiae probrum. Prae-
ponderavit tamen in contemplatore virtutum animo servandae
honestatis cupido, obtuditque cladis formidinem impensior
laudis aviditas : ne solidus gloriae fulgor meticulosa fati
declinatione corrumperetur. Animadvertebat quoque tantum
paene inter ignobilem vitam et splendidam mortem discriminis
interesse, quantum dignitas a contemptu distare cognoscitur.
Tanta autem Hermutrudae charitate tenebatur : ut majorem
futurae ejus viduitatis, quam propriae necis solicitudinem animo
insitam gestaret : omnique studio circumspiceret : qualiter ei
secundas nuptias ante belli ingressum conscisceret. Quam
obrem Hermutruda virilem professa fiduciam, ne in acie
quidem se eum deserturam spopondit : detestabilem inquiens
foeminam, quae marito morte conseri formidaret. Quam

Amlethi
caedes.

promissionis novitatem parum executa est. Nam quum
Amlethus apud Jutiam a Vigleto acie interemptus fuisset,
ultro in victoris praedam, amplexumque concessit. Ita votum

he drove into exile ; and the tale is, that Fialler retired to a
spot called Undensakre, which is unknown to our peoples.
After this, Wiglek, recruited with the forces of Skaane and
Zealand, sent envoys to challenge Amleth to a war. Amleth,
with his marvellous shrewdness, saw that he was tossed
between two difficulties, one of which involved disgrace and
the other danger. For he knew that if he took up the
challenge he was threatened with peril of his life, while to
shrink from it would disgrace his reputation as a soldier.
Yet in that spirit ever fixed on deeds of prowess the desire
to save his honour won the day. Dread of disaster was
blunted by more vehement thirst for glory ; he would not
tarnish the unblemished lustre of his fame by timidly skulking
from his fate. Also he saw that there is almost as wide a
gap between a mean life and a noble death as that which is
acknowledged between honour and disgrace themselves. Yet
he was enchained by such love for Hermutrude, that he was
more deeply concerned in his mind about her future widowhood
than about his own death, and cast about very zealously how
he could decide on some second husband for her before the
opening of the war. Hermutrude, therefore, declared that
she had the courage of a man, and promised that she would
not forsake him even on the field, saying that the woman
who dreaded to be united with her lord in death was abominable. But she kept this rare promise ill ; for when Amleth had
been slain by Wiglek in battle in Jutland, she yielded herself
up unasked to be the conqueror's spoil and bride. Thus all

omne foemineum fortunae varietas abripit : temporum mutatio
dissolvit : et muliebris animi fidem lubrico nixam vestigio
fortuiti rerum casus extenuant : quae sicut ad pollicendum
facilis, ita ad persolvendum segnis : variis voluptatis irritamentis
astringitur atque ad recentia semper avidius expetenda,
veterum immemor : anhela, praeceps cupiditate dissultat. Hic
Amlethi exitus fuit : qui si parem naturae atque fortunae
indulgentiam expertus fuisset, aequasset fulgore superos :
Herculea virtutibus opera transscendisset. Insignis ejus
sepultura ac nomine campus apud Jutiam extat.

vows of women are loosed by change of fortune and melted by the shifting of time; the faith of their soul rests on a slippery foothold, and is weakened by casual chances; glib in promises, and as sluggish in performance, all manner of lustful promptings enslave it, and it bounds away with panting and precipitate desire, forgetful of old things, in the ever hot pursuit after something fresh. So ended Amleth. Had fortune been as kind to him as nature, he would have equalled the gods in glory, and surpassed the labours of Hercules by his deeds of prowess. A plain in Jutland is to be found, famous for his name and burial-place.

LE
CINQVIESME
TOME DES HISTOIRES
Tragiqves,

Contenant plusieurs Discours memorables, la plus part recueilly des histoires aduenues de nostre temps.

Le tout reueu, corrigé, & augmenté, outre les precedentes impressions : Par F. DE **BEL-LEFOREST** *Commingeois.*

A PARIS,

Chez Gabriel Buon, au clos Bruneau, à l'enseigne de sainct Claude.

1582.

AVEC PRIVILEGE DV ROY.

THE

HYSTORIE
OF HAMBLET

LONDON :

Imprinted by *Richard Bradocke*, for *Thomas Pauier*,
and are to be sold at his shop in Corne-hill, neere to
the Royall Exchange.

1608.

ARGUMENT

Le desir de regner conduit les hommes à devenir meurtriers, et traistres.

Ce n'est d'aujourdhuy, ny d'un seul jour que l'envie regnant à tellement aveuglé les hommes, que sans respect de sang ny d'obligation, ils se ont oubliez jusqu'à là, que de souiller leur vertu premiere, en espandant le sang, duquel à plus juste tiltre, ils deussent estre defenseurs. Car quelle autre impression avoit saisy le cœur de Romule, lors que souz couleur d'une telle quelle loy, il ensanglanta ses mains du sang de son propre frere, sinon ceste abominable convoitise? Laquelle si sagement, et en toutes ses occurrences, bon heurs, et circonstances estoit consideree, je ne sçache homme qui

Condition miserable de ceux qui regnent.

n'aymast mieux vivre à son ayse, et en son privé, sans charge, qu'estant craint et honoré de tous, avoir aussi les charges de tous sur les espaules, servir aux fantasies d'un peuple, craindre à tous propos, et de mesme se voir exposé à mille occasions de crainte, et le plus souvent assailly, lors qu'il se pense tenir fortune comme l'esclave de ses fantasies. Et toutesfois les hommes achetent une telle misere et vie calamiteuse, pour la

THE ARGUMENT

I⟨T⟩ is not at this present, neither yet a small time since, that envy raigning in the worlde hath in such sort blinded men, that without respect of consanguinitie, friendship, or favour whatsoever, they forget themselves so much as that they spared not to defile their hands with the blood of those men, who by all law and right they ought chiefly to defend and cherish. For what other impression was it that entered into Romulus heart, when, under pretence of I know not what lawe, he defiled his hands with the blood of his owne brother, but the abhominable vice of desire to raigne ? which, if in all the accurrences, prosperities, and circumstances thereof, it were well wayed and considered, I know not any man that had not rather live at his ease, and privately without charge, then, being feared and honored of all men, to beare all the charge and burden upon his shoulders ; to serve and please the fantasies of the common people ; to live continually in feare, and to see himself exposed to a thousand occasions of danger, and most commonly assailed and spoiled when hee thinkes verily to hold Fortune as slave to his fantasies and will, and yet buyes such and so great misery for the vaine

The desire of rule causeth men to become traytors and murtherers.

The miserable condition of such as rule over others.

167

gloire caduque de ce monde, au prix de leurs amis, et font
prodigue largesse de leur conscience, laquelle ne s'esmeut pour
meurtre, trahison, fraude, ou meschanceté qu'ils commettent,
pourveu que la voye leur soit ouverte, laquelle les face parvenir

Romule a
peu de
raison occist
son frere.

à ceste miserable felicité, que de commander sur tout un
peuple, ainsi que j'ay dict de Romule, lequel avec un forfaict
abhominable, se prepara la voye au ciel, et non avec la Vertu,

Ciceron au
Paradoxes.

ainsi que chante l'ambitieux Orateur, et sedicieux harangueur
dé Rome, qui trouvoit les degrez du Ciel, et le chemin de la
Vertu és trahisons, ravissements, et massacres, faicts par celuy
qui le premier posa les fondements de leur ville.   Et sans
nous esloigner des Romains, qui incita les enfans d'Ance

Tarquin
l'ancien
occis à
Rome.

Martie à massacrer Tarquin l'ancien, sinon ce desir de regner
mesme, lequel avoit esguillonné ledict l'ancien d'en frustrer
les vrays et legitimes heritiers ?   Qui conduit Tarquin le superbe à souiller traittreusement ses mains du sang de son beau-

Servie Tul-
li occis par
son gendre.

pere Servie Tullie, que ce desir sans bride, ny justice d'oc-
cuper la principauté de Rome ?   Ceste façon de faire ne se
discontinua onc en la cité chef de l'Empire : veu que et

Rome sub-
jette à sedi-
tion, et
pourquoy.

durant qu'elle estoit gouvernee par les plus grands et plus
sages, souz l'election et suffrages du peuple, on y a veu infinité
de seditions, troubles, pillages, rançonnemens, confiscations, et
massacres, procedans de ce seul fondement, et principe, lequel
saisist les hommes allichez de l'esperance de se faire chef de

and fraile pleasures of this world, with the losse of his owne
soule ; making so large a measure of his conscience, that it is
not once mooved at any murther, treason, deceit, nor wickednes whatsoever he committed, so the way may be opened and
made plaine unto him, whereby hee may attaine to that miserable felicitie, to command and governe a multitude of men
(as I said of Romulus), who, by a most abhominable action,
prepared himselfe a way to heaven (but not by vertue).

Romulus,
for small or
no cause,
killed his
brother.

The ambitious and seditious Orator of Rome supposed the
degrees and steps to heaven, and the wayes to vertue, to
consist in the treasons, ravishments, and massacres committed
by him that first layd the foundations of that citty. And
not to leave the hystories of Rome, what, I pray you, incited
Ancius Martinus to massacre Tarquin the Elder, but the desire
of raigning as a king, who before had bin the onely man to
move and solicite the saide Tarquinius to bereave the right
heires and inheriters thereof ? What caused Tarquinius the
Proud traiterously to imbrue his hands in the blood of Servius
Tullius, his father in law, but onely that furnish and unbridled desire to be commander over the cittie of Rome?
which practise never ceased nor discontinued in the said principall cittie of the empire, as long as it was governed by the
greatest and wisest personages chosen and elected by the
people ; for therein have been seen infinite numbers of seditions, troubles, pledges, ransommings, confiscations and
massacres, onely proceeding from this ground and principle,
which entereth into mens hearts, and maketh them covet and

Cicero in his
Paradoxes.

Tarquin the
elder slaine
in Rome.

Servius
Tullius
slaine by
his sonne
in law.

Wherefore
Rome was
subject to
seditions.

toute une republique.   Et apres que le peuple fut privé de sa
liberté, et que l'Empire se veit soumis à la volonté et fantasie

Plusieurs
parvenuz à
l'Empire par
meurtre.
d'un seul qui commandoit sur tous, je vous prie feuilletez moy
les livres, lisez diligemment les historiens, et regardez les
moyens tenuz par la pluspart pour parvenir à telle puissance,
et verrez les poisons, assasinats, et meurtres secrets faciliter
la voye à ceux, qui n'osoient l'attenter publiquement ou ne
pouvoient parvenir à guerre ouverte.   Et d'autant que
l'histoire que je pretens vous reciter, est apuyee sur la
trahison de frere conte frere, je ne veux m'esloigner aussi du
sujet : voulant neantmoins vous faire veoir, qu'encore cela a
eu place de long temps, qu'on s'est attaché à son sang le plus
proche pour se faire grand : et qu'il y en a eu que ne pouvans
attendre le temps juste des succes, ont advancé la mort à leurs

Absalon
conspira
contre
David son
pere.
parens, ainsi que vouloit faire Absalon au sainct Roy David
son pere et comme on lit de Domitian, qui empoisonna
son frere Tite le plus courtois, et liberal Prince qui jamais
tinst l'Empire de Rome.   Et Dieu scait si de nostre
temps les exemples de telle meschanceté nous manquent,
et si les fils ne conspirent contre le salut de leur pere :

Zelin fit
mourir son
pere
Bajazeth.
veu que Sultan Zelin Roy des Turcs, fut si homme de
bien que de ne pouvoir attendre que Bajazeth son pere
mourust de sa belle mort naturelle, si encor il n'y eust

desirous to be heads and rulers of a whole common wealth. And after the people were deprived of that libertie of election, and that the empire became subject to the pleasure and fantasie of one man, commanding al the rest, I pray you peruse their bookes, and read diligently their hystories, and do but looke into the meanes used by the most part of their kings and emperours to attaine to such power and authoritie, and you shall see how poysons, massacres, and secret murthers, were the meanes to push them forwards that durst not openly attempt it, or else could not compasse to make open warres. And for that the Hystory (which I pretend to shew unto you) is chiefly grounded upon treason, committed by one brother against the other, I will not erre far out of the matter ; thereby desiring to shew you, that it is and hath been a thing long since practised and put in use by men, to spill the blood of their neerest kinsmen and friends to attaine to the honour of being great and in authoritie ; and that there hath bin some, that being impatient of staying till their just time of succes-sion, have hastened the death of their owne parents : as Absolon would have done to the holy king David, his father ; and as wee read of Domitian, that poysoned his brother Titus, the most curtious and liberall prince that ever swayed the empire of Rome. And God knowes we have many the like examples in this our time, where the sonne conspired against the father ; for that Sultan Zelin, emperour of Turkes, was so honest a man, that fearing Bajazeth, his father, would die of his naturall death, and that thereby he should have stayd

Divers
attained to
the empire
by murther.

Absolon
conspired
against
David his
father.

Zelim slew
his father
Bajazeth.

Soliman fait
estrangler
son fils
Mustapha.

Rustain
Bassa cor-
rompus par
les Juifs.

Grand mal-
heur de no-
stre temps.

aidé pour s'emparer du royaume. Sultan Soliman
successeur de Zelin, quoy qu'il n'ayt rien attentté contre
celuy qui l'avoit engendrè si est ce que sollicite d'une fraieur
d'estre chassé de son siege, et portant envie à la vertu de
Mustapha son fils, esguillonné à se faire, si par Rustain Bassa,
gaigné par les presens des Juifs, ennemis de ce jeune Prince,
il le feit estrangler avec une corde d'arc, sans vouloir ouyr les
justifications de celuy qui onc ne luy avoit fait offense.
Laissons les Turcs comme barbares, et le throsne desquels
est ordinairement estably par l'effusion du sang de ceux, qui
les atouchent de plus pres de consanguinité, et alliance pour
considerer quelles tragedies ont esté jouees pour ce mesme cas
de la memoire de noz peres en Ecosse et Angleterre, et avec
quelle charité se sont caressez les plus proches parens
ensemble. Si vous n'aviez les histoires en main, si la
memoire n'en estoit comme toute fresche, si un Roy n'estoit
mort hors de saison, et si les plus tyrans, et qui n'ont aucun
droict és terres et seigneuries de leurs souverains, si les enfans
ne conspiroyent la mort de leurs peres, les femmes celles de
leurs espoux, si tout cela n'estoit presque cogneu à chascun,
j'en ferois un long discours : mais les choses estant si claires,
la verité tant descouverte, le peuple presque abbreuvé de telles
trahisons, je passeray outre pour suyvre mon project, et
monstrer que si l'iniquité d'un frere a faict perdre la vie à
celuy qui luy estoit si proche, aussi la vengeance ne s'en est
esloignee : mais quelle vengeance ? la plus gaillarde, sagement
conduite, et bravement executee, que homme sçauroit imaginer,

too long for the empire, bereaved him of his life; and Sultan Soliman, his successor, although he attempted not any thing against his father, yet being mooved with a certaine feare to bee deposed from his emperie, and bearing a hatred to Mustapha, his son (incited therunto by Rustain Bassa, whom the Jewes, enemies to the yong prince, had by gifts procured thereunto), caused him to be strangled with a bowe string, without hearing him (that never had offended his father) once speake to justifie his innocencie.   But let us leave the Turkes, like barbarians as they are, whose throne is ordinarily established by the effusion of the blood of those that are neerest of kindred and consanguinitie to the empire, and consider what tragedies have bin plaid to the like effect in the memorie of our ancestors, and with what charitie and love the neerest kindreds and friends among them have bin intertained.   One of the other, if you had not the hystories extant before you, if the memorie were not in a manner fresh, and known almost to every man, I would make a long discourse thereof; but things being so cleare and evident, the truth so much discovered, and the people almost, as it were, glutted with such treasons, I will omit them, and follow my matter, to shew you that, if the iniquitie of a brother caused his brother to loose his life, yet that vengeance was not long after

(margin note:) Soliman caused Mustapha, his sonne, to be hanged.

(margin note:) Great mischiefe in our age.

Dieu tardif
à ire, mais
vengeur
toutesfois,
voy
Plutarque
opuscule de
la tardine
vengeance
de Dieu.

à fin que les traistres cognoissent que jaçoit que la punition de leurs forfaicts soit retardee, si se peuvent ils asseurer, de jamais ne passer sans sentir la main puissante et vengeresse de Dieu, lequel estant tardif à courroux, ne laisse à la fin de donner les signes effroyables de son ire sur ceulx qui s'oubliants en leur devoir, espandent le sang innocent, et trahissent les chefz, ausquels ils doivent tout service, honneur et reverence.

Avec quelle ruse Amleth, qui depuis fut Roy de Dannemarch, vengea la mort de son pere Horuuendille, occis par Fengon son frere, et autre occurrence de son histoire.

HIST. TROISIESME.

Quoy que j'eusse deliberé dés le commencement de ce mien œuvre de ne m'esloigner, tant peu soit, des histoires de nostre temps, y ayant assez de sujets pleins de succez tragiques, si est-ce que partie pour ne pouvoir en discourir sans chatouiller plusieurs ausquels je ne voudroy desplaire, partie aussi que l'argument que j'ay en main m'a semblé digne d'estre offert à la noblesse Françoise, pour les grandes, et gaillardes occurrences qui y sont deduites, j'ay un peu esgaré mon cours de ce siecle, et sortant de France et pays voysins, suis allé visiter l'histoire Danoise afin qu'elle puisse servir et de

delayed; to the end that traitors may know, although the punishment of their trespasses committed be stayed for awhile, yet that they may assure themselves that, without all doubt, they shal never escape the puisant and revenging hand of God; who being slow to anger, yet in the ende doth not faile to shew some signes and evident tokens of his fearefull judgement upon such as, forgetting their duties, shed innocent blood, and betray their rulers, whom they ought chiefly to honour, serve, and reverence.

God stayeth his wrath, but yet revengeth wrong: read Plutarch Opuscules, of the slownesse of God's judgements.

THE PREFACE

Although in the beginning of this Hystorie I had determined not to have troubled you with any other matter than a hystorie of our owne time, having sufficient tragicall matter to satisfie the minds of men; but because I cannot wel discourse thereof without touching many personages whom I would not willingly displease, and partly because the argument that I have in hand, seemed unto me a thing worthy to bee offered to our French nobilitie, for the great and gallant accurrences therein set downe, I have somewhat strayed from my course, as touching the tragedies of this our age, and, starting out of France and over Neitherlanders countries, I have ventured to visit the hystories of Denmarke, that it may serve for an example of vertue and contentment to our nation (whom I specially seeke to please), and for whose satisfaction I have not left any flower whatsoever untasted, from whence I have not drawne the most perfect and delicate hony, thereby to bind them to my dili-

exemple de vertu, et de contentement aux nostres, ausquels
je tasche de complaire, et pour le rassasiement desquels je ne
laisse fleur qui ne soit goutee pour leur en tirer le miel'le plus
parfait et delicat, afin de les obliger à ma diligence : ne me
souciant de l'ingratitude du temps present, qui laisse ainsi en
arriere et sans recompence ceux, qui servent au public, et
honorent, par leur travail et diligence leur pays, et illustrent
la France d'autant que souuent la faulte vient plustost d'eux
que non des grands, lesquels ont d'autres affaires qui les des-
tournent de chose qui semble de peu de consequence.   Joinct
que je me tiens pour plus que satisfait en ce contentement et
grande liberté d'esprit, de laquelle je jouys estant aymé de la
noblesse, pour laquelle je travaille avec si peu de relache,
caressé des gens de sçavoir pour les admirer et leur faire
reverence, telle que leur excellence merite, et honoré du
peuple, duquel jaçoit que je ne cherche le jugement, pour ne
l'estimer assez suffisant de faire vivre le nom de quelque
homme illustre si me pense-je assez heureux d'avoir
atteint à ceste felicité, qu'il se trouve peu d'hommes qui
dasdaignent de lire mes œuvres.   Et y en a plusieurs qui
les admirent : comme d'autres, qui poussez d'envie blas-
ment et calomnient, ausquels je ne confesse estre grandement obligé.   Entant qu'ils sont cause que je veille
d'auantage, et que par mon trauail je suis plus aymé et
honoré que jamais, qui est le plaisir plus grand que j'aye, et

Gens de
letre mepri-
sez et sans
recompence
en ce temps.

Contente-
ment de
l'auteur de
cest œuvre.

gence herein; not caring for the ingratitude of the time present, that leaveth (as it were rejecteth) without recompence such as serve the common wealth, and by their travell and diligence honour their countrey, and illustrate the realme of France: so that oftentimes the fault proceedeth rather from them, then from the great personages that have other affaires which withdraw them from things that seeme of small consequence. Withall, esteeming my selfe more than satisfied in this contentment and freedome which I now injoy, being loved of the nobilitie, for whom I travell without grudging, favoured of men of learning and knowledge, for admiring and reverencing them according to their worthinesse, and honoured of the common people, of whom, although I crave not their judgement, as not esteeming them of abilitie to eternize the name of a worthy man, yet I account my selfe sufficiently happy to have attained to this felicitie, that few or no men refuse, or disdaine to reade my workes, many admiring and wondering thereat; as there are some that, provoked by envie, blame and condemne it. To whom I confesse my selfe much bound and beholding, for that by their meanes I am the more vigelant, and so by my travell much more beloved and honored then ever I was; which to mee is the greatest pleasure that I can injoy, and the most abundant treasures in my coffers, wherewith I am more satisfied and contented then (if without comparison) I enjoyed the greatest treasures in all Asia. Now, returning to our matter, let us beginne to declare the Hystorie.

la richesse la plus abondante de mes coffres, de laquelle
toutesfois je suis plus content que si sans nom je jouyssois
des tresors les plus grands qui soyent en l'Asie.   Revenant
donc à nostre propos, et recueillans un peu de loing le sujet
de nostre dire, faut sçavoir que longtemps au paravant
que le Royaume de Dannemarch receut la foy de Jesus, et
embrassast la doctrine et saint lavement des Chrestiens,
comme le peuple fut assez Barbare et mal civilisé, aussi
leurs Princes estoyent cruelz, sans foy ny loyauté, et qui
ne jouyent qu'au boutehors, taschans à se getter de leurs
sieges, ou de s'offencer, fust en leurs biens ou en l'honneur,
et le plus souvent en la vie, n'ayans guere de coustume de
mettre à rançon leurs prisonniers, ains les sacrifioyent à
la cruelle vengeance, imprimee naturellement en leurs ame.
Que s'il y avoit quelque bon Roy ou Prince, qui poussé
des instincts les plus parfaitz de nature, voulut s'addonner à
la vertu, et usast de courtoisie quoy que le peuple l'eut en
admiration (comme la vertu se rend admirable aux vicieux
mesme) si est ce que l'envie de ses voisins estoit si grande,
qu'on ne cessoit jamais jusqu' à tant que le monde fut
despeché de cest homme ainsi debonnaire.   Regnant donc

Danois jadis
fort rudes et
barbares.

Cruauté des
Danoys.

The Hystorie of Hamblet

Prince of Denmarke

CHAPTER I

How Horvendile and Fengon were made Governours of the Province of Ditmarse, and how Horvendile marryed Geruth, the daughter to Roderick, chief K. of Denmark, by whom he had Hamblet : ana how after his marriage his brother Fengon slewe him trayterously, and marryed his brothers wife, and what followed.

You must understand, that long time before the kingdome of Denmark received the faith of Jesus Christ, and imbraced the doctrin of the Christians, that the common people in those dayes were barbarous and uncivill, and their princes cruell, without faith or loyaltie, seeking nothing but murther, and deposing (or at the least) offending each other, either in honours, goods, or lives; not caring to ransome such as they tooke prisoners, but rather sacrificing them to the cruell vengeance naturally imprinted in their hearts : in such sort, that if ther were sometime a good prince or king among them, who beeing adorned with the most perfect gifts of nature, would adict himselfe to vertue, and use courtesie, although the people held him in admiration (as vertue is admirable to the most wicked) yet the envie of his neighbors was so great, that they never ceased untill that vertuous man were dispatched out of

The Danes in times past barbarous and uncivill.

The crueltie of the Danes.

179

en Dannemarch Rorique, apres qu'il eust apaisé les troubles
du pays, et chassé les Sueons et Sclaves de ses terres, il
departist les Provinces de son Royaume, y mettant des
Gouverneurs, qui depuis (anisi qu'il en est advenu en
France) ont porté tiltre de Ducz, Marquis et Contes: il
donna le gouvernement de Jutie (qui s'appelle vulgairement

à present Diethmarsen, et est assise sur le Chersonnese des
Cimbres, en celle estressisure de terre, qui avoisine la mer
comme une pointe, laquelle vers le North regarde le Royaume
de Norvege) à deux seigneurs vaillans hommes nommez
Horvvendille et Fengon, enfans de Gervvendille, lequel
avoit esté aussi Gouverneur de celle Province.   Or le plus
grand honneur que pouvoyent acquerir les hommes de sorte
en ce temps la, estoit en exerçant l'art d'escumeur et
pirate sur mer, assailans leurs voisins, et ravageant les terres
voisines.   Et tant plus accroissoit leur gloire et reputation,
comme ils alloyent voltiger par les Provinces, et Isles

lointaines : en quoy Horvvendille se faisoit dire le premier
de son temps, et le plus renommé de tous ceux qut escu-
moyent pour lors la mer, et havres de Septentrion.   La
grand renommee de cestui cy esmeut le cœur du Roy de

Norvege, nommé Collere, lequel se faschoit que Horvvendille
le surmontast en fait d'armes, et obscurcist la gloire qu'il
avoit desja aquise au fait de la marine : car c'estoit l'honneur,
plus que les richesses qui esguillonnoit ces Princes Barbares à

the world.   King Rodericke, as then raigning in Denmarke, after hee had appeased the troubles in the countrey, and driven the Sweathlanders and Slaveans from thence, he divided the kingdom into divers provinces, placing governours therein ; who after (as the like happened in France) bare the names of Dukes, Marqueses, and Earls, giving the government of Jutie (at this present called Ditmarsse) lying upon the countrey of the Cimbrians, in the straight or narrow part of land that sheweth like a point or cape of ground upon the sea, which neithward bordereth upon the countrey of Norway, two valiant and warlike lords Horvendile and Fengon, sonnes to Gervendile, who likewise had beene governour of that province.   Now the greatest honor that men of noble birth could at that time win and obtaine, was in exercising the art of piracie upon the seas, assayling their neighbours, and the countries bordering upon them ; and how much the more they used to rob, pill, and spoyle other provinces, and ilands far adjacent, so much the more their honours and reputation increased and augmented : wherin Horvendile obtained the highest place in his time, beeing the most renouned pirate that in those dayes scoured the seas and havens of the north parts : whose great fame so mooved the heart of Collere, king of Norway, that he was much grieved to heare that Horvendile surmounting him in feates of armes, thereby obscuring the glorie by him alreadie obtained upon the seas : (honor more than covetousnesse of riches (in those dayes) being the reason that provoked those barbarian princes to overthrow

Rodericke
king of
Denmarke.

Jutie at this
time, called
then Dit-
marsse.

Horvendile
a king and
a pirate.

Collere king
of Norway.

s'accabler l'un l'autre, sans qu'ils se souciassent de mourir de
la main de quelque vaillant homme.   Ce Roy magnanime
ayant deffié au combat, corps à corps, Horvvendille, y fut
receu avec pactes, que celuy qui seroit vaincu perdroit toutes les
richesses qui seroient en leurs vaisseaux, et le vainqueur feroit
enterrer honnestement celuy qui seroit occis au combat, car la
mort estoit le pris et salaire de celuy, qui perdroit la bataille.

Horvvendille   Que sert de tant discourir? le Roy (quoy que vaillant,
occist le
Roy Collere.   courageux, et adextre fut-il) en fin fut vaincu et occis par
le Danois, lequel luy feit dresser tout soudain un tombeau,
et luy feit des obseques dignes d'un Roy, suivant les façons
de faire et superstitions de leur siecle, et selon l'accord du
combat, despouillant la suite du Roy de leur richesses, ayant
fait mourir une seur du Roy defunct, fort gaillarde et
vaillante guerriere, et aiant couru toute la coste de Norvege,
et jusques aux Isles Septentrionalles, il s'en revinst chargé
d'honneur et de richesses, envoyant à son souverain le Roy
Rorique, la plus part du butin et despouilles, à fin de le
gaigner, et qu'estant si brave, il peust tenir le lieu des plus
favoris de sa majesté.   Le Roy alliché de ses presents, et
s'estimant heureux, d'avoir un si homme de bien pour subjet,
tacha avec une grande faveur, et courroisie et se rendre à
jamais obligé: car il luy donna pour femme Gerutthe sa fille,
de la quelle il sçavoit ce seigneur estre fort amoureux, et

and vanquish one the other, not caring to be slaine by the handes of a victorious person). This valiant and hardy king having challenged Horvendile to fight with him body to body, the combate was by him accepted, with conditions, that hee which should be vanquished should loose all the riches he had in his ship, and that the vanquisher should cause the body of the vanquished (that should bee slaine in the combate) to be honourably buried, death being the prise and reward of him that should loose the battaile : and to conclude, Collere, king of Norway (although a valiant, hardy, and couragious prince) was in the end vanquished and slaine by Horvendile, who presently caused a tombe to be erected, and therein (with all honorable obsequies fit for a prince) buried the body of king Collere, according to their aunicent manner and superstitions in these dayes, and the conditions of the combate, bereaving the kings shippes of all their riches ; and having slaine the kings sister, a very brave and valiant warriour, and over runne all the coast of Norway, and the Northern Ilands, returned home againe layden with much treasure, sending the most part thereof to his soveraigne, king Rodericke, thereby to procure his good liking, and so to be accounted one of the greatest favourites about his majestie.

Horvendile slew Collere.

The king, allured by those presents, and esteeming himselfe happy to have so valiant a subject, sought by a great favour and coutesie to make him become bounden unto him perpetually, giving him Geruth his daughter to his wife, of whom he knew Horvendile to bee already much inamored. And

voulut luy mesme la conduire, pour plus l'honnoter, jusques en
Jutie, ou les nopces furent celebree, selon la façon ancienne :
et pour trousser briefvement matiere, de ce mariage sortist

Amleth filz
de ce Roy
Horvven-
dille.

Amleth, duquel je pretens parler et pour lequel j'ay desseigné
le discours de l'histoire presente.   Fengon frere de ce genre
Royal, poussé d'un esprit d'envie, crevant de despit en son

Conspiration
de Fengon
contre son
frere Hor-
vvendille.

cœur, tant pour la grand' reputation aquise par Horvvendille
au maniement des armes, que solicité d'une sotte jalousie,
le voyant honnoré de l'alliance et amitié royalle, craignant
d'estre depossedé de sa part du gouvernement, ou plustost
desirant destre seul en la principauté, et obscurcir par ce
moyen, la memorre des victoires et conquestes de son frere,
delibera, comme que ce fust, de le faire mourir.   Ce qui luı
succeda assez aisement, nul ne se doubtant de luy, et chacun
pensant que d'un tel nœud d'alliance et consanguinité, ne
pourroit jamais sortir autre chose, que les effetz pleins de vertu
et courtoisie : mais comme j'ay dit le desir de regner, ne
respecte sang, ny amitié, et n'a soucy aucun de vertu : voire
il est sans respect, ny reverence des loix, ny de la majeste
divine, s'il ny est possible que celuy qui sans aucun droit
envahist le bien d'autruy, aye quelque opinion de la divinité.
Ne voila pas vn fin et rusé Conseiller ? mais il devoit penser
que la mere sachans les desseins du mary ne mettroit son fils
en adventure de mort.   Ainsi Fengon ayant gaigné secrette-

the more to honor him, determined himselfe in person to conduct her into Jutie, where the marriage was celebrated according to the ancient manner: and to be briefe, of this marriage proceeded Hamblet, of whom I intend to speake, and for his cause have chosen to renew this present hystorie

Fengon, brother to this prince Horvendile, who [not] onely fretting and despighting in his heart at the great honor and reputation wonne by his brother in warlike affaires, but solicited and provoked by a foolish jealousie to see him honored with royall aliance, and fearing thereby to bee deposed from his part of the government, or rather desiring to be onely governour, thereby to obscure the memorie of the victories and conquests of his brother Horvendile, determined (whatsoever happened) to kill him; which hee effected in such sort, that no man once so much as suspected him, every man esteeming that from such and so firme a knot of alliance and consanguinitie there could proceed no other issue then the full effects of vertue and courtesie: but (as I sayd before) the desire of bearing soveraigne rule and authoritie respecteth neither blood nor amitie, nor caring for vertue, as being wholly without respect of lawes, or majestie devine; for it is not possible that hee which invadeth the countrey and taketh away the riches of an other man without cause or reason, should know or feare God. Was not this a craftie and subtile counsellor? but he might have thought that the mother, knowing her husbands case, would not cast her sonne into the danger of death. But Fengon, having secretly assembled

Hamlet sonne to Horvendile.

Fengon, his conspiracie against his brother.

ment des hommes, se sentant assez fort pour executer son entreprinse, se rua un jour en un banquet, sur son frere lequel il occist autant traistreusement, comme cauteleusement il se purgea devant ses sujetz, d'un si detestable massacre : veu qu'avant que mettre la main sanguinolente, et parricide sur son frere, il avoit incestueusement souillé la couche fraternelle, abusant de la femme de celuy, duquel il devoit autant pour-chasser l'honneur, comme il en poursuivoit : et effectua la ruine : aussi il est bien vray, que l'homme, qui se laisse aller apres un vice, et forfait detestable estant la liaison des pechez fort grande, il ne se soucie en rien de s'abbandonner à un pire, et plus abhominable. Or couvrit il avec si grande ruse et cautelle, et souz un voile si fardé de simplicité, son audace, et mechanceté, que favori de l'honneste amitiè qu'il portoit à sa belle sœur, pour l'amour de laquelle il se disoit avoir ainsi puny son frere, que son peché trouva excuse à l'endroit du peuple, et fut reputé comme justice envers la noblesse : D'autant qu'estant Geruthe autant douce et courtoise, que Dame qui fut en tout les Royaumes du septentrion, et telle-ment que jamais n'avoit tant peu soit offencé homme de ses subjetz, soit du peuple, ou des courtisans, ce paillard, et infame meurtrier, calomnia le defunct, d'avoir voulu occir ceste Dame, et que s'estant trouvé sur le poinct qu'il taschoit de la massacrer, il avoit defendu la Dame et occis son frere, parant aux coups ruez sur la Princesse innocente, et sans fiel, ny malice quelconque. Il n'eust ja faute de tesmoins

Fengon occist son frere Hor-vvendille.

Ruse du meurtrier Fengon.

certain men, and perceiving himself strong enough to execute
his interprise, Horvendile his brother being at a banquet with
his friends, sodainely set upon him, where he slewe him as
traiterously, as cunningly he purged himselfe of so detestable
a murther to his subjects ; for that before he had any violent
or bloody handes, or once committed parricide upon his brother,
hee had incestuously abused his wife, whose honour hee ought
as well to have sought and procured as traiterously he pursued and effected his destruction.   And it is most certaine,
that the man that abandoneth himselfe to any notorious and
wicked action, whereby he becommeth a great sinner, he
careth not to commit much more haynous and abhominable
offences, and covered his boldnesse and wicked practise with
so great subtiltie and policie, and under a vaile of meere sim-
plicitie, that beeing favoured for the honest love that he bare
to his sister in lawe, for whose sake, hee affirmed, he had in
that sort murthered his brother, that his sinne found excuse
among the common people and of the nobilitie was esteemed
for justice : for that Geruth, being as courteous a princesse as
any then living in the north parts, and one that had never
once so much as offended any of her subjects, either commons
or courtyers, this adulterer and infamous murtherer, slaun-
dered his dead brother, that hee would have slaine his wife,
and that hee by chance finding him upon the point ready to
do it, in defence of the lady had slaine him, bearing off the
blows, which as then he strooke at the innocent princesse,
without any other cause of malice whatsoever.   Wherein hee

Fengon
killeth his
brother.

approuvans son faict, et qui deposerent selon le dire du calom-
niateur, mais c'estoyent ceux mesmes qui l'avoyent accompaigné, comme participans de la conjure et qu'au reste an
lieu de le poursuivre, comme parricide et incestueux, chacun
des courtisans luy applaudissoit, et le flattoit en sa fortune
prospere, et faisoient les Gentilshommes plus de compte des
faux rapporteurs, et honnoroyent les calomniateurs, plus que
ceux qui mettans en jeu les vertus du deffunct, eussent voulu
punir les brigans, et assasineurs de sa vie. Qui fut cause
que Fengon enhardy pour telle impunité, osa enor s'accoupler
par mariage, à celle qu'il entretenoit execrablement, durant la
vie du bon Horvvendille, souillant son non de double vice, et
chargeant sa conscience de double impieté, d'adultere incestueux, et de felonnie, et parricide. Et celle mal-heureuse
qui avoit receu l'honneur d'estre l'espouse d'un des plus
vaillans et sages Princes de Septentrion, souffrit de s'abaisser
jusques à telle villenie, que de luy faucer la foy: et qui
pis est, espouser encor celuy, lequel estoit le meurtrier
tiran de son espoux legitime: ce qui donna à penser à
plusieurs, qu'elle pouvoit avoir causé ce meurtre pour jouir
librement de son adultere. Que sçauroit on voir de plus
effronté, qu'une grande, depuis qu'elle s'esgare en ses
honestetez? Ceste Princesse, qui au commencement estoit

Calomnia-
teurs plus
honorez en
court que
la verite.

Mariage
incestueux
de Fengon
avec sa
belleseur.

wanted no false witnesses to approove his act, which deposed
in like sort, as the wicked calumniator himselfe protested,
being the same persons that had born him company, and
were participants of his treason; so that insteed of pursuing
him as a parricide and an incestuous person, al the courtyers
admired and flattered him in his good fortune, making more
account of false witnesses and detestable wicked reporters,
and more honouring the calumniators, then they esteemed
of those that seeking to call the matter in question, and admiring the vertues of the murthered prince, would have
punished the massacrers and bereavers of his life.   Which
was the cause that Fengon, boldned and incouraged by such
impunitie, durst venture to couple himselfe in marriage with
her whom hee used as his concubine during good Horvendiles life, in that sort spotting his name with a double vice,
and charging his conscience with abhominable guilt, and
two-fold impietie, as incestuous adulterie and parricide murther : and that the unfortunate and wicked woman, that had
receaved the honour to bee the wife of one of the valiantest
and wiseth princes in the north, imbased her selfe in such
vile sort, as to falsifie her faith unto him, and which is worse,
to marrie him, that had bin the tyranous murtherer of her
lawfull husband ; which made divers men thinke that she
had beene the causer of the murther, thereby to live in her
adultery without controle.   But where shall a man finde a
more wicked and bold woman, then a great parsonage once
having loosed the bands of honor and honestie ?   This prin-

Slanderers more honoured in court then vertuous persons.

The incestuous marriage of Fengon with his brother's wife.

honnoree de chacun, pour ses rares vertus, et coutoisies, et

cherie de son espoux, dés aussi tost qu'elle preste l'oreille au

tyran Fengon, elle oublia, et le ranc qu'elle tenoit entre les

plus grands, et le devoir d'une espouse honneste, pour le saut

de sa partie.   Je ne veux m'amuser contre ce sexe, à cause

qu'il en y a assez qui s'estudient à la blasonner, courant sus à

toute espece de femmes, pour la faute de quelques unes : Bien

diray-je que, ou faudroit que nature eust osté l'opinion aux

hommes de s'accointer à icelles, ou leur donner l'esprit assez

rassis, pour supporter les traverses qu'ils en reçoivent, sans se

plaindre si souvent, et tant estrangement, puis que c'est leur

bestise qui les accable.   Car s'il est ainsi que la femme soit

un animal si imparfait, qu'ils le chantent, et qu'ils congnois-

sent ceste beste si indomptable, comme ils le crient : pour-

quoy sont ils si sots, que de la pousuyvre, et tant hebetez,

Si l'homme
est trompé
par la
femme, c'est
se propre
bestise.

cesse, who at the first, for her rare vertues and courtesses was honored of al men and beloved of her husband, as soone as she once gave eare to the tyrant Fengon, forgot both the ranke she helde among the greatest names, and the dutie of an honest wife on her behalfe.   But I will not stand to gaze and mervaile at women, for that there are many which seeke to blase and set them foorth, in which their writings they spare not to blame them all for the faults of some one, or few women.   But I say, that either nature ought to have bereaved man of that opinion to accompany with women, or els to endow them with such spirits, as that they may easily support the crosses they endure, without complaining so often and so strangely, seeing it is their owne beastlinesse that overthrowes them.   For if it be so, that a woman is so imperfect a creature as they make her to be, and that they know this beast to bee so hard to bee tamed as they affirme, why then are they so foolish to preserve them, and so dull and brutish as to trust their deceitfull and wanton imbraceings. But let us leave her in this extreamitie of laciviousnesse, and proceed to shewe you in what sort the yong prince Hamblet behaved himselfe, to escape the tyranny of his uncle.

If a man be decieved by a woman, it is his owne beastlinesse

et abrutiz, que de se fier en ses caresses ?   Geruthe s'estant

ainsi oubliee, le Prince Amleth se voyant en danger de sa vie,

abandonné de sa mere propre, delaissé de chacun, et asseuré

que Fengon ne le souffriroit guere longuement sans luy faire

tenir le chemin de Horwendille ; pour tromper les ruses du

tyran, qui le soupçonnoit pour tel, que s'il venoit à perfection

d'aage, il n'auroit garde se passer de poursuivre la vengeance

de la mort de son pere, il contrefeist le fol, avec telle ruse, et

subtilité, qu'il faignit d'avoir tout perdu le sens, et souz un

tel voile il couvrist ses desseins et defendist son salut, et vie,

des trahisons et embusches du tyran.   Et bien qu'il eust esté

à l'Escole du Prince Romain, qui pour se faindre fol, fut

nommé Brute, si est-ce qu'i en imitoit les façons, et la sagesse.

Car tous les jours estant au palais de la Royne, qui avoit

plus de soing de plaire à son paillard, que de soucy de venger

son mary, ou de remettre son fils en son heritage il se soüilloit

CHAPTER II

*How Hamblet counterfeited the mad man, to escape the tyrannie of his uncle,
and how he was tempted by a woman (through his uncles procurement)
who thereby thought to undermine the Prince, and by that meanes to finde
out whether he counterfeited madnesse or not : and how Hamblet would by
no meanes bee brought to consent unto her, and what followed.*

GERUTH having (as I sayd before) so much forgotten herself, the prince Hamblet perceiving himself to bee in danger
of his life, as beeing abandoned of his owne mother, and
forsaken of all men, and assuring himselfe that Fengon
would not detract the time to send him the same way his
father Horvendile was gone, to beguile the tyrant in his subtilties (that esteemed him to bee of such a minde that if he
once attained to mans estate he wold not long delay the time
to revenge the death of his father) counterfeiting the mad man
with such craft and subtill practises, that hee made shewe as
if hee had utterly lost his wittes : and under that vayle hee
covered his pretence, and defended his life from the treasons
and practises of the tyrant his uncle.   And all though hee
had beene at the schoole of the Romane Prince, who, because
hee counterfeited himselfe to bee a foole, was called Brutus,
yet hee imitated his fashions, and his wisedom.   For every
day beeing in the queenes palace, (who as then was more
carefull to please her whoremaster, then ready to revenge
the cruell death of her husband, or to restore her sonne to his

tout de villenie, se veautrant és balieüres et immondices de
la maison, et se frottant le visage de la fange des rues par
lesquelles il couroit comme un maniacle, ne disant rien, qui
ne ressentit son transport de sens, et pure frenaisie, et toutes
ses actions, et gestes, n'estoyent que les contenances d'un
homme qui est privé de toute raison et entendement, de sorte
qui ne servoit plus que de passetemps aux pages et courtisans
esventez, qui estoient à la suite de son oncle, et beaupere.
Mais le galant les marquoit avec intention de s'en venger
un jour avec tel effort, qu'il en seroit à jamais memoire.
Voila un grand traict de sagesse, et bon esprit en un jeune
Prince, que de pouvoir avec un si grand defaut à son avancement, et par son abaissement, et mespris, de faciliter la voye,
à estre un des plus heureux Roys de son aage : Aussi jamais
homme ne fut reputé avec aucune sienne action plus sage et
prudent, que Brute, faignant un grand desvoyement de son
esprit: veu que l'occasion de telle ruyne: fainte de son meileur,
ne proceda jamais d'ailleurs, que d'un bon conseil, et sage
deliberation, tant à fin de conserver ses biens, et eviter la rage
du tyran le Roy superbe, qu'aussi pour se faire une large voye
de chasser Tarquin, et affranchir le peuple oppressé souz le
joug d'une grande et miserable servitude.

Brute
reputé sage
pour contre-
faire le fol.
Voy Tite
Live, et
Halicar-
nasse.

inheritance), hee rent and tore his clothes, wallowing and lying in the durt and mire, his face all filthy and blacke, running through the streets like a man distraught, not speaking one worde, but such as seemed to proceede of madnesse and meere frenzie; all his actions and jestures beeing no other than the right countenances of a man wholly deprived of all reason and understanding, in such sort, that as then hee seemed fitte for nothing but to make sport to the pages and ruffling courtiers that attended in the court of his uncle and father-in-law. But the yong prince noted them well enough, minding one day to bee revenged in such manner, that the memorie thereof should remaine perpetually to the world.

Beholde, I pray you, a great point of a wise and brave spirite in a yong prince, by so great a shewe of imperfection in his person for advancement, and his owne imbasing and despising, to worke the meanes and to prepare the way for himselfe to bee one of the happiest kings in his age. In like sort, never any man was reputed by any of his actions more wise and prudent then Brutus, dissembling a great alteration in his minde, for that the occasion of such his devise of foolishnesse proceeded onely of a good and mature counsell and deliberation, not onely to preserve his goods, and shunne the rage of the proude tyrant, but also to open a large way to procure the banishment and utter ruine of wicked Tarquinius, and to infranchise the people (which were before oppressed) from the yoake of a great and miserable servitude.

Brutus esteemed wise, for counterfeiting the foole. Read Titus Livius and Halicarnassus.

David fait
le fol devant
le roy
Achu.

Aussi tant Brute, que cestuy-cy, ausquels vous pouvez adjouster le Roy David, qui faignist le forcené entre les Royteletz de Palestine, pour conserver sa vie, monstrent la leçon à ceux qui malcontents de quelque grand, n'ont les forces suffisantes pour s'en prevaloir, ny se venger de l'injure receuë.   Or quand je parle de se resentir d'un grand, duquel on aura esté outragé, il le faut entendre de celuy qui ne nous

I des Rom.
viii. 21.

est point souverain, contre lequel ne faut regimber, ny luy tramer aucune trahison, ou conspirer aucunement contre sa vie.

Celuy qui veut suyvre tel chemin, faut qu'il parle, face tout au plaisir de l'homme qu'il veut tromper, loüe ses actions, l'estime sur tout autre, et contrairie en toute chose à ce qu'il

Qu'est ce
que faire le
fol en court.

a en son esprit: car c'est veritablement faire le sot, et contrefaire le fol, quand il faut dissimuler, et baiser la main de celuy, que l'on voudroit sçavoir cent pieds sous terre, pour n'en sentir point les approches.   Si cela n'estoit du tout esloigné de la perfection du Chrestien, qui ne doibt avoir le fiel amer, ni les desirs confits en vengeance.

Amleth donc se façonnant à l'exercice d'une grande folie, faisoit des actes pleins de grand' signifiance, et respondoit si à propos, qu'un sage homme eust jugé bien tost de quel esprit est ce que sortoit une invention si gentile : car estant aupres du feu, et aiguisant des buchettes, en forme de poignars, et

And so, not onely Brutus, but this man and worthy prince, to whom wee may also adde king David, that counterfeited the madde man among the petie kings of Palestina to preserve his life from the subtill practises of those kings. I shew this example unto such, as beeing offended with any great personage, have not sufficient meanes to prevaile in their intents, or revenge the injurie by them received. But when I speake of revenging any injury received upon a great personage or superior, it must be understood by such an one as is not our soveraigne, againste whom wee maie by no meanes resiste, nor once practise anie treason nor conspiracie against his life : and hee that will followe this course must speake and do all things whatsoever that are pleasing and acceptable to him whom hee meaneth to deceive, practise his actions, and esteeme him above all men, cleane contrarye to his owne intent and meaning ; for that is rightly to playe and counterfeite the foole, when a man is constrained to dissemble and kisse his hand, whome in hearte hee could wishe an hundred foote depth under the earth, so hee mighte never see him more, if it were not a thing wholly to bee disliked in a christian, who by no meanes ought to have a bitter gall, or desires infected with revenge.   Hamblet, in this sorte counterfeiting the madde man, many times did divers actions of great and deepe consideration, and often made such and so fitte answeres, that a wise man would soone have judged from what spirite so fine an invention mighte proceede ; for that standing by the fire and sharpning sticks like poy-

David counterfeited the mad man before king Aches.

Rom.viii. 21

estocs, quelqu'un luy demanda en riant à quoy servoyent ces
petits bastons, et qu'il faisoit de ces buchettes : J'appreste,
dit-il, des dards acerez et sagettes poignantes, pour venger la
mort de mon pere.   Les fols, comme jay dit, acomptoient
cecy à peu de sens, mais les hommes accors, et qui avoyent
le nez long, commencent à soupçonner ce qui estoit, et
estimerent que sous ceste folie gisoit, et estoit cachee une
grande finesse, et telle qui pourroit vn iour estre prejudiciable
à leur Prince : disant que sous telle rudesse et simplicité il
voiloit une grande et cauteleuse sagesse, et qu'il celoit un
grand lustre de bon esprit, soubs l'obscurité de ceste fardee
subtilité.   A ceste cause donnerent conseil au Roy de tenter
par tout moyen s'il se pourroit faire, que ce fard fust descouvert,
et qu'on s'aperceust de la tromperie de l'adolescent.   Or ne
voyent ils ruse plus propre pour l'atraper, que s'il luy mettoient
quelque belle femme en lieu secret, laquelle taschast de le
gaigner avec ses caresses les plus mignardes et attrayantes,

desquelles elle se pourroit adviser.   D'autant que le naturel
de tout jeune homme, mesmement estant nourry a son aise,
est si transporté aux plaisirs de la chair, et se lance avec telle
impetuosité à la jouyssance, qui lui est octroyee, de ce qui
est excellemment beau, qu'il est presque impossible de couvrir
telle affection, ny d'en dissimuler les apprehensions par art,
ny industrie quelconque, ny de le fuir, quelque ruse qu'il
usast pour pallier sa malice : veu que s'offrant l'occasion, et
icelle secrete de la volupté la plus chatouilleuse, il faudroit

nards and prickes, one in smiling manner asked him wherefore he made those little staves so sharpe at the points? I
prepare (saith he) piersing dartes and sharpe arrowes to
revenge my fathers death.   Fooles, as I said before, esteemed
those his words as nothing; but men of quicke spirits, and
such as hadde a deeper reache began to suspect somewhat,
esteeming that under that kinde of folly there lay hidden a
greate and rare subtilty, such as one day might bee prejudi-
ciall to their prince, saying, that under colour of such rudenes
he shadowed a crafty pollicy, and by his devised simplicitye,
he concealed a sharp and pregnant spirit : for which cause they
counselled the king to try and know, if it were possible, how
to discover the intent and meaning of the yong prince ; and
they could find no better nor more fit invention to intrap him,
then to set some faire and beawtifull woman in a secret place,
that with flattering speeches and all the craftiest meanes she
could use, should purposely seek to allure his mind to have
his pleasure of her : for the nature of all young men, (especially such as are brought up wantonlie) is so transported with
the desires of the flesh, and entreth so greedily into the pleasures therof, that it is almost impossible to cover the foul
affection, neither yet to dissemble or hyde the same by art or
industry, much lesse to shunne it.   What cunning or subtilty so ever they use to cloak theire pretence, seeing occasion offered, and that in secret, especially in the most inticing

A subtill
answere
of Prince
Hamlet.

Nature
corrupted
in man.

que forcé des apetits, il succombast aux efforts, et puissance
de la partie sensuelle.

Ainsi furent deputez quelques courtisans, pour mener le
Prince en quelque lieu escarté, dans le boys, et lesquels luy
presentassent ceste femme, l'incitans à se souiller en ses baysers
et embrassemens, artifices assez frequent de nostre temps, non
pour essayer si les grands sont hors de leur sens, mais pour les
priver de force, vertu et sagesse, par le moyen de ses sansues
et infernales Lamies, produites par leurs serviteurs, ministres
de corruption.   Le pauvre Prince eust esté en danger de
succomber à cest assaut, si un Gentil-homme, qui du vivant
de Horvvendille, avoit esté nourry avec luy, ne se fust plus
monstré ami de la nourriture prinse avec Amleth, que affec-
tionné à la puissance du tyran, lequel pourchassoit les moyens
de envelopper le fils és pieges, esquels le pere avoit finy
ses jours.   Cestuy s'cacompagna des courtisans deputez pour
ceste trahison, plus avec deliberation d'instruire le Prince, de
ce qu'il avoit à faire, que pour luy dresser des embusches et
le traihir, estimant que le moindre indice qu'il donneroit de
son bon sens, suffiroit pour luy faire perdre la vie.   Cestuy-
cy avec certains signes feit entendre à Amleth, en quel peril
est ce qu'il se mettroit si en sorte aucune il obeissoit, aux
mignardes caresses, et mignotises de la Damoyselle, envoyee
par son oncle : ce que'stonant le Prince esmeu de la beauté

Ruse pour
descouvrir
les finesses
de Amleth.

Corrupreurs
de la
jeunesse es
courts des
grands.

sinne that rayneth in man, they cannot chuse (being constrayned by voluptuousnesse) but fall to naturall effect and working. To this end certaine courtiers were appointed to leade Hamblet into a solitary place within the woods, whether they brought the woman, inciting him to take their pleasures together, and to imbrace one another, but the subtill practises used in these our daies, not to try if men of great account bee extract out of their wits, but rather to deprive them of strength, vertue and wisedome, by meanes of such devilish practitioners, and intefernall spirits, their domestical servants, and ministers of corruption. And surely the poore prince at this assault had him in great danger, if a gentleman (that in Horvendiles time had been nourished with him) had not showne himselfe more affectioned to the bringing up he had received with Hamblet, then desirous to please the tirant, who by all meanes sought to intangle the sonne in the same nets wherein the father had ended his dayes. This gentleman bare the courtyers (appointed as aforesaide of this treason) company, more desiring to give the prince instruction what he should do, then to intrap him, making full account that the least showe of perfect sence and wisedome that Hamblet should make would be sufficient to cause him to loose his life : and therefore by certain signes, he gave Hamblet intelligence in what danger hee was like to fall, it by any meanes hee seemed to obaye, or once like the wanton toyes and vicious provocations of the gentlewoman sent thither by his uncle. Which much abashed the prince, as

Subtilties used to discover Hamblet's madness.

Corrupters of yong gentlemen in princes courts and great houses.

de la fille, fut par elle asseuré encor de la trahison : car elle
l'aymoit des son enfance, et eust esté bien marie de son
desastre et fortune, et plus de sortir de ses mains, sans jouyr
de celuy qu'elle aimoit plus que soymesme.   Ayant le jeune
seigneur trompé les courtisans, et la fille, soustenans qu'il ne
s'estoit avancé en sorte aucune à la violer, quoy qu'il dict du
contraire, chacun s'asseura que veritablement il estoit insensé,
et que son cerveau n'avoit force quelconque, capable d'apprehension raisonnable.

Entre toue les amis de Fengon, en y
avoit un qui sur tout autre se doutoit des ruses, et subtilitez
de ce fol dissimulé, lequel pour ceste raison dict, qu'il estoit
impossible qu'un galant si rusé, que ce plaisant, que contre-

then wholy beeing in affection to the lady, but by her he was
likewise informed of the treason, as being one that from her
infancy loved and favoured him, and would have been exceeding sorrowfull for his misfortune, and much more to leave
his companie without injoying the pleasure of his body, whome
shee loved more than herselfe.   The prince in this sort having
both deceived the courtiers, and the ladyes expectation, that
affirmed and swore that hee never once offered to have his
pleasure of the woman, although in subtilty hee affirmed the
contrary, every man there upon assured themselves that
without all doubt he was distraught of his sences, that his
braynes were as then wholly void of force, and incapable of
reasonable apprehension, so that as then Fengons practise took
no effect: but for al that he left not off, still seeking by al
meanes to finde out Hamblets subtilty, as in the next chapter
you shall perceive.

CHAPTER III

How Fengon, uncle to Hamblet, a second time to intrap him in his politick
madnes, caused one of his counsellors to be secretly hidden in the queenes
chamber, behind the arras, to heare what speeches passed between Hamblet
and the Queen; and how Hamblet killed him, and escaped that danger,
and what followed.

AMONG the friends of Fengon, there was one that above al
the rest doubted of Hamblets practises in counterfeiting the
madman, who for that cause said, that it was impossible that

faisoit le fol, fust descouvert avec des subtilitez si communes,
et lesquelles on pouvoit aisément descouvrir : et que par ainsi
il falloit inventer quelque moyen plus accort et subtil, et ou
l'astuce fust attrahyante, et l'attrait si fort, que le galant ny
sçeut user de ses accoustumees dissimulations.   De cecy il se
disoit sçavoir une voye propre pour executer leur dessein, et
de surprendre Amleth en ses ruses, et luy faire de luy-mesme
se prendre au filet, et declarer quelles sont les conceptions de
son ame.   Il faut (dit-il) que le Roy Fengon faigne s'en

Autre ruse
pour tromper
Amleth.

aller en quelque voyage, pour quelque affaire de grand importance, et que cependant on enferme Amleth seul avec sa
mere dans une chambre, dans laquelle soit caché quelqu'un
au desseu de l'un et de l'autre, pour ouyr et sentir leurs
propos, et les complots qu'ils prendront, pour les desseins
bastiz par ce fol sage et rusé compagnon.   Asseurant le Roy
que s'il y avoit rien de sage, ny arresté en l'esprit ny cerveau
du jeune homme, que facilement il se descouvriroit à sa mere,
sans craindre rien, et qu'il fieroit son conseil et deliberation
à la foy, et loyauté de celle qui l'avoit porté en ses flancs,
et nourry avec si grande diligence.

Cestuy mesme s'offrist pour estre l'espion, et tesmoin des
propos du fils avec la mere, à fin qu'on ne l'estimast tel qui

so craftie a gallant as Hamblet, that counterfeited the foole,
should be discovered with so common and unskilfull practises,
which might easily bee perceived, and that to finde out his
politique pretence it were necessary to invent some subtill and
crafty meanes, more attractive, whereby the gallant might
not have the leysure to use his accustomed dissimulation ;
which to effect he said he knewe a fit waie, and a most convenient meane to effect the kings desire, and thereby to intrap
Hamblet in his subtilties, and cause him of his owne accord
to fall into the net prepared for him, and thereby evidently
shewe his secret meaning.   His devise was thus, that King
Fengon should make as though he were to goe some long
voyage concerning affaires of great importance, and that in
the meane time Hamblet should be shut up alone in a chamber
with his mother, wherein some other should secretly be hidden
behind the hangings, unknowne either to him or his mother,
there to stand and heere their speeches, and the complots by
them to bee taken concerning the accomplishment of the dissembling fooles pretence ; assuring the king that if there were
any point of wisedome and perfect sence in the gallants spirit,
that without all doubte he would easily discover it to his
mother, as being devoid of all feare that she would utter or
make knowne his secret intent, beeing the woman that had
borne him in her bodie, and nourished him so carefully ; and
withall offered himselfe to be the man that should stand to
harken and beare witnesse of Hamblets speeches with his
mother, that hee might not be esteemed a counsellor in such

Another
subtilty used
to deceive
Hamblet.

donnoit un conseil, duquel il refusast estre l'executeur, pour
servir son Prince. Le Roy prinst grand plaisir à ceste
invention, comme le seul souuverain remede pour guerir le
Prince de sa folie : et ainsi en faisant un long voyage, sort
du palais, et s'en va pourmener à la chasse, là ou ce pendant
le conseil entra secrettement en la chambre de la Royne, se
cachant souz quelque loudier : un peu au paravant que le fils

**Cautelle
d'Amleth.**
y fust enclos avec sa mere. Lequel comme il estoit fin et
cauteleux, si tost qui fut dedans la chambre, se douta de
quelque trahison et surprinse, et que s'il parloit à sa mere
de quelque cas serieux, il ne fust entendu, continuant en ses
façons de faire, folles et niaises, se prist à chanter tout ainsi
qu'un coq, et batant tout ainsi des bras, comme cest oyseau
fait des aisles, sauta sur ce lourdier, ou sentant qu'il y avoit

**Fait cruel
d'Amleth sur
celuy qui le
vouloit
trahir.**
dessous quelque cas caché, ne faillit aussi tost d'y donner
dedans à tout son glaive, puis tirant le galant à demy mort,
l'acheva d'occir, et le mit en pieces, puis le feit bouillir, et
cuit qu'il est le jetta par un grand conduit de cloaque, par
ou sortoient les immondicitez, à fin qu'il servist de pasture
aux pourceaux. Ayant ainsi descouvert l'embusche, et puny
l'inventeur d'icelle il s'en revinst trouver la Royne, laquelle
se tourmentoit et plouroit voyant toute son esperance perdue :
car quelque faute qu'elle eust commise, si estoit elle angoissee
grandement, voyant que ce seul fils qui luy restoit, ne luy

a case wherein he refused to be the executioner for the behoofe
and service of his prince.   This invention pleased the king
exceeding well, esteeming it as the onelie and soveraigne
remedie to heale the prince of his lunacie ; and to that ende
making a long voyage, issued out of his pallace, and road to
hunt in the forrest.   Meane time the counsellor entred secretly

Hamblet's subtilty.

into the queenes chamber, and there hid himselfe behind the
arras, not long before the queene and Hamblet came thither,
who beeing craftie and pollitique, as soone as hee was within
the chamber, doubting some treason, and fearing if he should
speake severely and wisely to his mother touching his secret
practises he should be understood, and by that meanes inter-
cepted, used his ordinary manner of dissimulation, and began
to come like a cocke beating with his armes, (in such manner
as cockes use to strike with their wings) upon the hangings
of the chamber : whereby, feeling something stirring under
them, he cried, A rat, a rat! and presently drawing his

A cruell revenge taken by Hamblet upon him that would have betraid him.

sworde thrust it into the hangings, which done, pulled the
counsellour (halfe dead) out by the heeles, made an end of
killing him, and beeing slaine, cut his bodie in pieces, which
he caused to be boyled, and then cast it into an open vaulte
or privie, that so it mighte serve for foode to the hogges.   By
which meanes having discovered the ambushe, and given the
inventer thereof his just rewarde, hee came againe to his
mother, who in the meane time wepte and tormented her selfe
to see all her hopes frustrate, for that what fault soever she
had committed, yet was shee sore grieved to see her onely

servoit que de mocquerie, chacun luy reprochant sa folie, un trait de laquelle elle en avoit veu devant ses yeux : ce qui luy donna un grand elancement de conscience, estimant que les Dieux luy envoyassent ceste punition, pour s'estre incestu-

eusement accouplee avec le tyran meurtrier de son espoux, et lequel ne laissoit moyen aucun, qu'il ne cerchast pour mettre fin à la vie de son neveu, accusant l'indiscretion naturelle, qui est la guide ordinaire de celles qui ayment tant des plaisirs du corps, que voilant la voye à toute raison, n'advisent ce qui peut s'ensuyvir de leur legereté et grande inconstance, et comme un plaisir de peu de duree suffisoit pour luy causer un repentir à jamais, et luy faire maudire l'heure que onc ces apprehensions si volages luy avoient saisi l'esprit, ny bandé les yeulx pour rejetter l'honnesteté requise à Dame de son calibre, et à mespriser la saincte institution des Dames, qui l'avoyent precedé, et en sang, et en vertu. Se souvenoit du bon renom, et grandes louanges donnees par tous les Danoys à Rinde fille du Roy Rothere, la plus chaste de son temps,

et si pudique, que jamais elle ne voulut entendre à mariage d'aucun Prince, ny Chevalier, surpassant tout ainsi en vertu les Dames de son pays, comme elle les surmontoit en beauté, doux maintien et bonne grace.   Mais ainsi que la Royne se tourmentoit, voicy entrer Amleth, lequel ayant visité encor tous les coings de la chambre, comme se deffiant aussi bien

child made a meere mockery, every man reproaching her with
his folly, one point whereof she had as then seene before her
eyes, which was no small pricke to her conscience, esteeming
that the gods sent her that punishment for joyning incestuously in marriage with the tyrannous murtherer of her
husband, who like wise ceased not to invent all the means he
could to bring his nephew to his ende, accusing his owne
naturall indiscretion, as beeing the ordinary guide of those
that so much desire the pleasures of the bodie, who shutting
up the waie to all reason, respect not what maie ensue of
their lightnes and great inconstancy, and how a pleasure of
small moment is sufficient to give them cause of repentance
during their lives, and make them curse the daye and time
that ever any such apprehensions entred into theire mindes,
or that they closed their eies to reject the honestie requisite
in ladies of her qualitie, and to despise the holy institution of
those dames that had gone before her, both in nobilitie and
vertue, calling to mind the great prayses and commendations
given by the danes to Rinde, daughter to king Rothere, the
chastest lady in her time, and withall so shamefast that she
would never consent to marriage with any prince or knight
whatsoever; surpassing in vertue all the ladyes of her time,
as shee herselfe surmounted them in beawtie, good behaviour,
and comelines.   And while in this sort she sate tormenting
herselfe, Hamlet entred into the chamber, who having once
againe searched every corner of the same, distrusting his
mother as well as the rest, and perceiving himselfe to bee

Queene
Geruthe's
repentance.

Rinde and
princes of an
admirable
chastitie.

de sa mere que des autres, se voyant seul avec elle luy parla
fort sagement en ceste maniere.

Harangue d'Amleth à la Royne Geruthe sa mere.

Quelle trahison est cestecy, ô la plus infame de toutes
celles qui onc se sont prostituees à la volonté de quelque
paillard abominable, qui souz le fard d'un plus dissimulé vous
couvriez l'acte le plus meschant, et le crime le plus detestable,
que homme sçauroit imaginer, ny commettre ? Quelle fiance
peux-je avoir en vous, qui comme une lascive paillarde,
desreiglee sur toute impudicité, allez courant les bras tendus
apres celuy felon, et traistre tyran qui est le meurtrier de mon
pere, et caressez incestueusement le voleur du lict legitime
de vostre loyal espoux, mignardez impudiquement celuy qui
estoit le pere cher de fils miserable, et privé de tout confort,
si les Dieux ne luy font la grace de eschapper bien tost, d'une
captivité tant indigne du ranc qu'il tient, et de la noble race,
et illustre famille de ses ancestres et majeurs ? Est-ce à une
Royne et fille de Roy, de suivre les apetits des bestes et
que tout ainsi que les jumens s'accouplent à ceux, qui ont
vaincu leurs premiers marys, vous suyviez la volonté du Roy
abominable, qui a tué un plus vaillant et homme de bien que
luy, et à esteint, en massacrant Horvvendille, la gloire et
honneur des Danoys, lesquels sont aneantis, sans force ny
cœur de vaillance, depuis que le lustre de chevalerie a eu pris
fin par le plus poltron et cruel vilain de la terre ? Je ne veux

alone, began in sober and discreet manner to speak unto her, saying,

What treason is this, O most infamous woman! of all that ever prostrated themselves to the will of an abhominable whore monger, who, under the vail of a dissembling creature, covereth the most wicked and detestable crime that man could ever imagine, or was committed. Now may I be assured to trust you, that like a vile wanton adultresse, altogether impudent and given over to her pleasure, runnes spreading forth her armes joyfully to imbrace the trayterous villanous tyrant that murthered my father, and most incestuously receivest the villain into the lawfull bed of your loyall spouse, imprudently entertaining him in steede of the deare father of your miserable and discomforted soone, if the gods grant him not the grace speedilie to escape from a captivity so unworthie the degree he holdeth, and the race and noble familie of his ancestors. Is this the part of a queene, and daughter to a king? to live like a brute beast (and like a mare that yieldeth her bodie to the horse that hath beaten hir companion awaye), to followe the pleasure of an abhominable king that hath murthered a farre more honester and better man then himself in massacring Horvendile, the honor and glory of the Danes, who are now esteemed of no force nor valour at all, since the shining splendure of knighthood was brought to an end by the most wickedest and cruellest villaine living upon earth.

l'estimer mon parent et ne puis le regarder comme oncle, ny vous comme mere treschere, l'un ne ayant respecté le sang qui nous devoit unir plus estroictement qu'avec l'alliance de l'autre, qui aussi ne pouvoit avec son honneur, ny, sans soupçon d'avoir consenty, à la mort de son espoux, s'accorder jamais aux nopces de son cruel ennemy. Ah Royne Geruthe ! c'est à faire aux chiennes à se mesler avec plusieurs, et souhaiter le mariage et accouplement de divers masles : c'est la lubricité seule qui vous a effacé en l'ame la memoire des vaillances et vertuz du bon Roy : vostre espoux, et mon pere : c'est un desir effrené qui a conduit la fille de Rorique à embraser le tyran Fengon, sans respecter les ombres de Horvvendille, indigne de si estrange traictement, et que son frere l'occist traistreusement, et que sa femme le trahit laschement, laquelle il a tant bien traictee, et pour l'amour de laquelle il a jamais despouillé Norvege de richesses, et despeuplé d'hommes vaillans pour accroistre les thresors de Rorique, et randre Geruthe l'espouse du plus hardy Prince de l'Europe. Ce n'est pas estre femme, et moins Princesse, en laquelle doit reluire toute douceur, cour- toisie, compassion et amitié, que laisser ainsi sa chere geniture à l'abandon de fortune, et entre les mains sanglantes et meur- trieres d'un felon et voleur. Les bestes plus farouches n'en font pas ainsi : car les Lyons, Tigres, Onces, et Leopards com- battent pour la defence de leurs faons, et les oyseaux de bec, griffes et esles resistent à ceux qui veulent voler leurs petits, là ou vous m'exposez et livrez à mort en lieu de me defendre.

I, for my part, will never account him for my kinsman, nor once knowe him for mine uncle, nor you my deer mother, for not having respect to the blud that ought to have united us so straightly together, and who neither with your honor nor without suspicion of consent to the death of your husband could ever have agreed to have marryed with his cruell enemie.   O, queene Geruthe, it is the part of a bitch to couple with many, and desire acquaintance of divers mastiffes : it is licentiousnes only that hath made you deface out of your minde the memory of the valor and vertues of the good king your husband and my father : it was an unbrideled desire that guided the daughter of Roderick to imbrace the tyrant Fengon, and not to remember Horvendile (unworthy of so strange intertainment), neither that he killed his brother traiterously, and that shee being his fathers wife betrayed him, although he so well favoured and loved her, that for her sake he utterly bereaved Norway of her riches and valiant souldiers to augment the treasures of Roderick, and make Geruthe wife to the hardyest prince in Europe : it is not the parte of a woman, much lesse of a princesse, in whome all modesty, curtesse, compassion, and love ought to abound, thus to leave her deare child to fortune in the bloody and murtherous hands of a villain and traytor.   Bruite beasts do not so, for lyons, tygers, ounces and leopards fight for the safety and defence of their whelpes ; and birds that have beakes, claws, and wings, resist such as would ravish them of their yong ones ; but you, to the contrary, expose and deliver mee to death, whereas ye

N'est-ce pas me trahir, quand cognoissant la perversité d'un
tyran, et ses desseins, pleins de conseil de mort sur la race, et
image de son frere, vous n'ayez sçeu ou daigné trouver les
moyens de sauver vostre enfant ou en Suece, ou Norvege ou
plustost l'exposer aux Anglois, que le laisser la proye de
vostre infame adultere? Ne vous offencez, je vous prie,
Madame, si transporté de douleur, je vous parle si rigoureuse-
ment, et si je vous respecte moins que de mon devoir : car
vous m'ayant oublié, et mis à neant la memoire du defunct
Roy mon pere, ne faut s'esbahir, si aussi je sors des limites
de toute recognoissance.   Voyez en quelles destresses je suis
tombé, et à quel malheur m'a acheminé ma fortune, et vostre
trop grande legereté, et peu de sagesse, que je sois contrainct
de faire le fol, et imite les façons de faire d'un insensé pour
sauver ma vie, en lieu de m'adextrer aux armes, suyvre les
adventures, et tacher par tout moien de me faire cognoistre
pour le vray enfant du vailant, et vertueux Roy Horvvenle.
Ce n'est sans cause et juste occasion que mes gestes, contenances et parolles resentent le fol, et que je veux que chacun
me tienne pour privé de sens et cognoissance, veu que je sçay
bien que celuy qui n'a point faict conscience de tuer son
propre frere, accoustumé aux meurtres, et alliché au gouvernement sans avoir compaignon, qui luy contrerolles ses meschancetez et trahisons, ne se souciera guere de s'acharner avec

should defend me.   Is not this as much as if you should betray me, when you knowing the perversenes of the tyrant
and his intents, ful of deadly counsell as touching the race
and image of his brother, have not once sought, nor desired
to finde the meanes to save your child (and only son) by sending him into Swethland, Norway, or England, rather than to
leave him as a pray to youre infamous adulterer ? bee not
offended, I praye you, Madame, if transported with dolour
and griefe, I speake so boldely unto you, and that I respect
you lesse then duetie requireth ; for you, having forgotten mee,
and wholy rejected the memorye of the deceased K. my
father, must not bee abashed if I also surpasse the bounds and
limits of due consideration.   Beholde into what distresse I
am now fallen, and to what mischiefe my fortune, and your
over great lightnesse, and want of wisdome have induced mee,
that I am constrained to playe the madde man to save my
life, in steed of using and practising armes, following
adventures, and seeking all meanes to make my selfe knowne
to bee the true and undoubted heire of the valiant and
vertuous king Horvendile.   It was not without cause, and
juste occasion, that my gestures, countenances, and words,
seeme all to proceed from a madman, and that I desire to
have all men esteeme mee wholly deprived of sence and reasonable understanding, bycause I am well assured, that he that
hath made no conscience to kill his owne brother, (accustomed
to murthers, and allured with desire of governement without
controll in his treasons), will not spare, to save himselfe with

pareille cruauté sur le sang et reliques qui sont sorties de son
frere par luy massacré : ainsi, il vaut mieux faindre l'un, que
suyvre ce que nature me donne : les clers, et saincts rayons
de laquelle, j'absconse souz cest ombragement, tout ainsi que
le soleil ses flammes souz quelque grand nuage, durant les
ardeurs de l'esté.　Le visage de un insensé me duit, pour y
couvrir mes gaillardises, et les gestes d'un fol me sont propres,
àfin que sagement me conduisant, je conserve ma vie au pays
Danoys, et à la memoire du feu Roy mon pere.　Car les
desirs de le venger sont tellement gravez en mon coeur, que
si bien tost je ne meurs, j'espere d'en faire une telle, et si
haute vengeance, qu'il en sera à jamais parlé en ces terres.
Toutesfois faut il attendre le temps, et les moyens et occasions,
à fin que si je precipitois par trop les matieres, je ne causasse
ma ruine trop soudaine, et ne finisse plustost que donner
commencement aux effets de ce que mon cœur desseine.
Aussi faut il que contre un meschant desloyal, cruel et
descourtois homme, on use des plus gentiles inventions et
forbes, desquelles se peut adviser un bon esprit, pour ne
descouvrir point son entreprise : veu que la force n'estant
point de mon costé, c'est raison que les ruses, dissimulations, et secrettes menees y donnent ordre.　Au
reste, Madame, ne plourez point pour l'esgard de ma folie,
plustost gemissez la faute que vous avez commise, et vous
tourmentez pour celle infamie qui a souillee celle ancienne
renommee, et gloire qui rendoit illustre la Royne Geruthe :

Es grandes
entreprises
ne faut rien
precipiter.

Contre un
desloial, il
faut user de
cautelle.

the like crueltie, in the blood and flesh of the loyns of his brother by him massacred : and, therefore, it is better for me to fayne madnesse, then to use my right sences as nature hath bestowed them upon me ; the bright shining clearnes therof I am forced to hide under this shadow of dissimulation, as the sun doth hir beams under some great cloud, when the wether in sommer time overcasteth.   The face of a mad man serveth to cover my gallant countenance, and the gestures of a fool are fit for me, to the end that guiding my self wisely therein, I may preserve my life for the Danes, and the memory of my late deceased father ; for the desire of revenging his death is so engraven in my heart, that if I dye not shortly, I hope to take such and so great vengeance, that these countryes shall for ever speake thereof.   Neverthelesse, I must stay the time, meanes, and occasion, lest by making over great hast, I be now the cause of mine owne sodaine ruine and overthrow, and by that meanes end before I beginne to effect my hearts desire.   Hee that hath to doe with a wicked, disloyall, cruell, and discourteous man must use craft and politike inventions, such as a fine witte can best imagine, not to discover his interprise ; for seeing that by force I cannot effect my desire, reason alloweth me by dissimulation, subtiltie, and secret practises to proceed therein. To conclude, weepe not (madame) to see my folly, but rather sigh and lament your owne offence, tormenting your conscience in regard of the infamie that hath so defiled the ancient renowne and glorie that (in times past) honoured

We must use subtiltie to a disloyal person.

Faut plourer
pour ses
fautes et non
pour le vice
d'autruy.

car ce n'est les vices d'autruy qui doivent élancer noz consciences, ains faut se douloir de noz meffaits, et trop grandes
folies. Vous advisant au reste sur tout aussi cher que vous
avez la vie, que le Roy, ny autre ne soit en rien informé de
cecy, et me laissez faire au reste, car j'espere de venir à bout
de mon entreprise.

Quoy que la Royne se sentist piquer de bien pres, et
que Amleth la touchast vive-vivement ou plus elle se sentoit
interessee, si est-ce qu'elle oublia tout le desdain qu'elle eust
peu conccuoir, se voyant ainsi aigrement tancee et reprise,
pour la grande joye qui la saisit, cognoissant la gentilesse
d'esprit de son fils, et ce qu'elle pouvoit esperer d'une telle
et si grande sagesse : d'un costé elle n'osoit lever les yeulx
pour le regarder, se souvenant de sa faute, et de l'autre elle
eust volontiers embrassé son fils, pour les sages admonitions
qu'il luy avoit fait, et lesquelles eurent telle efficace, que sur
l'heure elle estaignist les flammes de convoitise, qui l'avoient
rendue amie de Fengon, pour planter encor en son cœur le
souvenir des vertus de son espoux legitime, lequel elle regretoit
en son cœur, voyant la vive image de sa vertu et sagesse en
cest enfant, representant le haut cœur de son pere. Ainsi
vaincue de ceste honneste passion, et fondant toute en l'armes,
apres avoir longuement tenus les yeux fichez sur Amleth,
comme ravie en quelque grande contemplation, et saisie de

queene Geruth; for wee are not to sorrowe and grieve at other mens vices, but for our owne misdeedes, and great folloyes. Desiring you, for the surplus of my proceedings, above all things (as you love your owne life and welfare) that neither the king nor any other may by any meanes know mine intent; and let me alone with the rest, for I hope in the ende to bring my purpose to effect.

Although the queene perceived herselfe neerly touched, and that Hamlet mooved her to the quicke, where she felt herselfe interested, neverthelesse shee forgot all disdaine and wrath, which thereby she might as then have had, hearing her selfe so sharply chiden and reprooved, for the joy she then conceaved, to behold the gallant spirit of her sonne, and to thinke what she might hope, and the easier expect of his so great policie and wisdome. But on the one side she durst not lift up her eyes to beholde him, remembering her offence, and on the other side she would gladly have imbraced her son, in regard of the wise admonitions by him given unto her, which as then quenched the flames of unbridled desire that before had moved her to affect K. Fengon, to ingraff in her heart the vertuous actions of her lawfull spouse, whom inwardly she much lamented, when she beheld the lively image and portraiture of his vertue and great wisedome in her childe, representing his fathers haughtie and valiant heart: and so, overcome and vanquished with this honest passion, and weeping most bitterly, having long time fixed her eyes upon Hamlet, as beeing ravished into some great and deepe con-

Wee must weepe for our owne faults and not for other mens.

quelque estonnement, en fin l'accollant, avec la mesme amitié qu'une mere vertueuse peut baiser, et caresser sa portee, elle luy usa de ce langage.

Geruthe á
son filz
Amleth

Je sçay bien (mon filz) que je t'ay fait tort en souffrant le mariage de Fengon, pour estre le cruel tiran et assassineur de ton pere, et de mon loyal espoux, mais quand tu considereras le peu de moyen de resistence, et la trahison de ceux du Palais, le peu de fiance que nous pouvons avoir aux courtisans tous faits à sa poste, et la force qu'il preparoit, là où j'eusse faict refus de son alliance, tu m'excuseras plustost que accuser de lubricité, ny d'inconstance, et moins me feras ce tort que de soupçonner que jamais Geruthe ait consenty à la mort de son espoux, te jurant par la haute majesté des Dieux, que s'il eust esté en ma puissance de resister au tyran, et qu'avec l'effusion de mon sang, et perte de ma vie, j'eusse peu sauver la vie de mon seigneur et espoux, je l'eusse fait d'aussi bon cœur, comme depuis j'ay plusieurs fois donné empeschement à l'accourcissement de la tienne, laquelle t'estant ravie, je ne veux plus demeurer en ce monde, puis que l'esprit estant sain, je voy les moyens plus aysez de la vengeance de ton pere. Toutesfois, mon filz, et doux amy, si tu as pitié de toy, et soin de la memoire de ton pere : et si tu veux rien faire pour celle qui ne merite point le nom de mere en ton endroict, je te

templation, and as it were wholy amazed, at the last imbracing him in her armes (with the like love that a vertuous mother may or can use to kisse and entertaine her owne childe), shee spake unto him in this manner.

I know well (my sonne) that I have done thee great wrong in marrying with Fengon, the cruell tyrant and murtherer of thy father, and my loyall spouse : but when thou shalt consider the small meanes of resistance, and the treason of the palace, with the little cause of confidence we are to expect or hope for of the courtiers, all wrought to his will, as also the power hee made ready, if I should have refused to like of him, thou wouldest rather excuse then accuse me of lasciviousnes or inconstancy, much lesse offer me that wrong to suspect that ever thy mother Geruthe once consented to the death and murther of her husband : swearing unto thee (by the majestie of the Gods) that if it had layne in my power to have resisted the tyrant, although it had beene with the losse of my blood, yea and my life, I would surely have saved the life of my lord and husband, with as good a will and desire as, since that time, I have often beene a meanes to hinder and impeach the shortning of thy life, which being taken away, I will no longer live here upon earth. For seeing that thy sences are whole and sound, I am in hope to see an easie meanes invented for the revenging of thy fathers death. Neverthelesse, mine owne sweet soone, if thou hast pittie of thy selfe, or care of the memorie of thy father (although thou wilt do nothing for her that deserveth

prie de conduire sagement tes affaires, n'estre hasté, ny trop
boüillant en tes entreprinses, n'y t'avancer plus que de raison
à l'effect de ton dessein.   Tu voys qu'il n'y a homme presque
en qui tu te puisses fier, ny moy femme à qui j'osasse avoir dit
un seul secret, lequel ne soit soudain rapporté à ton adversaire,
lequel combien qu'il feigne de m'aimer, pour joüir de mes
embrassemens, si est-ce qu'il se deffie, et craint de moy, à ta
cause : et n'est si sot qu'il se puisse bien persuader, que tu sois
fol, ou incensé : or si tu fais quelque acte qui ressente rien de
serieux, et prudent, tant secrettement le sçaches tu executer,
si est-ce que soudain il en aura les nouvelles : et me crains
encor que les Demons ne luy signifient ce qui s'est passé à
present entre nous, tant fortune nous est contraire, et poursuit
noz aises, ou que ce meurtre que tu as commis, ne soit cause
de nostre ruine, duquel je feindray ne sçavoir rien, comme
aussi je tiendray secrette, et ta sagesse, et ta gaillarde entreprinse.   Priant les Dieux (mon fils) que guidans ton cœur,
dressans tes conseils, et bien heurans ton entreprinse, je te voye
jouyssant des biens qui te sont deuz, et de la couronne de
Dannemarch, que le tyran ta ravie, à fin que j'aye le moyen
de me resiouïr en ta prosperité, et me contenter, voyant
avec qu'elle hardiesse tu auras pris vengeance du meurtrier de

not the name of a mother in this respect), I pray thee, carie thine affayres wisely : bee not hastie, nor over furious in thy interprises, neither yet advance thy selfe more then reason shall moove thee to effect thy purpose.   Thou seest there is not almost any man wherein thou mayest put thy trust, nor any woman to whom I dare utter the least part of my secrets, that would not presently report it to thine adversarie, who, although in outward shew he dissembleth to love thee, the better to injoy his pleasures of me, yet hee distrusteth and feareth mee for thy sake, and is not so simple to be easily perswaded that thou art a foole or mad ; so that if thou chance to doe any thing that seemeth to proceed of wisedome or policie (how secretly soever it be done) he will presently be informed thereof, and I am greatly afraide that the devils have shewed him what hath past at this present between us, (fortune so much pursueth and contrarieth our ease and welfare) or that this murther that now thou has committed be not the cause of both our destructions, which I by no meanes will seeme to know, but will keepe secret both thy wisedome and hardy interprise ; beseeching the Gods (my good soone) that they, guiding thy heart, directing thy counsels, and prospering thy interprise, I may see thee possesse and injoy that which is thy right, and weare the crowne of Denmarke, by the tyrant taken from thee ; that I may rejoyce in thy prosperitie, and therewith content my self, seeing with what courage and boldnesse thou shalt take vengeance upon the murtherer of thy father, as also upon all

ton pere, et de ceux qui luy ont donné faveur, et main forte
pour l'executer.   Madame, respondit Amleth, j'adjousteray
foy à vostre dire, et ne veux m'enquerir plus outre de voz
affaires : vous priant que selon l'amitié que vous devez à vostre
sang, vous ne faciez plus de compte de ce paillard mon ennemy,
lequel je feray mourir, quoy que tous les Demons le tinssent
en leur garde, et ne sera en la puissance de ses courtisans, que
je n'en despeche le monde, et qu'eux mesmes ne l'accom-
paignent aussi bien à sa mort, comme ils ont esté les pervers
conseilles de la mort de mon pere, et les compaignons de sa
trahison, assassinat, et cruelle entreprinse.   Aussi est-il raison
que tout ainsi que traitreusement ils ont faict mourir, leur
Prince, qu'avec pareille, mais plus juste, finesse, ils payent les
interestz de leur felonnie.   Vous sçavez Madame, comme

Hothere vostre ayeul, et pere du bon Roy Rorique ayant
vaincu Guimon, le feit brusler tout vif, à cause que auparavant

ce cruel paillard avoit usé de tel traictement à l'endroit de
Gevare son seigneur, qu'il prinst de nuict, et par trahison.
Et qui est celuy qui ne sçache que les trahistres, et parjures,

ne meritent point qu'on leur garde foy ny loyauté quelconque,
et que les pactes faicts avec un assassineur se doivent estimer
comme toilles d'araignes, et tenir en mesme rang, comme
chose non promise ?   Mais quand bien j'auray dressé la main
contre Fengon, ce ne sera trahison ny felonnie, luy n'estant
point mon Roy n'y Seigneur : ains justement le puniray comme

those that have assisted and favoured him in his murtherous
and bloody enterprise.   Madame (sayd Hamlet) I will put my
trust in you, and from henceforth meane not to meddle
further with your affayres, beseeching you (as you love your
owne flesh and blood) that you will from hence foorth no
more esteeme of the adulterer, mine enemie whom I wil
surely kill, or cause to be put to death, in despite of all the
devils in hel : and have he never so manie flattering courtezans
to defend him, yet will I bring him to his death, and they
themselves also shall beare him company therein, as they
have bin his perverse counsellors in the action of killing my
father, and his companions in his treason, massacre and cruell
enterprise.   And reason requireth that, even as trayterously
they then caused their prince to bee put to death, that with
the like (nay well, much more) justice they should pay the
interest of their fellonious actions.

You know (Madame) how Hother your grandfather,
and father to the good king Roderick, having vanquished
Guimon, caused him to be burnt, for that the cruell vilain
had done the like to his lord Gevare, whom he betrayed in
the night time.   And who knoweth not that traytors and
perjured persons deserve no faith nor loyaltie to be observed
towardes them, and that conditions made with murtherers ought
to bee esteemed as cobwebs, and accounted as if they were
things never promised nor agreed upon : but if I lay handes
upon Fengon, it will neither be fellonie nor treason, hee being
neither my king nor my lord, but I shall justly punish him

Hother,
father to
Rodericke.

Guimon
burnt
his Lord
Gevare.

We must
observe
neither faith-
fulnesse or
fidelitie to
traytors or
parricides.

mon vassal, qui s'est forfait desloyaument contre son seigneur, et souverain Prince. Et puis que la gloire est le salaire des vertueux, l'honneur, et le prix de ceux qui font service à leur Prince naturel, pourquoy le blasme n'accompagnera il les traistres, et la mort ignominieuse, ceux qui osent mettre la main violente sur les Roys sacrez, et qui sont les amis et compaignons des Dieux, et ceux qui representent leur majesté, et image? En somme la gloire estant la couronne de vertu, et le prix de la constance, puis qu'elle ne s'accompaigne point avec l'infelicité, et qu'elle fuit la coüardise, et s'esloigne des esprits avilliz, et abbatus, il faut ou qu'une fin glorieuse mette fin à mes jours, ou qu'ayant les armes au poing, chargé de triomphe et victoire, je ravisse la vie à ceux qui rendent la mienne mal heureuse, et obscurcissent les rayons de celle vertu que je tiens du sang et memoire illustre de mes predecesseurs. Et dequoy sert vivre, où la honte, et l'infamie, sont les bourreaux qui tourmentent nostre conscience, et la poltronnerie est celle qui retarde le cœur des gaillardes entreprises, et destourne l'esprit des honnestes desirs de gloire et louange, qui sera à jamais durable? Je sçay que c'est sottement faict, que de cueillir un fruict avant saison, Et de tascher de joüir d'un bien, duquel on ne sçait si la joüissance nous en est deuë: Mais je m'attends de faire si bien, et espere tant en la fortune, qui a guidé jusques icy les actions de ma vie, que je ne mourray ja, sans me venger de mon ennemy, et que luy mesme sera

Gloire est le salarie des vertueux.

Roys sont l'image des Dieux.

L'honneur s'esloigne des couards, et fait neans.

Vie miserable qui est accompaignee d'infamie.

as my subject, that hath disloyaly behaved himselfe against his lord and soveraigne prince. And seeing that glory is the rewarde of the vertuous, and the honour and praise of those that do service to their naturall prince, why should not blame and dishonour accompany traytors, and ignominious death al those that dare be so bold as to lay violent hands upon sacred kings, that are friends and companions of the gods, as representing their majestie and persons. To conclude, glorie is the crown of vertue, and the price of constancie; and seeing that it never accompanieth with infelicitie, but shunneth cowardize and spirits of base and trayterous conditions, it must necessarily followe, that either a glorious death will be mine ende, or with my sword in hand, (laden with tryumph and victorie) I shall bereave them of their lives that made mine unfortunate, and darkened the beames of that vertue which I possessed from the blood and famous memory of my predecessors. For why should men desire to live, when shame and infamie are the executioners that torment their consciences, and villany is the cause that withholdeth the heart from valiant interprises, and diverteth the minde from honest desire of glorie and commendation, which indureth for ever? I know it is foolishly done to gather fruit before it is ripe, and to seeke to enjoy a benefit, not knowing whither it belong to us of right; but I hope to effect it so well, and have so great confidence in my fortune (that hitherto hath guided the action of my life) that I shall not dye without revenging my selfe upon mine enemie, and

l'instrument de sa ruine, et me guidera à executer ce, que de moymesme je n'eusse osé entreprendre. Apres cecy Fengon comme s'il fust venu de quelquel loingtain voyage arrive en court, et s'enquerant de celuy qui avoit entreprise la charge d'espion, pour surprendre Amleth en sa sagesse dissimulee, fut bien estonné n'en pouvant oyr ny vent, ny nouvelle : et pour ceste cause, demanda au fol s'il sçavoit point qu'estoit devenu celuy qu'il luy nomma.

Le Prince qui n'estoit menteur, et qui en quelque response que jamais il feit durant sa fainte folie, ne s'estoit onc esgaré de la verité ; comme aussi tout esprit genereux est mortel ennemy de la mensonge, luy respondit, que le courtisan qu'il cherchoit s'en estoit allé par les privez, là où suffoqué par les immondices du lieu, les pourceaux s'y rencontrans en avoyent remply leur ventre.

L'esprit genereux ne sçait mentir.

On eust plustost creu autre chose, que ce massacre, fait par Amleth : toutesfois Fengon ne se pouvoit asseurer, et luy

that himselfe shall be the instrument of his owne decay, and to execute that which of my selfe I durst not have enterprised.

After this, Fengon (as if hee had beene out some long journey) came to the court againe, and asked for him that had received the charge to play the intilligencer, to entrap Hamlet in his dissembled wisedome, was abashed to heare neither newes nor tydings of him, and for that cause asked Hamlet what was become of him, naming the man. The prince that never used lying, and who in all the answers that ever he made (during his counterfeit madnesse) never strayed from the trueth (as a generous minde is a mortal enemie to untruth) answered and sayd, that the counsellor he sought for was gone downe through the privie, where being choaked by the filthynesse of the place, the hogs meeting him had filled their bellyes.

CHAPTER IIII

How Fengon the third time devised to send Hamblet to the king of England, with secret letters to have him put to death: and how Hamblet, when his companions slept, read the letters, and instead of them counterfeited others, willing the king of England to put the two messengers to death, and to marry his daughter to Hamblet, which was effected; and how Hamblet escaped out of England.

A MAN would have judged any thing, rather then that Hamblet had committed that murther, nevertheless Fengon

sembloit tousjours, que ce fol luy jouëroit quelque mauvais
tour, il l'eust volontiers occis, mais il craignoit le Roy
Rorique son aieul, et qu'aussi il n'ozoit offencer la Royne mere
du fol, qu'elle aymoit, et caressoit, quoy que elle monstrast
un grand creve-cœur de le voir ainsi transporté de son sens.

Ainsi voulant s'en depescher, il tascha de s'ayder du
ministere d'un estranger, et feit le Roy des Anglois le
ministre du massacre de l'innocence simulee, aymant mieux
que son amy soüiliast son renom, avec une telle meschanceté,
que de tomber en infamie par l'exploit d'une si grande,
cruauté vers lequel se resolut de l'envoyer, et le prier
par lettre d'en despecher le monde. Amleth entandant
qu'on l'envoioit en la grand Bretaigne, vers l'Anglois,
se douta tout aussi tost de l'occasion de ce voyage, pour
ce ayant parlé à la Royne, la pria de ne faire aucun signe
d'estre fachee de ce depart, plustost feignist d'en estre
joyeuse, comme deschargee de la presence de celuy lequel,
jaçoit qu'elle l'aimast, si mouroit elle de dueil, le voyant en si
piteux estat, et privé de tout usage de raison : encor suplia
il la Roine, qu'a son depart elle tapisast la salle, et affichast
avec des clouds les tapiseries contre le mur, et luy gardast ces
tisons, qu'il avoit aguisez par le bout, lors qu'il dist qu'il
faisoit des sagettes pour venger la mort de son pere : en fin
l'admonesta, que l'an accomply, elle celebrast ses obseques et

could not content himselfe, but still his minde gave him that
the foole would play him some tricke of liegerdemaine, and
willingly would have killed him, but he feared king Rodericke,
his grandfather, and further durst not offend the queene,
mother to the foole whom she loved and much cherished,
shewing great griefe and heavinesse to see him so transported
out of his wits. And in that conceit, seeking to bee rid of
him, determined to finde the meanes to doe it by the ayde of a
stranger, making the king of England minister of his massa-
creing resolution, choosing rather that his friende should
defile his renowne with so great a wickednesse, then himselfe
to fall into perpetuall infamie by an exploit of so great crueltie,
to whom hee purposed to send him, and by letters desire him
to put him to death.

Hamblet, understanding that he should be sent into England,
presently doubted the occasion of his voyage, and for that
cause speaking to the queene, desired her not to make any
shew of sorrow or griefe for his departure, but rather counterfeit a gladnesse, as being rid of his presence ; whom, although
she loved, yet she dayly grieved to see him in so pittifull
estate, deprived of all sence and reason : desiring her further,
that she should hang the hall with tapestrie, and make it fast
with nayles upon the walles, and keepe the brands for him
which hee had sharpened at the points, then, when as he said
he made arrowes to revenge the death of his father : lastly,
he counselled her, that the yeere after his departure being
accomplished, she should celebrate his funerals ; assuring her

funerailles, l'asseurant, qu'en ceste mesme saison, elle le verroit
de retour, et tel qu'elle seroit contente et plusque satisfaicte
de son voyage.   Auquel avec luy furent envoyez deux des
fideles ministres de Fengon, portans des lettres, gravees dans
du boys, qui portoyent la mort de Amleth, ainsi qu'ill a commandoit à l'Anglois : mais le rusé Prince Danois, tandis que
ses compaignons dormoyent ayant visité le pacquet, et cogneu
la grande trahison de son oncle, et la meschanceté des

Ruse et
quautelle
d'Amleth
pour sauver
sa vie.

courtisans qui le conduisoient à la boucherie, rasa les lettres
mentionans sa mort, et au lieu y grava et cisa un commandement à l'Anglois de faire pendre et estrangler ses compaignons :
et non content de tourner sur eux la mort ordonnee pour sa
teste: il y adjousta que Fengon commandoit au Roy insulaire
de donner au nepveu du Roy sa fille en mariage.   Arrivez
qu'ils sont en la grand Bretaigne, les messagers se presentent
au Roy, et luy donnent les lettres de leur seigneur, lequel
voiant le contenu d'icelles, dissimula le tout attendant son

Roys
familiers le
temps passé.

opportunité de mettre en effect la volonté de Fengon.
Ce pendant il traita les Danois fort gratieusement, et leur fait
c'est honneur, que de les recevoir à sa table, d'autant que les
Roys d'alors n'estoient pas si supersticieux que maintenant,
et ne tenoyent leur presence si chere, n'y n'estoient si chiches
de leur familiarité, qu'on les voit en ce temps, ou les Roytelets
et Seigneurs de peu de consequence, sont aussi difficiles à

Roys de
Perse ne se
laissoient
voir.

estre accostez, qu'estoient jadis les Monarques des Perses, ou
comme l'on dict encor du grand Roy de l'Etiopie, qui ne
permet qu'on voye à descouvert sa face, laquelle il couvre

that at the same instant she should see him returne with great contentment and pleasure unto her for that his voyage. Now, to beare him company were assigned two of Fengons faithfull ministers, bearing letters ingraved in wood, that contained Hamlets death, in such sort as he had advertised the king of England. But the subtile Danish prince (beeing at sea) whilst his companions slept, having read the letters, and knowne his uncles great treason, with the wicked and villainous mindes of the two courtyers that led him to the slaughter, raced out the letters that concerned his death, and in stead thereof graved others, with commission to the king of England to hang his two companions; and not content to turne the death they had devised against him upon their owne neckes, wrote further, that king Fengon willed him to give his daughter to Hamlet in marriage. And so arriving in England, the messengers presented themselves to the king, giving him Fengons letters; who having read the contents, sayd nothing as then, but stayed convenient time to effect Fengons desire, meane time using the Danes familiarly, doing them that honour to sit at his table (for that kings as then were not so curiously, nor solemnely served as in these our dayes,) for in these dayes meane kings, and lords of small revenewe are as difficult and hard to bee seene, as in times past the monarches of Persia used to bee: or as it is reported of the great king of Aethyopia, who will not permit any man to see his face,

Hamblets craft to save his life.

ordinairement du'n voile.   Comme ses messagers sont à table
et s'esjouissoient parmi les Anglois, le cauteleux Amleth, tant
s'en faut qu'il s'esjouist avec la troupe, qu'il ne voulut toucher
viande ny breuvage quelconque, qu'on servit à la table
Royale, non sans l'esbahissement des assistans, lesquels
estoyent estonnez de voir un adolescens estranger ne tenir
compte des viandes exquses, ny des breuvages delicieux pre-
sentez au banquet, et les avoit tout ainsi rejetez comme chose
sale, de mauvais goust, et encor plus mal apprestee.   Le Roy
qui sur l'heure dissimula ce quil en pensoit, feit conduire ses
hostes en leur chambre, enjoingnant à un sien loyal de se
cacher dedans, pour luy rapporter les propos tenuz par les
estrangers en se couchant.

Or ne furent ils si tost dans la chambre, qu'estans sortis
ceux qui avoyent la charge de les traicter, les compaignons de
Amleth ne luy demandassent pour quelle occasion, il avoit
desdaigné, et les viandes et la boisson qu'on luy avoit presenté
à table, et n'avoit honoré la table d'un si grand Roy qui les
avoit recueilliz, avec telle honnesteté et courtoisie : disoyent
en oultre qu'il avoit tort, et faisoit deshonneur à celuy qui
l'envoyoit, comme s'il mandoit en Bretaignes des hommes,
qui se craignoyent d'estre empoisonnez par un Roy tant

honnorable.   Le Prince qui n'avoit rien fait sans raison, leur
respondit tout soudain, et quoy pensez vous que je vueille
manger le pain trempé avec le sang humain, et soiller mon
gosier de rouilleure de fer, et user de la chair qui sent la puanteur,
et corruption des corps humains, ja tous pourris et corrompuz,

which ordinarily hee covereth with a vaile. And as the
messengers sate at the table with the king, subtile Hamlet
was so far from being merry with them, that he would not
taste one bit of meate, bread, nor cup of beare whatsoever, as
then set upon the table, not without great wondering of the
company, abashed to see a yong man and a stranger not to
esteeme of the delicate meates and pleasant drinkes served at
the banquet, rejecting them as things filthy, evill of tast, and
worse prepared. The king, who for that time dissembled
what he thought, caused his ghests to be conveyed into their
chamber, willing one of his secret servantes to hide himselfe
therein, and so to certifie him what speeches past among the
Danes at their going to bed.

Now they were no sooner entred into the chamber, and
those that were appointed to attend upon them gone out, but
Hamlets companions asked him, why he refused to eate and
drinke of that which hee found upon the table, not honouring
the banquet of so great a king, that entertained them in
friendly sort, with such honour and courtesie as it deserved?
saying further, that hee did not well, but dishonoured him
that sent him, as if he sent men into England that feared to
bee poysoned by so great a king. The prince, that had done
nothing without reason and prudent consideration, answered
them, and sayd: What, think you, that I wil eat bread dipt
in humane blood, and defile my throate with the rust of yron,
and use that meat that stinketh and savoureth of mans flesh,
already putrified and corrupted, and that senteth like the

et qui rapporte au goust d'une charongne de long temps jettee à la voyrie ? Et comment voulez vous que je respecte le Roy qui a un regard d'esclave et une Royne, laquelle en lieu d'une grande Majesté a faict trois chose dignes d'une femme de vil estat, et qui sont plus propres à quelque chambriere qu'a une Dame de son calibre. Et ayant dict cecy, il avança plusieurs propos injurieux et piquans, tant comme le Roy, et Royne, que les autres qui avoyent assisté à ce banquet et festin, pour la reception des Ambasades de Dannemarch, Amleth ne dit rien qui ne fust veritable, ainsi que pourrez entendre cy apres, veu qu'en ce temps là tous ces pays Septentrionaux, estans souz l'obeissance de Sathan, il y avoit une infinité d'enchanteurs : et n'estoit fils de bonne mere, qui n'en sçavoit assez pour sa provision, si comme encor en la Gothie et Biarmie, il se trouve infinité qui sçavent plus de choses que la sainteté de la religion Chrestienne ne permet, comme lisant les histoires de Norvege et Gouthie, vous verrez assez facilement. Et ainsi Amleth, vivant son pere, avoit esté endoctriné en celle science, avec laquelle le malin esprit abuse les hommes et advertissoit ce Prince (comme il peut) des choses ja passees. Je n'ay affaire icy de discourir des parties de divination en l'homme, et si ce Prince, pour la vehemence de la melancholie, avoit receu ces impressions, devinant ce qu'autre ne luy avoit jamais declairé, ainsi que les Philosophes qui traitent de la judiciaire, donnent la force de telle prediction à ceux, qui influez de

Pais Septentrionaux pleins d'enchanteurs.

Gothie et Biarmie royaumes Septentrionaux. Voy l'histoyre de Jean et Olaus le grand.

savour of a dead carryon, long since cast into a valt? and
how woulde you have mee to respect the king, that hath the
countenance of a slave; and the queene, who in stead of
great majestie, hath done three things more like a woman
of base parentage, and fitter for a waiting gentlewoman then
beseeming a lady of her qualitie and estate.   And having
sayd so, used many injurious and sharpe speeches as well
against the king and queene, as others that had assisted at
that banquet for the intertainment of the Danish ambassadors;
and therein Hamblet said trueth, as hereafter you shall heare,
for that in those dayes, the north parts of the worlde, living
as then under Sathans lawes, were full of inchanters, so that
there was not any yong gentleman whatsoever that knew not
something therein sufficient to serve his turne, if need required:
as yet in those dayes in Gothland and Biarmy, there are
many that knew not what the Christian religion permitteth,
as by reading the histories of Norway and Gothland, you
maie easilie perceive: and so Hamlet, while his father lived,
had bin instructed in that devilish art, whereby the wicked
spirite abuseth mankind, and advertiseth him (as he can) of
things past.

It toucheth not the matter herein to discover the parts of
devination in man, and whether this prince, by reason of his
over great melancholy, had received those impressions, devining
that, which never any but himselfe had before declared, like
the philosophers, who discoursing of divers deep points of
philosophie, attribute the force of those divinations to such

Saturne, chantent souvent des choses, lesquelles cessant une telle fureur, ils ne peuvent eux mesmes entendre qui en sont les prononceurs.   Et c'est pourquoy Platon dit, plusieurs vaticinateurs et Poetes devins apres que l'effort, et impetuosité de leur fureur se refroidit, à peine entendent ils ce qu'ils escrivent, jaçoit qu'en traitant ces choses durant leur transport, ils discourent si bien de ce qu'ils demeslent, que les auteurs et versez és arts, par ceux la mis en avant en louent le discours, et subtile dispute.   Aussi ne me soucie de mettre en jeu, ce que croyent plusieurs qu'une ame toute convertie en raison, devient la maison et domicile des demons moyens, par le moyen desquels il apprend la science et secret des choses naturelles et humaines : et moins tiens-je compte des gouverneurs supposez du monde, par les Magitiens, par le moyen desquels ils se vantent d'effectuer des choses merveilleuses : jacoit que ce soit choses miraculeuse, que Amleth peut deviner, ce que puis apres on veit estre plus que veritable, si (comme je vous ay dit) le diable n'avoit la congnoissance parfaite des choses passees : car de vous accorder que l'advenir luy soit notoire, jamais je ne trouveray une faute si lourde ny ne tomberay en si grand erreur, si vous ne voulez mesurer les predictions faites par conjecture, aussi asseurees que celles qui sont gardees par l'esprit de Dieu, et annoncees par les saincts Prophetes, lesquels ont gousté la science meruriileuse, et à eux seuls declaree des merveilles, et secrets du tout puissant. Et ne faut que ces imposteurs, qui veulent tant donner de divinité à l'ennemy de Dieu et pere de mensonge, que de luy

Effect de l'ame convertie en raison.

Demons gouverneurs du monde.

Les Diables scauent bien le passé mais le futur ils l'ignorent.

as are saturnists by complection, who oftentimes speake of
things which, their fury ceasing, they then alreadye can hardly
understand who are the pronouncers ; and for that cause Plato
saith, many deviners and many poets, after the force and
vigour of their fier beginneth to lessen, do hardly understand
what they have written, although intreating of such things,
while the spirite of devination continueth upon them, they doe
in such sorte discourse thereof that the authors and inventers
of the arts themselves by them alledged, commend their dis-
courses and subtill disputations.   Likewise I mean not to
relate that which divers men beleeve, that a reasonable soul
becometh the habitation of a meaner sort of devels, by whom
men learn the secrets of things natural ; and much lesse do I
account of the supposed governors of the world fained by
magitians, by whose means they brag to effect mervailous
things.   It would seeme miraculous that Hamlet shold divine
in that sort, which after prooved so true (if as I said before)
the devel had not knowledg of things past, but to grant it he
knoweth things to come I hope you shall never finde me
in so grose an error.   You will compare and make equall
derivation, and conjecture with those that are made by the
spirit of God, and pronounced by the holy prophets, that
tasted of that marvelous science, to whome onely was declared
the secrets and wondrous workes of the Almighty.   Yet
there are some imposturious companions that impute so much
devinitie to the devell, the father of lyes, that they attribute

Saul faict
revoquer
l'ame de
Samuel I
des Roys. 28.

attribuer la verité de ce qui doit succeder aux hommes, me
mettent en avant le fait de Saul, avec la devineresse : veu
qu'un exemple estant en l'escriture, et mesme ameiné pour la
condemnation d'un meschant, n'est puissant pour donner loy
de vigeur universelle : car eux mesmes confessent qu'ils
peuvent predire non suyvant la cause universelle : des choses,

Comme les
Magiciens
peuvent de
viner.

mais par les signes emprains és causes semblables, qui sont
tousjours mesmes, et peuvent par ses conjectures donner
jugement des effets à venir.

Mais estant tout cecy appuyé d'un si foible baston, que la
conjecture, et ayant un si maigre fondement, que quelque sotte
et tardive experience, et les fictions en estant volontaires, se
seroit une grand folie à l'homme de bon esprit, et mesmement à celuy qui embrasse la pureté de la doctrine, et ne
cherche que leur pur effect de la verité de s'arrester à pas
une reigle de ces verisimilitudes, ou escrits plein de fallace.

Les enchan-
teurs font
des choses
merveil-
leuses.

Quant aux operations magiques, je leur en accorderay une
partie, voyant les histoires pleinnes de telles illusions, et que
la saincte Bible en fait foy, et en defend l'usage, voire les
loix des gentils, et ordonnances des Empereurs y ont

Mahometh
defend en sa
loy l'arc de
Magie.

pourveu par leurs ordonnances, tellement que Mahomet im-
posteur, et amy des Diables, avec l'astuce desquels il abbusa
presque tout l'Orient, a estably grosses peines à ceux qui
s'adonnoyent à ces arts illicites, et damnables. Desquels
esloignans le propos, reviendrons à Amleth institué en ces
folies, suyvans la coustume de son pays : les compaignons

unto him the truth of the knowledge of thinges that shall happen unto men, alledging the conference of Saul with the witch, although one example out of the Holy Scriptures, specially set downe for the condemnation of wicked man, is not of force to give a sufficient law to all the world; for they themselves confesse that they can devine, not according to the universal cause of things, but by signes borrowed from such like causes, which are all waies alike, and by those conjectures they can give judgement of thinges to come, but all this beeing grounded upon a weake support, (which is a simple conjecture) and having so slender a foundation, as some foolish or late experience the fictions being voluntarie. It should be a great folly in a man of good judgment, specially one that imbraceth the preaching of the gospell, and seeketh after no other but the trueth thereof, to repose upon any of these likelihoods or writings full of deceipt.

As touching magical operations, I will grant them somewhat therein, finding divers histories that write thereof, and that the Bible maketh mention, and forbiddeth the use thereof: yea, the lawes of the gentiles and ordinances of emperors have bin made against it in such sort, that Mahomet, the great hereticke and friend of the devell, by whose subtiltyes hee abused most part of the east countries, hath ordained great punishments for such as use and practise those unlawfull and damnable arts, which, for this time leaving of, let us returne to Hamblet, brought up in these abuses, according to the manner of his country, whose companions

duquel oyans sa responce, luy reprochoient sa folie disoient qu'il n'en pouvoit donner plus grans indice, qu'en mesprisant ce qui estoit louable, et rejettant ce que tous receuoient comme necessaire, et qu'au reste il s'estoit bien lourdement oublié, accusant ainsi un tel, et si excellent homme que le Roy, et vituperer la Royne des plus illustres, et sages princesses, qui fust és Isles voysines, le menaçans au reste de le faire chastier, selon le merite de son outrecuidance. Mais luy continuant en sa folie dissimulee, se mocquoit d'eux, et disoit qu'il n'avoit rien fait, ny proposé qui ne fut bon, et plus que veritable. D'autre part le Roy adverty, qu'il est de tout cecy, par celuy qui les avoit escoutés, jugea soudain que Amleth parlant ainsi ambiguement, ou estoit fol jusque à la haute game, ou des plus sages de son temps respondant si soudain, et si à propos à ce que les compaignons s'estoyent enquis sur ses façons de faire : et pour en sçavoir mieux la verité, commanda qu'on feist venir le boulanger qui avoit fait le pain de sa bouche, auquel comme il s'enquist en quel lieu est ce qu'on avoit cueilly le grain, duquel on faisoit le pain pour son ordinaire, et si en ce champ y avoit point aucun signe ny indice de bataille ny combat, pour y avoir du sang humain espars. A quoy fut respondu que non loin de là, estoit un camp tout chargé des ossements d'hommes occis jadis en quelque cruelle rencontre, veu le taz amoncellé qu'on y pouvoit encore apercevoir, et que pour estre la terre plus grasse et fertille à cause de l'humeur et gresse des morts, on y semoit

hearing his answere reproached him of folly, saying that hee
could by no meanes show a greater point of indiscretion, then
in despising that which is lawfull, and rejecting that which
all men receaved as a necessary thing, and that hee had not
grossely so forgotten himselfe as in that sort to accuse such
and so excellent a man as the king of England, and to slander
the queene, being then as famous and wise a princes as any at
that day raigning in the ilands thereabouts, to cause him to
be punished according to his deserts ; but he, continuing in
his dissimulation, mocked him, saying that hee had not done
any thing that was not good and most true.   On the other
side, the king being advertised thereof by him that stood to
heare the discourse, judged presently that Hamlet, speaking so
ambiguously, was either a perfect foole, or else one of the
wisest princes in his time, answering so sodainly, and so much
to the purpose upon the demaund by his companions made
touching his behaviour ; and the better to find the trueth,
caused the babler to be sent for, of whome inquiring in what
place the corne grew whereof he made bread for his table,
and whether in that ground there were not some signes or
newes of a battaile fought, whereby humaine blood had
therein been shed ? the babler answered that not far from
thence there lay a field ful of dead mens bones, in times past
slaine in a battaile, as by the greate heapes of wounded sculles
mighte well appeare, and for that the ground in that parte
was become fertiler then other grounds, by reason of the fatte
and humours of the dead bodies, that every yeer the farmers

tous les ans le plus beau bled qu'on pouvoit choisir pour son service, Le Roy voyant la verité correspondre aux parolles du jeune Prince, s'enquist encor ou est ce qu'on avoyt nourry les pourceaux, la chair desquels avoit esté servie sur table, et congueut que estans eschapez de leur tect et estable, ils s'estoyent rassasiez de la chanrongne et corps d'un larron justicié pour ses forfaits et demerites C'est icy que le prince Angloys s'estonne et voulut sçavoir de quelle eau estoit ce que la Biere servie à table avoit esté composee : tellement que faisant creuser bien avant le ruisseau, duquel on s'estoit aidé à faire leur boisson, on trouvades espees et armes rouilees, qui donnoyent ce mauvais goust au breuvage. Il sembleroit advis

Merlin prophete des Angloys.

que je vous feisse icy des comptes de Merlin que lon feinct avoir parlé avant qu'il eust un an accompli : maïs si vous advisez de pres tout ce qui est desja dit, n'est guere difficile à deviner, quoy que le ministere de sathan y eust peu servir, donnant les responces soudaine à cest adolescent : veu qu'il ny à rïen icy que choses naturelles, A telles qui estoyent desja en la cognoissance de ce qui est, et ne falloit songer sur ce qui devoit advenir. Tout cecy espluché, le Roy fut esmeu encor d'une curiosité de sçavoir pourquoy le seigneur Danoys avoit dit que le Roy avoit regard d'un esclave, car il soupçonnoit que l'autre luy reprochast la villeté de son sang, et quil voulust dire que jamais Prince n'avoit esté l'auteur de son engeance : et afin d'esclercir ce doubte il sadressa à sa Mere, et l'ayant conduicte secrettement en une chambre,

used there to have in the best wheat they could finde to
serve his majesties house.   The king perceiving it to be true,
according to the yong princes wordes, asked where the hogs
had bin fed that were killed to be served at his table ? and
answere was made him, that those hogs getting out of the
said fielde wherein they were kepte, had found the bodie of a
thiefe that had beene hanged for his demerits, and had eaten
thereof : whereat the king of England beeing abashed, would
needs know with what water the beer he used to drinke of
had beene brued ? which having knowne, he caused the river
to bee digged somewhat deeper, and therin found great store
of swords and rustie armours, that gave an ill savour to the
drinke.   It were good I should heere dilate somewhat of
Merlins prophesies, which are said to be spoken of him
before he was fully one yeere old ; but if you consider wel
what hath al reddy been spoken, it is no hard matter to divine
of things past, although the minister of Sathan therein played
his part, giving sodaine and prompt answeres to this yong
prince, for that herein are nothing but natural things, such as
were wel known to be true, and therefore not needfull to
dreame of thinges to come.   This knowne, the king, greatly
moved with a certaine curiositie to knowe why the Danish
prince saide that he had the countenance of a slave, suspecting thereby that he reproached the basenes of his blood, and
that he wold affirme that never any prince had bin his sire,
wherin to satisfie himselfe he went to his mother, and
leading her into a secret chamber, which he shut as soone as

laquelle il ferma sur eux, la pria de luy dire sur son honneur
à qu'il il devoit rendre graces d'estre né en ce monde.　La
bonne Dame asseuree que jamais aucun n'avoit rien sceu de
ses amours, ny forfaiture, luy jura que le Roy seul se pouvoit
vanter sans autre d'avoir jouy de ses embrassemens.　Luy qui
desja estoit abrevé de l'opinion des responces veritables du
Danois menace sa mere, de luy faire dire par force, ce que
de bon gré ne luy vouloit confesser, entendist qu'elle d'autre-
fois se soumettant à un esclave, l'avoit rendu le pere du Roy
de la grand Breraigne ; dequoy si le Roy fut estonné, et
camuz, je le l'aisse à penser à ceux qui s'estiment plus gens
de bien que tout autre, et cuidans qu'il n'y ayt rien que
reprendre en leur maison, s'enquierent plus qu'il ne faut pour
entendre aussi ce que point ne desirent : toutesfois dissiulant
son mal talent, et rongeant son frein, pour ne vouloir point se
scandaliser en publiant la lubricité de sa mere, ayma mieux
laisser un grand peché impuny, que se rendre contemptible à
ses subjetz, qui peut estre l'eussent rejetté, comme ne voulans
un bastard qui commandast à une si belle province.

　　Comme donc il estoit marry de ouir sa confusion, il print
grand plaisir à la subtilité, et gentillesse d'esprit du jeune
Prince, le vinst trouver, et s'enquist de luy pourquoy est-ce
qu'il avoit repris en la Royne trois choses plus requises à un
esclave, et resentans leur servitude, que rien de Roy, et qui

La Mere de
l'Angloys
confesse son
fils estre
Bastard.

Curiosité
trop grande
preiudicable
à l'homme.

they were entred, desired her of her honour to shewe him of whome he was ingendred in this world. The good lady, wel assured that never any man had bin acquainted with her love touching any other man then her husband, sware that the king her husband onely was the man that had enjoyed the pleasures of her body; but the king her sonne, alreadie with the truth of the Danish princes answers, threatned his mother to make her tell by force, if otherwise she would not confesse it, who for feare of death acknowledged that she had prostrated her body to a slave, and made him father to the king of England; whereat the king was abashed, and wholy ashamed. I give them leave to judge who esteeming themselves honester than theire neighbours, and supposing that there can be nothing amisse in their houses, make more enquirie then is requisite to know the which they would rather not have known. Neverthelesse dissembling what he thought, and biting upon the bridle, rather then he would deprive himselfe by publishing the lasciviousnes of his mother, thought better to leave a great sin unpunished, then thereby to make himselfe contemptible to his subjects, who per-adventure would have rejected him, as not desiring to have a bastard to raigne over so great a kingdome.

But as he was sorry to hear his mothers confession, on the other side he tooke great pleasure in the subtilty and quick spirit of the yong prince, and for that cause went unto him to aske him, why he had reproved three things in his queene convenient for a slave, and savouring more of basenes then of

eust une majesté propre pour une grande Princesse. Ce Roy
non content d'avoir receu un grand desplaisir, pour se sçavoir
estre bastard, et d'avoir ouy avec quelles injures il attaquoit
celle que le plus il aimoit en ce monde, voulut aussi entendre
ce qui luy despleut autant que son malheur propre, à sçavoir
que la Royne sa femme estoit fille d'une chambriere, et luy
specifia quelques sottes contenances d'icelle, qui declaroyent
assez non seulement de quel sang, et condition elle estoit
sortie, ains encor que ses humeurs correspondoyent à la
vilenie et villeté de ses parens, la mere de laquelle il luy
asseura estre encor detenue en servitude. Le Roy admirant

Trahison
tombe sur la
teste de
celuy qui la
veut faire.

ce jeune homme, et contemplant en lui quelque cas de plus
grand que le commun des hommes, luy donna sa fille en
mariage, suyvant les tablettes falcifiees par le cauteleux
Amleth, et des l'endemain il feit prendre les deux serviteurs
du Roy Fengon, comme satisfaisant à la volonté de son grand

Astuce
d'Amleth.

amy : mais Amleth, quoy que le jeu luy pleust, et que
l'Anglois ne luy peut faire chose plus agreable, feignit d'en

Astuce
d'Amleth.

estre fort marry, et menaça le Roy de se resenrir de l'injure :
pour lequel appaiser, l'Angloys luy donna une grande somme
d'or, que le Prince feit fondre, et mettre dans des bastons
qu'il avoit fait creuser pour c'est effect, et pour s'en servir
ainsi qu'orrez cy apres : car de toutes les Royalles richesses
il n'emporta rien en Dannemarch, que ces bastons, prenans
son chemin à son pays, si tos que l'an fut accomply, ayant

royaltie, and far unfit for the majesty of a great prince? The
king, not content to have receaved a great displeasure by
knowing him selfe to be a bastard, and to have heard with
what injuries he charged her whom hee loved best in all the
world, would not content himself untill he also understood
that which displeased him, as much as his owne proper disgrace, which was that his queen was the daughter of a
chambermaid, and with all noted certaine foolish countenances she made, which not onely shewed of what parentage
she came, but also that hir humors savored of the basenes and
low degree of hir parents, whose mother, he assured the
king, was as then yet holden in servitude. The king
admiring the young prince, and behoulding in him some
matter of greater respect then in the common sort of men,
gave him his daughter in marriage, according to the counterfet letters by him devised, and the next day caused the two
servants of Fengon to be executed, to satisfie, as he thought,
the king's desire. But Hamlet, although the sport plesed
him wel, and that the king of England could not have done
him a greater favour, made as though he had been much
offended, threatning the king to be revenged, but the king, to
appease him, gave him a great sum of gold, which Hamlet
caused to be molten, and put into two staves, made hollow
for the same purpose, to serve his tourne there with as neede
should require; for of all other the kings treasures he took
nothing with him into Denmark but onely those two staves,
and as soone as the yeere began to bee at an end, having

plustost obtenu congé du Roy son beau pere, avec promesse
de revenir le plustost pour accomplir le mariage d'entre luy,
et la Princesse Angloise.

Diverses
humeurs de
courtisans.

        Arrivé qu'il fut en la maison et
palais de son oncle, dans lequel on celebroit ces propres
funerailles et entrant en la sale, ou le dueil estoit demené ce
ne fut sans donner un grand estonnement à chacun, n'y ayant
personne qui ne le pensast estre mort, et d'entre lesquels la
plus part n'en fussent joyeux pour le plaisir qu'il sçavoyent
que Fengon recevoit d'une si plaisante perte, et peu qui se
contristoyent, se souvenant de la gloire du deffunct Horvvendille, les victoires duquel ils ne pouvoyent oublier, et
moins effacer de leur memoire rien qui sortist du sien,
lesquels s'esjouïrent grandement, voyans que le renom avoit
failly à ceste fois, et que le tiran n'auroit encor le passetemps
du vray heritier de Jutie, mais que plustost les Dieux luy
randroyent son bon sens, pour le bien de sa Province.

somewhat before obtained licence of the king his father in law to depart, went for Denmarke; then, with all the speed hee could to returne againe into England to marry his daughter, and so set sayle for Denmarke.

CHAPTER V

How Hamblet, having escapea out of England, arrived in Denmarke the same aay that the Danes were celebrating his funerals, supposing him to be dead in England; and how he revenged his fathers death upon his uncle and the rest of the courtiers; and what followed.

HAMBLET in that sort sayling into Denmark, being arrived in the contry, entered into the pallace of his uncle the same day that they were celebrating his funeralls, and going into the hall, procured no small astonishment and wonder to them all, no man thinking other but that hee had beene deade: among the which many of them rejoyced not a little for the pleasure which they knew Fengon would conceave for so pleasant a losse, and some were sadde, as remembering the honourable king Horvendile, whose victories they could by no meanes forget, much lesse deface out of theire memories that which apperteined unto him, who as then greatly rejoyced to see a false report spread of Hamlets death, and that the tyrant had not as yet obtained his will of the heire of Jutie, but rather hoped God would restore him to his sences againe for the good and welfare of that province.   Their amazement at the

L'esbahissement converty que fust en risee, chacun de
ceux qui assistoyent au banquet funebre de celuy qu'on tenoit
pour mort, se moquoit de son compaignon pour avoir esté si
simplement deceuz, et gaussans le Prince, de ce que avec le
voyage, il n'avoit rien recouvert de son bon sens, luy deman-
derent qu'estoyent devenuz ceux qui avoyent voiagé avec luy
en la grande Bretaigne : ausquels il respondit, en monstrant les
deux bastons creusez, ou il avoit mis l'or fondu, que l'Anglois
luy donna pour l'apaise sur le meurtre de ses compaignons,
voicy et l'un et l'autre de ceux qui m'ont accompaigne.

Plusieurs qui cognoissent des-ja les humeurs du pelerin,
s'asseurent soudain qu'il leur avoit joué quelque tour de
maistre, et que pour se delivrer de peril, les avoit lancez dans
la fosse pour luy preparee, si que craignant de suivre leurs
voyes, et courir quelque mauvaise fortune, s'absenterent du
Palais, et bien pour eux, veu les esplanades de ce Prince le
jour de ses funerailles, qui fut le dernier pour ceux, qui
s'esjouissoient pour sa ruine. Car comme chacun fut en-
tentif à faire grand chere, et semblast que l'arrivvee
d'Amleth leur donnast plus d'occasion de haucer le gobelet,
le Prince faissoit aussi l'estat, et office d'eschanson et gentil-
homme servant, ne laissant jamais les hanaps vuides, et
abbreva la noblesse de telle sorte, que tous estans chargez
de vin, et offusquez de viandes, fallut que se couchassent au
lieu mesme ou ils avoient pris le repas, tant les avoit abestis et

last beeing tourned into laughter, all that as then were assistant
at the funerall banquet of him whome they esteemed dead,
mocked each at other, for having beene so simply deceived,
and wondering at the prince, that in his so long a voyage he
had not recovered any of his sences, asked what was become
of them that had borne him company into Greate Brittain?
to whome he made answere (shewing them the two hollow
staves, wherein he had put his molten golde, that the King
of England had given him to appease his fury, concerning the
murther of his two companions), and said, Here they are
both.   Whereat many that already knew his humours, presently conjectured that hee had plaide some tricke of legerde-
mane, and to deliver himselfe out of danger, had throwne
them into the pitte prepared for him; so that fearing to follow
after them and light upon some evil adventure, they went
presently out of the court.   And it was well for them that
they didde so, considering the tragedy acted by him the same
daie, beeing accounted his funerall, but in trueth theire last
daies, that as then rejoyced for their overthrow; for when
every man busied himselfe to make good cheare, and Hamlets
arivall provoked them more to drinke and carouse, the prince
himselfe at that time played the butler and a gentleman
attending on the tables, not suffering the pots nor goblets to
bee empty, whereby hee gave the noble men such store of
liquor, that all of them being ful laden with wine and gorged
with meate, were constrained to lay themselves downe in the
same place where they had supt, so much their sences were

Yvrognerie
vice commun
aux peuples
ou sep-
tentrion.

privez de sens, et de force de trop boire, vice assez familier,
et à l'Alemant, et à toutes ces nations et peuples Septentrionaux, Amleth, voyant l'oportunite si grande pour faire
son coup, et se venger de ses adversaires, et ensemble laisser,
et les actions, et le geste, et la'billement d'un incensé, ayant
l'occasion à propos, et qui luy offroit sa chevelure, ne faillit
de l'empoigner, ains voyant ces corps assoupis de vin, gisans
par terre comme pourceaux, les uns dormans, les autres
vomissans le trop de vin que par trop goulement il avoyent
avallé, feit tomber la tapisserie tendue par la salle sur eux,
laquelle il cloua par le pavé de la sale, qui estoit tout d'aiz, et
aux coingz il mit les tisons qu'il avoit aguisez, et desquels a

Estrange
vengeance
prise par
Amleth.

esté parlé cy dessus, qui servoyent d'attaches, les liant avec
telle façon, que quelque effort qu'ils feissent, il leur fut
impossible de se despestrer, et soudain il mit le feu par les
quatre coings de la maison Royalle : de sorte que de ceux
qui estoyent en la sale, il n'en eschappa pas un seul, qui ne
purgeast ses fautes par le feu, et ne dessechast le trop de
ligueur qu'il avoit avallee mourans trestous enveloppez dans
l'ardeur inevitable des flammes. Ce que voyant l'Adolescent,
devenu sage, et sachant que son oncle s'estoit retiré avant la
fin du banquet, en son corps de logis, separé du lieu exposé
aux flammes, s'en y alla, si que entrant en sa chambre, se

dulled, and overcome with the fire of over great drinking (a vice common and familiar among the Almaines, and other nations inhabiting the north parts of the world) which when Hamlet perceiving, and finding so good opportunitie to effect his purpose and bee revenged of his enemies, and by the means to abandon the actions, gestures, and apparel of a mad man, occasion so fitly finding his turn, and as it were effecting it selfe, failed not to take hold therof, and seeing those drunken bodies, filled with wine, lying like hogs upon the ground, some sleeping, others vomiting the over great abundance of wine which without measure they had swallowed up, made the hangings about the hall to fall downe and cover them all over; which he nailed to the ground, being boorded, and at the ends thereof he stuck the brands, whereof I spake before, by him sharpned, which served for prickes, binding and tying the hangings in such sort, that what force soever they used to loose themselves, it was unpossible to get from under them: and presently he set fire to the foure corners of the hal, in such sort, that all that were as then therein not one escaped away, but were forced to purge their sins by fire, and dry up the great aboundance of liquor by them received into their bodies, all of them dying in the inevitable and mercilesse flames of the whot and burning fire: which the prince perceiving, became wise, and knowing that his uncle, before the end of the banquet, had withdrawn himselfe into his chamber, which stood apart from the place where the fire burnt, went thither, and entring into the chamber, layd hand

saisit de l'espee du meurtrier de son pere, et y laissa la sienne
au lieu, qu'on luy avoit clouee avec le fourreau, durant le
banquet: puis s'adressant à Fengon, lui dit: Je me'stonne,
Roy desloyal, comme tu dors ainsi à ton aise, tandis que ton
Palais est tout en feu, et que l'embrasement d'iceluy, a bruslé
tous les courtisans, et ministres de tes cruautez, et detestables
tyrannies: et ne sçais comme tu es si asseuré de ta fortune,
que de reposer, voyant Amleth si pres de toy, et armé des
pieux qu'il aiguisa, il y a long temps, et qui à present est tout
prest de se venger du tort, et injure traistresse par toy faite à
son seigneur et pere. Fengon cognoissant à la verité la
descouverte des ruses de son nepveu, et l'oyant parler de sens
rassis, et qui plus est, luy voyant le glaive nud en main, que
desja il hauçoit pour le priver de vie, sauta legerement du lict,
gettant la main à l'espee clouée, de son nepveu, laquelle
comme il s'efforçoit de desgaigner, Amleth luy donna un
grand coup sur le chinon du col, de sorte qu'il luy feit voler
la teste par terre, disant: c'est le salaire deu à ceux qui te
ressemblent, que de mourir ainsi violemment: et pour ce va,
et estant aux enfers, ne faux de compter à ton frere, que tu
occis meschamment, que c'est son fils qui te faict faire ce
message, à fin que soulagé par ceste memoire, son ombre
s'appaise parmy les esprits bien-heureux, et me quitte de celle
obligation qui m'astraignoit à poursuivre ceste vengeance sur

Mocquerie
poignante
d'Amleth à
son Oncle.

Fengon
occis par
Amleth son
neveu.

upon the sword of his fathers murtherer, leaving his own in the place, which while he was at the banket some of the courtiers had nailed fast into the scaberd, and going to Fengon said : I wonder, disloyal king, how thou canst sleep heer at thine ease, and al thy pallace is burnt, the fire thereof having burnt the greatest part of thy courtiers and ministers of thy cruelty, and detestable tirannies ; and which is more, I cannot imagin how thou sholdst wel assure thy self and thy estate, as now to take thy ease, seeing Hamlet so neer thee armed with the shafts by him prepared long since, and at this present is redy to revenge the traiterous injury by thee done to his lord and father.

A mocke but yet sharp and stinging, given by Hamlet to his uncle.

Fengon, as then knowing the truth of his nephews subtile practise, and hering him speak with stayed mind, and which is more, perceived a sword naked in his hand, which he already lifted up to deprive him of his life, leaped quickly out of the bed, taking holde of Hamlets sworde, that was nayled into the scaberd, which as hee sought to pull out, Hamlet gave him such a blowe upon the chine of the necke, that hee cut his head cleane from his shoulders, and as he fell to the ground sayd, This just and violent death is a just reward for such as thou art : now go thy wayes, and when thou commest in hell, see thou forget not to tell thy brother (whom thou trayterously slewest), that it was his sonne that sent thee thither with the message, to the ende that beeing comforted thereby, his soule may rest among the blessed spirits, and quit mee of the obligation that bound me to

mon sang mesme puis que c'estoit par luy, que javois perdu
ce qui me lioit à telle consanguinité et alliance. Homme
pour vray hardy et courageux, et digne d'eternelle louange,
qui s'armant d'une folie cauteleuse, et dissimulant accorte-
ment un grand desvoyement de sens, trompa souz telle
simplicité les plus sages, fins, et rusez : conservant non seulement sa vie des efforts et embusches du tyran, ains qui plus
est vengeant avec un nouveau genre de punition, et non
excogité supplice la mort de son pere, plusieurs annees apres
l'execution : de sorte que conduisant ses affaires avec telle
prudence, et effectuant ses desseins avec une si grande hardiesse, et constance, il laisse un jugement indecis entre les
hommes de bon esprit, lequel est le plus recommandable en
luy, ou sa constance et magnanimité, ou la sagesse, en
desseignant, et accortise, en mettant ses desseins au parfaict
accomplissement de son oeuvre de long temps premedité. Si
jamais la vengeance sembla avoir quelque face et forme de
justice, il est hors de doute, que la pieté et affection qui nous
lie à la souvenance de nos peres, poursuivis injustement, est
celle qui nous dispense à cercher les moyens de ne laisser
impunie une trahison, et effort outrageux et proditoire : veu
que jaçoit que David fut un sainct, et juste Roy, homme
simple, et courtois, et debonnaire, si est-ce que mourant il
enchargea à son fils Salomon, luy succedant à la couronne, de
ne laisser descendre au tombeau quelque certain, qui l'avoit
outragé ; non que le Roy, et prochain de la mort, et prest à
rendre compte devant Dieu, fust soigneux, ny desireux

Louange
d'Amleth
tuans le ty-
ran.

Vengeance
juste, ou est
ce que doit
estre
consideree.

Intention de
David com-
mandant
ceste
vengeance.

pursue his vengeance upon mine owne blood, that seeing it was by thee that I lost the chiefe thing that tyed me to this aliance and consanguinitie.   A man (to say the trueth) hardie, couragious, and worthy of eternall comendation, who arming himself with a crafty, dissembling, and strange shew of beeing distract out of his wits, under that pretence deceived the wise, pollitike, and craftie, thereby not onely preserving his life from the treasons and wicked practises of the tyrant, but (which is more) by an new and unexpected kinde of punishment, revenged his fathers death, many yeeres after the act committed : in no such sort that directing his courses with such prudence, and effecting his purposes with so great boldnes and constancie, he left a judgement to be decyded among men of wisdom, which was more commendable in him, his constancy or magnanimitie, or his wisdom in ordring his affaires, according to the premeditable determination he had conceaved.

Commendation of Hamlet for killing the tyrant.

If vengeance ever seemed to have any shew of justice, it is then, when pietie and affection constraineth us to remember our fathers unjustly murdered, as the things wherby we are dispensed withal, and which seeke the means not to leave treason and murther unpunished : seeing David a holy and just king, and of nature simple, courteous, and debonaire, yet when he dyed he charged his soone Salomon (that succeeded him in his throane) not to suffer certaine men that had done him injurie to escape unpunished.   Not that this holy king (as then ready to dye, and to give account before God of all

How just vengeance ought to be considered.

Davids intent in commanding Salomon to revenge him of some of his enemies.

d'aucune vengeance, mais àfin de donner ceste leçon à ceux qui viendroyent apres eux, que ou le public est interessé, le desir de vengeance, ne peut porter, tant s'en faut tiltre de condemnation, que plustost il est loüable, et digne de recommandation et recompense.

Car autrement ny les bons Roys de Juda, ny autres apres eux, eussent poursuivy la mort de ceux qui avoient offencez leurs majeurs, si Dieu mesme n'eut en eux inspiré et graué ce desir. De cecy font foy les loix Atheniennes, erigeans des statues, en l'honneur de ceux qui vengeans le tort et injure faits à la republique, massacroyent hardiment les tyrans, et ceux qui troubloient l'aise des citoyens. Le Prince Danoys s'estant vengé si hautement, n'osa de prime face declarer son dessein au peuple, ains delibera d'user de ruses, pour luy faire entendre ce qu'il avoit executé, et la raison qu'il avoit esmeu à ce faire : si que accompaigné de ceux qui restoyent encor des amis de feu son pere, il attendoit ce que le peuple feroit sur ceste soudaine, et effroiable occurrence. Les villes voisines desirans cognoistre d'où procedoient les flammes qu'on avoit veu la nuict, viennent le matin, et voyant la maison du Roy toute en cendre, et les corps demy bruslez, parmy les ruines de l'edifice, il n'y eut citoien qui ne se trouvast grandement esbahy, appercevant que de tout le bastiment, ny paressoit rien plus que les flammes n'eussent

Loix d'Athenes à l'avantage de ceux qui tuoient les tyrans.

Diverses affections d'un peuple.

his actions) was carefull or desirous of revenge, but to leave this example unto us, that where the prince or countrey is interested, the desire of revenge cannot by any meanes (how small soever) beare the title of condemnation, but is rather commendable and worthy of praise : for otherwise the good kings of Juda, nor others had not pursued them to death, that had offended their predecessors, if God himself had not inspired and ingraven that desire within their hearts. Hereof the Athenian lawes beare witnesse, whose custome was to erect images in remembrance of those men that, revenging the injuries of the commonwealth, boldly massacred tyrants and such as troubled the peace and welfare of the citizens.

Hamblet, having in this manner revenged himselfe, durst not presently declare his action to the people, but to the contrary determined to worke by policie, so to give them intelligence, what he had done, and the reason that drewe him thereunto : so that beeing accompanied with such of his fathers friends that then were rising, he stayed to see what the people would doe when they shoulde heare of that sodaine and fearefull action. The next morning the townes bordering there aboutes, desiring to know from whence the flames of fire proceeded the night before they had seene, came thither, and perceiving the kings pallace burnt to ashes, and many bodyes (most part consumed) lying among the ruines of the house, all of them were much abashed, nothing being left of the palace but the foundation. But they were

devoré jusques aux fondemens. Plus les estonna voyant le
corps du Roy tout ensanglanté, et le tronc d'iceluy d'un
costé, et la teste de l'autre : c'est icy que les uns s'aigrissent,
sans sçavoir contre qui, les autres l'armoient, voians un
spectacle si piteux : d'autres s'esjouissoient, sans en oser
faire semblant : les uns detestoient la cruauté, et d'autres
plaignoient le desastre de leur Prince, mais la pluspart se
souvenans du meurtre commis en Horvvendille, recognoissoient
un juste jugement d'enhaut, qui avoit accablé la teste superbe
de ce tyran : ainsi estans diverses les opinions de ceste
multitude, chacun ignorant qu'elle seroit l'issue de ceste
tragedie, nul ne bougea, ou attenta de faire esmotion quelconque, chacun craignant sa peau, et se defiant de son voisin,
l'estimant estre consentant à la conjuration et massacre.

Deffiance
empesche
souvent les
combats.

Amleth voyant ce peuple ainsi
coy, et les plus grans sans s'esmouvoir, et tous ne cerchans
que de sçavoir simplement la cause de ceste ruine et deffaite,
ne voulant laisser couler le temps, ains s'aidant de la com-

much more amased to beholde the body of the king all
bloody, and his head cut off lying hard by him ; whereat some
began to threaten revenge, yet not knowing against whom ;
others beholding so lamentable a spectacle, armed themselves,
the rest rejoycing, yet not daring to make any shewe thereof ;
some detesting the crueltie, others lamenting the death of
their Prince, but the greatest part calling Horvendiles murther
to remembrance, acknowledging a just judgement from above,
that had throwne downe the pride of the tyrant.   And in
this sort, the diversities of opinions among that multitude of
people being many, yet every man ignorant what would be
the issue of that tragedie, none stirred from thence, neither
yet attempted to move any tumult, every man fearing his
owne skinne, and distrusting his neighbour, esteeming each
other to bee consenting to the massacre.

CHAPTER VI

*How Hamlet, having slaine his Uncle, and burnt his Palace, made an Oration
to the Danes to shew them what he done ; and how they made him King
of Denmark ; and what followed.*

HAMLET then seeing the people to be so quiet, and most
part of them not using any words, all searching onely and
simply the cause of this ruine and destruction, not minding
to loose any time, but ayding himself with the commodotie

modité d'iceluy s'avança avec sa suite : et estant en l'assemblee
des citoyens, leur parla en ceste sorte.

Harangue d'Amleth aux Danoys.

S'il y a quelqu'un d'entre vous, Messieurs, de Dannemarch,
qui aye encore fresche memoire du tort fait au puissant Roy
Horvvendille, qu'il ne s'esmeuve en rien voyant la face
confuse et hydeusement espouventable de la presente calamité :
S'il y a aucun qui aye la fidelité pour recommandee, et cherisse
l'affection qu'on doit à ses parens, et trouve bonne la souvenance des outrages faicts à ceux qui nous ont produits au
monde, que celuy ne s'ebahisse, contemplant un tel massacre,
et moins s'offence en advisant une si effroyable ruine, et
d'hommes et des plus superbes edifices, de tout le pays : car
la main qui a executé ceste justice, ne pouvoit en chevir à
meilleur marché, et ne luy estoit loisible d'autrement se
prevaloir, qu'en ruinant, et l'insensible, et le sensible, pour
garder la memoire d'une si equitable vengeance. Je voy
bien, Messieurs, (et suis joyeux de cognoistre une telle vostre
si affectionnee devotion) que vous estes marris, ayans devant
voz yeux Fengon ainsi mutilé, et celuy sans teste, que d'autres-
fois vous avez recogneu pour chef, mais je vous prie penser
que ce corps n'est le corps d'un Roy, ains d'un tyran
execrable, et d'un parricide plus que detestable. Ah !
Danoys, le spectacle estoit bien plus hideux, lors que vostre
Roy Horvvendille fut massacré par un sien frere : quoy frere ?
mais bien plustost par le bourreau le plus abhominable que

thereof, entred among the multitude of people, and standing in the middle spake unto them as followeth.

If there be any among you (good people of Denmark) that as yet have fresh within your memories the wrong done to the valiant king Horvendile, let him not be mooved, nor thinke it strange to behold the confused, hydeous, and fearfull spectacle of this present calamitie : if there be any man that affecteth fidelitie, and alloweth of the love and dutie that man is bound to shewe his parents, and find it a just cause to call to remembrance the injuryes and wrongs that have been done to our progenitors, let him not be ashamed beholding this massacre, much lesse offended to see so fearfull a ruine both of men and of the bravest house in all this countrey : for the hand that hath done this justice could not effect it by any other meanes, neither yet was it lawfull for him to doe it otherwise, then by ruinating both sensible and unsensible things, thereby to preserve the memorie of so just a vengeance.

I see well (my good friends) and am very glad to know so good attention and devotion in you, that you are sorrie (before your eyes) to see Fengon so murthered, and without a head, which heeretofore you acknowledged for your commander ; but I pray you remember this body is not the body of a king, but of an execrable tyrant, and a parricide most detestable. Oh Danes! the spectacle was much more hydeous when Horvendile your king was murthered by his brother. What should I say a brother! nay, rather by the

le soleil contemple. C'est vous, qui avez veu les membres d'Horvvendille mutilez, et qui avec larmes et souspirs, avez accompaigné au cercueil son corps deffiguré, blessé en mille lieux, et bourrelé en cent mille sortes. Et qui doubte, (puis que l'experience vous l'a faict cognoistre) que le tyran en accablant vostre Roy legitime, ne tendoit qu'à ruiner, et abbatte la liberté ancienne, de ses concitoyens? Aussi fut-ce une seule main, laquelle s'acharnant sur Horvvendille, le despouilla de vie cruellement, et par mesme moyen, injustement vous osta la liberté, et anciennes franchises. Qui est celuy si despourveu de sens, qui ayme mieux choisir une miserable servitude, et se plaist plus d'en estre accablé, que d'embrasser la face joyeuse, de quelque liberté proposee, et livree, sans qu'il luy faille rien avanturer, pour avoir la jouissance? Et qui est l'insensé qui se delecte plus en la tyrannie de Fengon, qu'en la douceur, et courtoisie renouvellee d'Horvvendille? S'il est ainsi que par clemence et affabilité les cœurs plus rogues et farouches sont adoucis, et rendus traitables, et que le mauvais traictement rend un peuple insuportable et seditieux: que ne voyez vous la debonnaireté du premier, pour la paren-gonner aux cruautez et insolences de ce second, autant cruel et barbare, que son frere a esté doux plaisant et accostable? Souvienne vous, Danois, souvienne vous, qu'elle estoit l'amitié d'Horvvendille envers vous, avec qu'elle equité il a gouverné les affaires du royaume, et avec quelle humanité, et courtoisie, il vous a defendus et cheris, et lors je m'asseure que le plus grossier d'entre vous, se souviendra et cognoistra qu'on luy a

La douceur des Rois dompte les cœurs des peuples farouches.

most abhominable executioner that ever beheld the same.   It
was you that saw Horvendiles members massacred, and that
with teares and lamentations accompanied him to the grave ;
his body disfigured, hurt in a thousand places, and misused
in ten times as many fashions.   And who doubteth (seeing
experience hath taught you) that the tyrant (in massacring
your lawfull king) sought onely to infringe the ancient
liberties of the common people ? and it was one hand onely,
that murthering Horvendile, cruelly dispoyled him of life,
and by the same meanes unjustly bereaved you of your ancient
liberties, and delighted more in oppression then to embrace
the plesant countenance of prosperous libertie without ad-
venturing for the same.   And what mad man is he that
delighteth more in the tyrany of Fengon then in the clemencie
and renewed courtesie of Horvendile ?   If it bee so, that by
clemencie and affabilitie the hardest and stoutest hearts are
molified and made tractable, and that evill and hard usage
causeth subjects to be outragious and unruly, why behold you
not the debonair cariage of the first, to compare it with the
cruelties and insolencies of the second, in every respect as cruell
and barbarous as his brother was gentle, meeke, and courteous ?
Remember, O you Danes, remember what love and amitie
Horvendile shewed unto you ; with what equitie and justice
he swayed the great affaires of this kingdome, and with what
humanitie and courtisie he defended and cherished you, and
then I am assured that the simplest man among you will both
remember and acknowledge that he had a most peaceable,

osté un Roy trespaisible, et pere tresjuste, et equitable, pour mettre en sa place un tyran, et asseoir sur son throsne le meurtrier de son frere, lequel à perverti tout droict, aboly les loix de nos majeurs, souillé la memoire de nos ancestres et pollu par sa meschanceté l'integrité de ceste province, sur le col de laquelle il a mis le joug fascheux d'une lourde servitude, abolissant celle liberté, en laquelle Horvvendille vous maintenoit, et vous souffroit vivre à vostre aise. Et serez vous marris de voir la fin de voz malheurs, et que ce miserable, accablé du fardeau de ses forfaits paye à present l'usure du parricide commis en la personne de son frere, et soit luy mesme le vengeur de l'outrage, fait au fils d'Horvvendille, qu'il vouloit priver de son heritage, ostant au pays de Dannemarch un successeur legitime, pour en saisir quelque voleur estranger, et captiver ceux que mon pere à jettez hors de misere et servitude ? Et qui est l'homme, jouissant le moins du monde de quelque prudence, qui accompte un bien fait à injure, et mesure les plaisirs à l'esgal de quelque tort, et evident outrage ? Ce seroit bien grand folie et temerité aux Princes et vaillans chefs de guerre, de s'exposer à peril et hazard de leur vie, pour le soulagement d'un peuple, si pour toute recompense et action de graces, ils n'en raportoient que la haine, et indignation de la multitude, qui eust servy à Hothere d'accabler le tyran Baldere, si pour et au lieu de recognoissance, les Sueson et Danois l'eussent chassé, pour

just, and righteous king taken from him, to place in his
throane a tyrant and murtherer of his brother : one that
hath perverted all right, abolished the auncient lawes of our
fathers, contaminated the memories of our ancestors, and by
his wickednesse polluted the integritie of this kingdome, upon
the necke thereof having placed the troublesome yoak of
heavie servitude, abolishing that libertie wherein Horvendile
used to maintaine you, and suffered you to live at your ease.
And should you now bee sorrie to see the ende of your
mischiefes, and that this miserable wretch, pressed downe
with the burthen of his offences, at this present payeth the
usury of the parricide committed upon the body of his
brother, and would not himselfe be the revenger of the
outrage done to me, whom he sought to deprive of mine
inheritance, taking from Denmark a lawfull successor, to
plant a wicked stranger, and bring into captivitie those that
my father had infranchised and delivered out of misery and
bondage ?   And what man is he, that having any sparke of
wisdom, would esteem a good deed to be an injury, and
account pleasures equal with wrongs and evident outrages ?
It were then great folly and temerity in princes and valiant
commanders in the wars to expose themselves to perils and
hazards of their lives for the welfare of the common people,
if that for a recompence they should reape hatred and indignation of the multitude.   To what end should Hother have
punished Balder, if, in steed of recompence, the Danes and
Swethlanders had banished him to receive and accept the

caresser les successeurs de celuy qui ne pourchassoit que leur
ruine ? Qui sera celuy, ayant si peu de sentiment, de raison
et justice, qui soit marry de voir que la trahison paye son
autheur, et qu'un forfaict face sentir la penitence de sa felonnie,
à celuy mesme qui en aura esté l'occasion ? Qui fut onc
dolent de voir exterminé le cruel meurtrier des innocens, ou
qui pleure sur le juste massacre, faict en un tyran usurpateur,
meschant, et sanguinaire ? Je vous voy tous attentifs et
estonnez, pour ignorer l'autheur de vostre delivrance : et
marris, que ne sçavez à qui vous devez rendre graces d'un
tel, et si grand benefice, que l'accablement d'un tyran, et la
ruyne du lieu, qui estoit le magazin de ses meschancetez, et
le vray asile et retraite de tous les voleurs, et traistres de ce
royaume : mais voicy devant vous celuy, qui a effectué un
bien tant necessaire, c'est moy (messieurs) c'est moy, qui
confesse avoir prins vengeance, pour l'outrage faict à Mon-
seigneur, et Pere, et pour l'assujetissement et servitude, en
laquelle je voyois reduire la Province, de laquelle je suis le
juste successeur, et heritier legitime. C'est moy qui a mis
à effect tout seul l'œuvre, auquel vous me deviez tenir la
main, et m'y donner faveur et ayde, et seul ay accomply, ce
que vous tous pouviez justement parachever, avec raison, et
sans tiltre aucun de felonnie. Il est bien vray que je me fie
tant de vostre bonne volonté, envers le deffunct Horvvendille,
et que la memoire de ses vertus, est encor si vivement imprimee

successors of him that desired nought but his ruine and overthrowe? What is hee that hath so small feeling of reason
and equitie, that would be grieved to see treason rewarded
with the like, and that an evill act is punished with just de-
merit in the partie himselfe that was the occasion? who was
ever sorowfull to behold the murtherer of innocents brought
to his end, or what man weepeth to see a just massacre done
upon a tyrant, usurper, villaine, and bloody personage?

I perceive you are attentive, and abashed for not krowing
the author of your deliverance, and sorry that you cannot tell
to whom you should bee thankefull for such and so great a
benefit as the destruction of a tyrant, and the overthrow of
the place that was the storehouse of his villanies, and the true
receptacle of all the theeves and traytors in this kingdome:
but beholde (here in your presence) him that brought so good
an enterprise to effect. It is I (my good friends), it is I, that
confesse I have taken vengeance for the violence done unto
my lord and father, and for the subjection and servitude that
I perceived in this countrey, whereof I am the just and lawfull successor. It is I alone, that have done this piece of
worke, whereunto you ought to have lent me your handes,
and therein have ayded and assisted me. I have only accomplished that which all of you might justly have effected,
by good reason, without falling into any point of treason or
fellonie. It is true that I hope so much of your good willes
towards the deceased king Horvendile, and that the remem-
brances of his vertues is yet so fresh within your memories,

en vostre ame, que si je vous eusse requis de secours, vous n'eussiez ja refusé vostre assistance; et moyens à vostre naturel Prince. Mais il m'a pleu de le faire tout seul, me semblant tresbon de punir les meschans, sans hazarder la vie de mes amis; et loyaux citoyens, ne voulant soumettre les espaules d'aurruy, à supporter ce faix, puis que je m'en faisois fort d'en venir à bout, sans exposer personne en peril, et gaster, en le publiant, le dessein que j'ay mis à fin avec si grande felicité. J'ay redigé en cendre les courtisans, compagnons des forfaits et trahisons du tyran, mais j'ay laissé Fengon, à fin que ce soit vous qui punissez le tronc, et charongne morte, puis que vivant il n'est peu tombes en voz mains, pour en faire entiere la punition et vengeance et rassasier vostre colere, sur les os de celuy qui s'est repeu de vos richessses, et a espandu le sang de vos freres et amis. Courage donc, mes bons amis, dressez le bucher pour ce Roy usurpateur, brulez son corps abhominable, cuisez ses membres lascifs, et espandez en l'air les cendres de celuy qui a esté nuisible à tout le monde, chassez loing de vous ses estincelles impitoyables, afin que ny la cruche d'argent, ou cristal, ny un sacré tombeau soient le repos des reliques, et ossements d'un homme si detestable. Faites qu'on ne voye une seule trace de parricide, et que vostre pays ne soit pollu de la seule presence du moindre membre qui soit de ce tyran sans pieté, que les voisins n'en sentent point la contagion, et nostre terre l'infection

that if I had required your aide herein, you would not have denied it, specially to your naturall prince. But it liked mee best to doe it my selfe alone, thinking it a good thing to punish the wicked without hazarding the lives of my friends and loyall subjects, not desiring to burthen other mens shoulders with this weight; for that I made account to effect it well inough without exposing any man into danger, and by publishing the same should cleane have overthrowne the device, which at this present I have so happily brought to passe. I have burnt the bodyes of the courtiers to ashes, being companions in the mischiefs and treasons of the tyrant; but I have left Fengon whole, that you might punish his dead carkasse (seeing that when hee lived you durst not lay hands upon him), to accomplish the full punishment and vengeance due unto him, and so satisfie your choller upon the bones of him that filled his greedy hands and coffers with your riches, and shed the blood of your brethren and friends. Bee joyfull, then (my good friends); make ready the nosegay for this usurping king: burne his abhominable body, boyle his lascivious members, and cast the ashes of him that hath beene hurtfull to all the world into the ayre: drive from you the sparkes of pitie, to the end that neither silver, nor christall cup, nor sacred tombe may be the restfull habitation of the reliques and bones of so detestable a man: let not one trace of a parricide be seene, nor your countrey defiled with the presence of the least member of this tyrant without pity, that your neighbors may not smell the contagion, nor our

pollue d'un corps condamné pour ses demerites : j'ay faict
mon debvoir, en le vous rendant tel, c'est à vous à mettre fin
à l'œuvre, et adjouster la derniere main au devoir à quoy
vostre office vous appelle : car c'est ainsi qu'il faut honorer
les Princes abominables. Et telles doivent estre les funerailles
d'un tyran, parricide, et usurpateur, et du lit et du patrimoine
qui ne luy appartenoit en rien : lequel ayant desnué son pays
de liberté, c'est raison que sa terre luy refuse giste, pour
l'eternel repos de ses ossemens. Ah ! mes bons amis, puis
que vous sçavez le tort que on m'a faict, quelles sont mes
angoisses, en quelle misere j'ay vescu depuis la mort du Roy
mon seigneur, puis que mieux que moy toutes ces choses
vous avez cogneuës et goustees, lors que encore je ne pouvoye
gouster parfaictement l'outrage que je soufroy : que me
servira-il de le vous reciter ? De quel proufit en sera le
discours, devant ceux qui le sçachans, crevoyent de despit de
voir si grand mon desastre et malheur ; et despitoient la fortune,
qui accabloit ainsi un enfant Royal, que de le priver de sa
majesté : jaçoit que pas un de vous n'osast faire semblant de
tristesse ? Vous sçavez comme mon beau pere a conspiré ma
mort, et a tasché en plusieurs sortes de m'accabler, comme
j'ay esté abandonné laschement par la Royne ma mere, et
mocqué de mes amis, mesprisé de mes propres subjets, j'ay
jusques icy vescu chargé de dueil, et tout confit en larmes,
ayant le temps de ma vie tousjours accompaigné de craintes
et soupçons, et n'attendant à tout propos que l'heure que le

land the polluted infection of a body condemned for his wickednes. I have done my part to present him to you in this sort; now it belongs to you to make an end of the worke, and put to the last hand of dutie whereunto your severall functions call you; for in this sort you must honor abhominable princes, and such ought to be the funerall of a tyrant, parricide, and usurper, both of the bed and patrimony that no way belonged unto him, who having bereaved his countrey of liberty, it is fit that the land refuse to give him a place for the eternal rest of his bones.

O my good friends, seeing you know the wrong that hath bin done unto mee, what my griefs are, and in what misery I have lived since the death of the king, my lord and father, and seeing that you have both known and tasted these things then, when as I could not conceive the outrage that I felt, what neede I recite it unto you? what benefit would it be to discover it before them that knowing it would burst (as it were with despight) to heare of my hard chance, and curse Fortune for so much imbasing a royall prince, as to deprive him of his majesty, although not any of you durst so much as shew one sight of sorrow or sadnes? You know how my father in law conspired my death, and sought by divers meanes to take away my life; how I was forsaken of the queen my mother, mocked of my friends, and dispised of mine own subjects : hetherto I have lived laden with griefe, and wholy confounded in teares, my life still accompanied with fear and suspition, expecting the houre when the sharp

glaive trenchant mist fin, et à ma vie et a mes angoisses
et soucis, en tout miserables. Combien de fois, faignant
l'insensé, vous ay je ouy plaindre mon desastre, et vous
lamenter en secret de me voir desherité, et sans aucun, qui
vengeast la mort de mon pere, ou punist le forfaict de mon
incestueux oncle, et beau pere plein de meurtres, et massacres ?
Ceste charité me donnoit cœur, et ces voz affectionnees com-
plaintes, me faisoyent voir evidemment vostre bon vouloir,
qui aviez presenté la calamité de vostre Prince, et engravé
en vostre coeur le desir de vengeance de la mort de celuy, qui
meritoit de vivre plus longuement.

Et quel sera le cœur si dur et peu maniable, ny l'esprit tant
severe, cruel, et rigoureux qui ne s'amolisse par la souvenance
de mes passions, et angoisses, et n'aye pitié d'un enfant orpbe-
lin, et ainsi abandonné de tout le monde ? Quels seront les
yeux si taris et sans humeur, qui encor ne distillent quelques
larmes, voyans un pauvre Prince assailly des siens, trahy par
sa mere, poursuivy par son oncle, et si fort accablé, que le
peuple qui l'ayme n'ayt osé luy monstrer les effects de sa
charité, et devotion bien affectionnee ? Ah ! messieurs, ayez
compassion de celuy que vous avez nourry, et que vostre cœur
sente quelque elancement pour la memoire de mes infortunes.
Je parle à vous qui estes innocens de toute trahison, et ne
souillastes onc ny vos mains, ny vostre esprit, ou desir du
sang du grand et vertueux Roy Horwendille. Ayez pitié de
la Royne jadis vostre Dame, et ma treshonoree mere, forcee
par le tyran, et soyez joyeux de veoir finy, et esteint l'object

sword would make an ende of my life and miserable an-
guishes.   How many times, counterfeiting the mad man,
have I heard you pitty my distresse, and secretly lament to
see me disinherited? and yet no man sought to revenge the
death of my father, nor to punish the treason of my incestuous
uncle, full of murthers and massacres.   This charitie ministred
comfort, and your affectionate complaints made me evidently
see your good wills, that you had in memorie the calamity of
your prince, and within your harts ingraven the desire of
vengeance for the death of him that deserved a long life.
And what heart can bee so hard and untractable, or spirit to
severe, cruel, and rigorous, that would not relent at the remembrance of my extremities, and take pitty of an orphan
child, so abandoned of the world? What eyes were so voyd
of moysture but would distill a field of tears, to see a poore
prince assaulted by his owne subjects, betrayed by his mother,
pursued by his uncle, and so much oppressed that his friends
durst not shew the effects of their charitie and good affection?
O (my good friends) shew pity to him whom you have
nourished, and let your harts take some compassion upon
the memory of my misfortunes!   I speak to you that are
innocent of al treason, and never defiled your hands, spirits,
nor desires with the blud of the greate and vertuous king
Horvendile.   Take pity upon the queen, sometime your
soveraign lady, and my right honorable mother, forced by
the tyrant, and rejoyce to see the end and extinguishing of

de son deshonneur, et lequel la contraignoit à estre peu pitoy-
able à l'endroit de son mesme sang, voire d'embrasser le
meurtrier de son cher espoux, portant sur elle un double
fardeau, d'infamie, et d'inceste, et de souffrance pour
l'avillissement de sa moytié, et ruyne de sa race. C'a
esté l'occasion, Messieurs, pour laquelle j'ay fainte ceste
sottise, et ay voilé mes desseins souz la fard d'une grande
folie, laquelle a couvé ma sagesse et prudence pour esclorre
le fruit de ceste vengeance, laquelle si elle est d'assez
d'efficace, et si est parvenue à son parfait accomplissement,
vous en serez les juges Car de cecy, et de tout autre chose
concernant mon proufit, et le maniment des affaires, c'est a
vostre sage advis et conseil que je m'en r'aporte, et sous lequel
je pretens me assujetir. Aussi estes vous ceux qui foulez
aux pieds les estincelles meurtrieres de mon pere, et mesprisez
les cendres de celuy qui a pollu, et violé la femme, et espouse
de son frere, par luy massacré, qui a commis felonnie contre
son seigneur, qui a traistreusement assailly la majesté de son
Roy, et esclavé injustement sous une grand' servitude son païs,
et vous ses loiaux citoiens, à qui ravissant la liberté, n'a craint
d'adjouster inceste au parricide, detesté par tout le monde.
C'est aussi à vous que le devoir et raison commandent de
garantir, et defendre Amleth, qui est le ministre et executeur
de si juste vengeance, et qui jaloux de son honneur, et de
vostre reputation, s'est ainsi hazardé, esperant que vous luy
servirez de peres et defenseurs, serez ses tuteurs, et le
regardans en pitié luy rendrez son bien, et legitime heritage.

the object of her dishonor, which constrained her to be lesse pitiful to her own blood, so far as to imbrace the murtherer of her own dear spouse, charging her selfe with a double burthen of infamy and incest, together with injuring and dis-annulling of her house, and the ruine of her race. This hath bin the occasion that made me counterfet folly, and cover my intents under a vaile of meer madnes, which hath wisdom and pollicy therby to inclose the fruit of this vengeance, which, that it hath attained to the ful point of efficacy and perfect ac-complishment, you yourselves shall bee judges; for touching this and other things concerning my profit, and the managing of great affairs, I refer my self to your counsels, and there unto am fully determined to yeeld, as being those that trample under your feet the murtherers of my father, and despise the ashes of him that hath polluted and violated the spouse of his brother, by him massacred; that hath committed felony against his lord, traiterously assailed the majesty of his king, and odiously thralled his contry under servitude and bondage, and you his loyall subjects, from whom he, bereaving your liberty, feared not to ad incest to parricide, detestable to al the world. To you also it belongeth by dewty and reason commonly to defend and protect Hamlet, the minister and ex-ecutor of just vengeance, who being jealous of your honour and your reputation, hath hazarded himself, hoping you will serve him for fathers, defenders, and tutors, and regarding him in pity, restore him to his goods and inheritances. It is

C'est moy qui ay osté le diffame de mon pays, et estaint le feu qui embrassoit voz fortunes, j'ay lavé les tasches, qui denigroient la reputation de la Royne, accablant et le tyran, et la tyrannie, et trompant les ruses du plus cauteleux affineur de l'univers, et par mesme moyen donné fin à ses meschancetez, et imposture. J'estois marry de l'injure faicte, et à mon pere, et à ma chere patrie, et ay occis celuy qui usoit de commandement plus rigoureux sur vous qu'il n'est juste ny seant qu'on en use sur les hommes, qui ont commandé aux plus braves nations de la terre.

Estant donc tel envers vous, c'est raison que vous recognoissez le plaisir, et me sachez gré du bien que j'ay faict à la posterité, et que reverant mon esprit et sagesse, vous meslisez pour Roy, s'il vous semble que j'en sois digne. Vous me voyez autheur de vostre salut, heritier de l'Empire de mon pere, ne forlignant et devoyant aucunement de ses vertueux actes non meurtrier, violateur, ny parricide, ny homme qui jamais n'offensay aucun que les vicieux, legitime successeur du Royaume, et juste vengeur d'un crime sur tout autre le plus grief et punissable. C'est à moy, à qui vous devez le benefice de vostre liberté recouvree, et de l'avilissement de celle tyrannie qui tant vous affligeoit : qui ay foulé aux pieds le joug du tyran, et ruiné son trosne, et osté le sceptre des mains à celuy, qui abusoit d'une sainte puissance. Mais c'est à vous à recompenser ceux qui ont bien merité : vous sçavez quel est le salaire et retribution d'un tel merite et estant en

I that have taken away the infamy of my contry, and extinguished the fire that imbraced your fortunes. I have washed the spots that defiled the reputation of the queen, overthrowing both the tirant and the tiranny, and beguiling the subtilties of the craftiest deceiver in the world, and by that meanes brought his wickednes and impostures to an end. I was grieved at the injurie committed both to my father and my native country, and have slaine him that used more rigorus commandements over you, then was either just or convenient to be used unto men that have commaunded the valiantest nations in the world. Seeing, then, he was such a one to you, it is reason that you acknowledge the benefit, and thinke wel of for the good I had done your posterity, and admiring my spirit and wisdome, chuse me your king, if you think me worthy of the place. You see I am the author of your preservation, heire of my fathers kingdome, not straying in any point from his vertuous action, no murtherer, violent parricide, nor man that ever offended any of you, but only the vitious. I am lawfull successor in the kingdom, and just revenger of a crime above al others most grievous and punishable : it is to me that you owe the benefit of your liberty receaved, and of the subversion of that tyranny that so much afflicted you, that hath troden under feete the yoke of the tirant, and overwhelmed his throne, and taken the scepter out of the hands of him that abused a holy and just authoritie ; but it is you that are to recompence those that have well deserved, you know what is the reward of so greate

vos mains à le distribuer, c'est aussi de vous que je redemande
le pris deu de ma vertu, et la recompence de ma victoire.

Ceste harangue du jeune Prince esmeut de telle sorte le
cœur des Danois, et gaigna si bien les affections de la noblesse
que les uns plouroient de pitié, les autres de grand'joye,
voyans la sagesse et gaillardise d'esprit d'Amleth : et ayans
mis fin à leur tristesse tous d'un consentement le declairerent
Roy de Jutie, et Chersonne ce qui est à present le propre
pays qu'on nomme Dannemarch.   Ayant celebré les festes
de son couronnement, et receu les hommages et fidelitez de
ses subjetz, il passa en la grande Bretaige pour aller querir son
espouse, et se resjouyr avec son beau pere sur sa presente bonne
fortune : mais il s'en fallut bien peu que l'Anglois ne parfeit
ce à quoy jamais Fengon n'avoit sçeu attaindre avec toute
ses ruses :

Amleth fait
Roy d'une
partie de
Danne-
march.

Fengon et
l'Anglois
quel serment
avoyent fait
ensemble.

Car dés que Amleth fut en
Bretaigne, il raconta les moyens qu'il avoit tenus à regaigner
sa perte, si que l'Anglois entendant la mort de Fengon, de-

desert, and being in your hands to distribute the same, it is of you that I demand the price of my vertue, and the recompence of my victory.

This oration of the yong prince so mooved the harts of the Danes, and wan the affections of the nobility, that some wept for pity, other for joy, to see the wisedome and gallant spirit of Hamlet; and having made an end of their sorrow, al with one consent proclaimed him king of Jutie and Chersonnese, at this present the proper country of Denmarke. And having celebrated his coronation, and received the homages and fidelities of his subjects, he went into England to fetch his wife, and rejoyced with his father in law touching his good fortune; but it wanted little that the king of England had not accomplished that which Fengon with all his subtilties could never attaine.

Hamlet king of one part of Denmark.

CHAPTER VII

How Hamlet, after his coronation, went into England; and how the king of England secretly would have put him to death; and how he slew the king of England, and returned againe into Denmarke with two wives; and what followed.

HAMLET, being in England, shewed the king what meanes hee had wrought to recover his kingdom; but when the king of England understood of Fengons death, he was both

meura estonné, et confuz en son ame, se sentant assailly de
deux puissantes passions, veu que jadis luy et Fengon, ayans
esté compaignon d'armes s'estoyent juré reciproquement la
foy, que s'il advenoit que l'un d'eux fut occis par quiconque
ce fust, que l'autre (espousant la querelle) ne cesseroit tant
qu'il en eut pris la vengeance, ou se fust mis en devoir de ce
faire.   Or l'amitié juree, et le serment incitoyent, ce Roy
Barbare à massacrer Amleth, puis l'alliance se presentant
devant ses yeux, et contemplant l'un mort, quoy que son amy,
l'autre en vie, et l'espoux de la fille, il effaçoit ce desir de
vengeance : mais à la fin le devoir et conscience d'un serment,
et foy promise gaignerent le dessus, et conclud ce Roy en son
esprit la mort de son gendre, laquelle entreprinse fut cause de
sa mort, et du saccagement de toute l'Isle Angloise, par la
cruauté, et despit esmeu du Roy des Danoys.   J'ay laissé le
discours de ceste bataille tout à escient, pour ne servir de
guere à nostre propos, et que aussi je ne veux vous tenir si
longuement, me contentant de vous faire veoir quelle fut la
fin de ce vaillant et sage Roy, qui se vengeant de tant d'ennemis, et descouvrant toutes les trahisons brassees contre son
salut, et vie, en fin servit de jouet à fortune, et d'exemple aux
grans, qui se fient trop és felicitez de ce monde, lesquelles ont
bien peu de stabilité, et sont de peu de duree.

Or l'Anglois voyant que peu facilement il pourroit se

Conscience
de l'Anglois
ne voulant
faucer sa
foy.
Mor du
Roy Anglois
et sac de son
Isle.

abashed and confused in his minde, at that instant feeling himselfe assailed with two great passions, for that in times past he and Fengon having bin companions together in armes, had given each other their faith and promises, by oath, that if either of them chanced to bee slaine by any man whatsoever, hee that survived (taking the quarrel upon him as his owne) should never cease till he were revenged, or at the leaste do his endeavour.   This promise incited the barbarous king to massacre Hamlet, but the alliance presenting it selfe before his eies, and beholding the one deade, although his friend, and the other alive, and husband to his daughter, made him deface his desire of revenge.   But in the end, the conscience of his oath and promise obtained the upper hand, and secretly made him conclude the death of his sonne in law, which enterprise after that was cause of his own death, and over-running of the whole country of England by the cruelty and despight conceived by the king of Denmarke.   I have purposely omitted the discourse of that battaile, as not much pertinent to our matter, as also, not to trouble you with too tedious a discourse, being content to shew you the end of this wise and valiant king Hamlet, who revenging himselfe upon so many enemies, and discovering all the treasons practised against his life, in the end served for a sport to fortune, and an example to all great personages that trust overmuch to the felicities of this world, that are of small moment, and lesse continuance.

The king of England perceiving that hee could not easilie

prevaloir du Roy son gendre, et qu'aussi il ne vouloit violer les droits et loix d'hospitalité il delibera de faire qu'un estranger seroit le vangeur de son injure, et accompliroit le serment juré à Fengon, sans qu'il souillast ses mains du sang du mary de sa fille, ny poullust sa maison, en massacrant traitreussement son hoste.

A lire ceste histoire il sembleroit veoir en Amleth un Hercule envoyé çà et là par Euristee, (sollicité par Junon) de tous costez du monde, la ou il sçauroit estre quelque peril evident, pour l'y precipiter, et luy faire perdre la vie : ou bien que ce fust Bellerophon mandé à Jobatez, pour l'ex- poser à la mort, ou (laissant les fables) un Uire destiné par David pour servir de butte. Et de blanc pour faire passer la colere des Barbares.

Urie expose par David II Rois 11.

Car l'Anglois (estant franchement morte sa femme) quoy qu'il ne se souciast point de se lier à femme quelconque, pria son gendre, de faire un voyage pour luy en Escosse, et l'amadoua avec ce mot que sa singuliere prudence l'avoit induit à le preferer à tout autre en telle legation, s'asseurant qu'il estoit impossible, que Amleth, le plus subtil, et accort homme du monde, sceut rien entreprendre, sans le conduire à son effect.

Arrogante chastetè d Herme- trude Royne d'Escosse.

Or la Royne d'Escosse fille vierge, et d'un hautain courage, mesprisoit les nopces de chacun, et n'estimoit homme digne de son acointance, de sorte qu'avec ceste si arrogante opinion, il n'y venoit amoureux aucun pour la soliciter, à qui elle ne feit perdre la vie.

effect his desire upon the king, his son in lawe, as also not being willing to break the laws and rights of hospitality, determined to make a stranger the revenger of his injury, and so accomplish his oath made to Fengon without defiling his handes with the blood of the husband of his daughter, and polluting his house by the traiterous massacring of his friend. In reading of this history, it seemeth, Hamlet should resemble another Hercules, sent into divers places of the world by Euristheus (solicited by Juno) where he knew any dangerous adventure, thereby to overthrow and destroy him; or else Bellerophon sent to Ariobatus to put him to death; or (leaving prophane histories) an other Urias, by king David appointed to bee placed in the fore front of the battaile, and the man that should bee first slain by the barbarians. For the king of Englands wife being dead not long before (although he cared not for marrying an other woman) desired his sonne in lawe to make a voyage for him into Scotland, flattering him in such sort, that he made him beleeve that his singular wisdome caused him to preferre him to that ambassage, assuring himselfe that it were impossible that Hamlet, the subtillest and wisest prince in the worlde, should take any thing in the world in hand without effecting the same.

Now the queen of Scots beeing a maid, and of a haughty courage, despised marriage with al men, as not esteeming any worthy to be her companion, in such manner that by reason of this arrogant opinion there never came any man to desire

Mais la fortune du Prince Danois fut si bonne que
Hermetrude (car tel estoit le nom de la Royne Escossoise)
oyant parler d'Amleth, et comme il venoit pour l'Anglois la
demander à mariage, oublia tout son orgueil, et despouilla son
naturel farouche, avec intention de rendre sien le Prince le
plus accompli, duquel elle eust jamais ouy parler, et priver la
Princesse Angloise d'un mariage, que seule elle se pensoit
meriter.   Ainsi ceste Amazone sans amitié, parant l'estomach

Hermetrude
devient
amoureuse
d'Amleth.

à Cupidon, de se sommettant de son gré aux assaux de sa
concupiscence, arrivé le Dannoys voulut veoir les lettres du
vieillard d'Angleterre, et se moquant des fols apetits de celuy
duquel le sang estoit à demy glacé tenoit l'œil fiché sur ce
jeune et plaisant Adonis de Septentrion s'estimant bien
heureuse, qu'une telle proye luy fut tombee en main, et de
laquelle elle se faisoit forte d'en avoir les despouilles.

Et de fait elle qui jamais n'avoit peu estre vaincue par
la grace, gentillesse, vaillance, ni richesses d'aucun Prince, ny
chevalier grand seigneur, est à present mise à bas par le seul
renom des ruses du Danoys, lequel, sachant avoir fiancé la
fille de l'Anglois, elle arraisonna luy parlant ainsi.

Je n'eusse jamais attendu un si grand heur, ny des Dieux,
ny de la fortune que de voir en mes terres le Prince plus
accomply, qui soit en toutes les marches Septentrionales, et
lequel s'est rendu louable et estimé parmy toutes les nations,
tant voisines qu'estrangeres, pour le seul respect de sa vertu,

her love but she caused him to loose his life : but the Danish kings fortune was so good, that Hermetrude (for so was the queens name) hearing that Hamlet was come thither to intreat a marriage between her and the king of England, forgot all her pride, and dispoiling herselfe of her sterne nature, being as then determined to make him (being the greatest prince as then living) her husband, and deprive the English princesse of her spouse, whome shee thought fit for no men but herself; and so this Amazon without love, disdaining Cupid, by her free wil submitted her haughtie mind to her concupiscence. The Dane arriving in her court, desired she to see the old king of Englands letters, and mocking at his fond appetites, whose blood as then was half congealed, cast her eies upon the yong and plesant Adonis of the North, esteeming her selfe happy to have such a pray fallen into her hands, wherof she made her ful account to have the possession : and to conclude, she that never had been overcome by the grace, courtesie, valor, or riches of anie prince nor lord whatsoever, was as then vanquished with the onelie report of the subtilties of the Dane; who knowing that he was already fianced to the daughter of the king of England, spake unto him and said : I never looked for so great a blisse, neither from the gods nor yet from fortune, as to behold in my countries the most compleate prince in the North, and he that hath made himselfe famous and renowned through all the nations of the world, as well neighbours as strangers, for the only respect of

sagesse, et bon-heur, luy servans beaucoup en la poursuite et effect des choses par luy deseignees : et me sens grandement redevable au Roy Anglois, quoy que sa malice ne cherche ny mon avancement, ny le bien de vous Monsieur de m'avoir tant honnoree, que de m'envoyer un si excellent homme, pour capituler avec moy du mariage d'entre luy, qui est ja vieux et casse, ennemy et mortel des miens, avec moy qui suis telle que chacun voit, et qui ne desire m'accointer d'homme de si basse qualité que celuy que vous avez dit estre fils d'un esclave.

Mais d'autre costé, je mesbais que le fils de Horvvendille, et petit fils du grand Roy Rorique, celuy qui par sa folle sagesse et feinte sottise à surmonté les forces et ruses de Fengon, et s'est emparé du Royaume de son adversaire, se soit avili jusques à là, qu'ayant esté bien sage et advisé en toutes ses actions, au chois de la compaignie de son lict, il se soit forvoyé, et luy qui par son excellence et lustre, surpassa l'humaine capacité, se soit abaissé jusques à prendre pour femme, celle qui sortant d'une race servile, a beau avoir un Roy pour pere, veu que tousjours la vilité de son sang, luy fera monstrer quelles sont les vertus, et noblesse ancienne de sa race.

Est-ce à vous, Monsieur à ignorer, que la liaison maritale, ne doit estre mesuree par quelque folle opinion d'une beauté exterieure, mais plustost par le lustre de la vertu, et antiquité de race, honnoree pour sa prudence, et qui jamais ne degenera de l'integrité de ses ancestres ? Aussi la beauté exterieure

Les mariages se doivent mesurer à la vertu et race, et non à la beauté.

his vertue, wisdom, and good fortune, serving him much in the pursuite and effect of divers thinges by him undertaken, and thinke myselfe much beholding to the king of England (although his malice seeketh neither my advancement nor the good of you, my lord) to do me so much honor as to send me so excellent a man to intreate of a marriage (he being olde, and a mortal enemy to me and mine) with mee that am such a one as every man seeth, is not desirous to couple with a man of so base quality as he, whom you have said to be the son of a slave.   But on the other side, I marvel that the son of Horvendile, and grand-child to king Roderick, he that by his foolish wisedom and fained madnesse surmounted the forces and subtilties of Fengon, and obtained the kingdom of his adversary, should so much imbase himselfe (having otherwise bin very wise and wel advised in all his actions) touching his bedfellow; and hee that for his excellency and valor surpasseth humane capacity, should stoope so lowe as to take to wife her that, issuing from a servile race, hath only the name of a king for her father, for that the basenes of her blood will alwaies cause her to shewe what are the vertues and noble qualities of her ancestors. And you, my lord, said she, are you so ignorant as not to know that mariage should not bee measured by any foolish opinion of an outward beautie, but rather by vertues, and antiquitie of race, which maketh the wife to be honored for her prudence, and never degenerating from the integritie of his ancestors : exterior beauty also is nothing, where perfection

n'est rien, ou la perfection de l'esprit ne donne accomplissement, et orne ce qui au corps se flestrit, et perd par un accident et occurrence de peu d'effect : joinct que telles mignotises en ont deceu plusieurs, et les attrayans, comme gluantes amorces, les ont precipitez és abismes de leur ruine, deshonneur, et accablement. C'estoit à moy à qui cest advantage estoit deu, qui suis Royne, et telle qui me puis esgaler en noblesse, avec les plus grans de l'Europe, qui ne suis en rien moindre, soit en antiquité de sang, ou valeur des parens et abondance de richesses.

Et ne suis seulement Royne, mais telle que recevant qui bon me semblera pour compaignon de ma couche, je peux luy faire porter tiltre de Roy et luy donner, avec mes embrassemens, la jouissance d'un beau Royaume et grand' Province. Advisez Monsieur, combien j'estime vostre alliance, qui ayant de coustume de poursuivre, avec le glaive, ceux qui s'osoyent enhardir de pourchasser mon acointance, cest à vous seul à qui je fais present, et de mes baisers, et accollade, et de mon sceptre, et couronne. Qui est l'homme, s'il n'est de marbre, qui refusast un gage si precieux que Hermetrude avec le Royaume descosse ? Acceptez, gentil Roy, acceptez ceste Royne, qui avec une si grande amitié vous pourchasse tant de bien, et peut vous donner plus d'aise en un jour, que jamais l'Angloise ne sçauroit vous apprester de contentement et plaisir toute sa vie : et quoy qu'elle me surpasse en beauté, si est-ce que le sang en estant vil et roturier, il est plus seant à un te Roy, que vous de choisir

of the mind doth not accomplish and adorn that which is outwardly seen to be in the bodie, and is lost by an accident and occurrence of small moment : as also such toyes have deceived many men, and drawing them like enticing baits, have cast them headlong into the gulf of their ruine, dishonor, and utter overthrow.   It was I to whom this advantage belonged, being a queen, and such a one as for nobility may compare my selfe with the greatest princes in Europe, being nothing inferiour unto any of them, neither for antiquitie of blood, nobilitie of parents, nor abundance of riches ; and I am not only a queene, but such a one as that, receiving whom I will for my companion in bed, can make him beare the title of a king, and with my body give him possession of a great kingdome, and goodly province.   Think then, my Lord, how much I account of your alliance, who being accustomed with the sword to pursue such as durst imbolden themselves to win my love, it is to you only to whom I make a present both of my kisses, imbracings, scepter, and crown : what man is he, if he be not made of stone, that would refuse so precious a pawn as Hermetrude, with the kingdome of Scotland ? accept, sweete king, accepte this queene, who with so great love and amitie, desireth your so great profit, and can give you more contentment in one day then the princesse of England wold yeeld you pleasure during her life : although shee surpass me in beauty, her bloud beeing base it is fitter

Hermetrude moins belle, mais noble et illustre, que l'Angloise
de grand beauté, mais sortie d'une race incognue, et sans non
quelconque. Or pensez si le Danoys oiant des raisons si
vallables, et sentant attaindre au poinct que luy mesme avoit
descouvert, puis esmeu de courroux, pour la trahison de son
beau pere, qui l'avoit là envoyé pour le faire mourir, et en fin
caressé, baisé et mignardé par ceste Royne, et jeune, et passable-
ment belle, s'il ne fust assez facile à estre converty, et à oublier
l'affection de sa premiere espouse, pour avec ceste cy empieter
l'Escosse, et se faire la voye à estre seigneur de toute la grand
Bretaigné. Tant y a qu'il l'espousa, et l'emmena avec luy

La fille
d'Angleter à
son espoux,
l'ayant
laisse-pour
un autre.

à la court de l'Anglois, ce qui esmeut d'avantage l'autre à
chercher les moiens de le faire mourir, et l'eust mis a effect,
si sa fille, et lespouse d'Amleth plus soigneuse de celuy qui
l'avoit mesprisee que du salut de son pere, ne luy eut descouvert l'entreprinse en luy disant. Je sçay bien, Monsieur,
que les allichemens d'une effrontee, et les attraiz d'une femme
sans vergoigne quelconque estans plus lascifs, que les chastes
embrassemens d'une femme legitime et pudique, sont plus
chatouilleux, et de tant plus charment les sens des jeunes
hommes : mais je ne puis prendre pour argent content ce
vostre mespris, qui me laissa sans aucune raison, ny faute pre-
cedente congneue en vostre loyalle espouse, avez trouvee bonne
l'alliance de celle, qui un jour sera cause de vostre ruine. Or
quoy qu'une juste jalousie, et courroux raisonnable me dispence à ne tenir non plus de compte de vous, que vous faites

for such a king as you are to chuse Hermetrude, lesse beautiful but noble and famous, rather then the English lady with great beawtie, but issuing from an unknown race, without any title of honor.

Now think if the Dane, hearing such forcible resons and understanding that by her which he half doubted, as also moved with choller for the treason of his father in law, that purposely sent him thether to loose his life, and being welcomed, kist, and playd withal by this queen, yong and reasonable fair, if he were not easie enough to be converted, and like to forget the affection of his first wife, with this to enjoy the realme of Scotland, and so open the waie to become king of all Greate Britain : that, to conclude, he marryed her, and led her with him to the king of Englands court, which moved the king from that time forward much more to seek the meanes to bereave him of his life ; and had surely done it, if his daughter, Hamlets other wife, more careful of him that had rejected her then of her fathers welfare, had not discovered the enterprise to Hamlet, saying : I know well, my Lord, that the allurements and perswasions of a bold and altogether shameles woman, being more lascivious then the chast imbracements of a lawful and modest wife, are of more force to intice and charm the sences of yong men ; but for my part, I cannot take this abuse for satisfaction, to leave mee in this sorte without all cause, reason, or precedent faulte once known in mee, your loyall spouse, and take more pleasure in the aliance of her who one day will be the cause

de moy, qui ne suis digne qu'on mesprise de telle sorte, si
estce que la charité maritale aura bien plus de force en mon
endroit, que non pas le desdain conceu, pour veoir qu'une
concubine tienne ma place, et qu'une femme estrangere jouisse
en ma presence des embrassemens de mon loyal espoux.
Ceste injure, Monsieur, que quoy de grande, et pour laquelle
venger plusieurs Dames de grand renom ont jadis causé la
mort et ruine de leurs maris, ne me gardent de vous advertir
de ce que lon trame contre vous, et vous prier de vous tenir
sur vos gardes veu qu'on ne machine rien moins que vostre
mort, laquelle advenant, je ne sçaurois gueres plus vous suivre.
Plusieurs raisons m'induisent à vous cherir, et icelles de grand
consequence, mais sur tout me soigne-je de vous, me sentant
un gage de vostre fait remuer dans mes entrailles, pour le
respect duquel sans (sans tant vous oublier) vous devez plus
faire de compte de moy, que non de vostre concubine : laquelle

j'aimeray, puis que vous luy portez amitié, me suffissant que
vostre fils l'ait en haine, et detestation, pour le tort qu'elle
fait à sa mere : car il est impossible, que passion, ny trouble
aucun de l'ame puisse amortir ces premieres flammes d'amour,
qui m'ont faite vostre, ny que j'oublie voz anciens desirs, à
poursuivre tant instamment la fille du Roy d'Angleterre :
et n'est en la puissance de l'envie de ma larronesse de vostre
cœur, ny de la cholere de mon pere, de m'empescher de vous

of your ruine and overthrow.   And although a just cause of jealousye and reasonable motion of anger, dispence with mee at this time to make no more account of you then you do of me, that am not worthy to be so scornfully rejected; yet matrimoniall charitie shal have more force and vigour in my hart, then the disdaine which I have justly conceived to see a concubine hold my place, and a strange woman before my face injoy the pleasures of my husband.   This injury, my Lord, although great and offensive, which to revenge divers ladies of great renown have in times past sought and procured the death of their husbands, cannot so much restrain my good wil, but that [I] may not chuse but advertise you what treason is devised against you, beseeching you to stand upon your guard, for that my fathers onely seeking is to bereave you of your life, which if it happen, I shall not long live after you.   Manie reasons induce me to love and cherish you, and those of great consequence, but especially and above all the rest, I am and must bee carefull of you, when I feele your child stirring in my wombe; for which respecte, without so much forgetting yourselfe, you ought to make more account of me then of your concubine, whome I will love because you love her, contenting my selfe that your sonne hateth her, in regard of the wrong she doth to his mother; for it is impossible that any passion or trouble of the mind whatsoever can quench those fierce passions of love that made me yours, neither that I shold forget your favours past, when loyallie you sought the love of the daughter of the king of England.

contregarder, aussi bien de vostre faint hoste, comme par cy
devant vous avez, en faignant, obvié aux desseins, et machin-
ations traitresses de vostre oncle Fengon, estant le complot
arresté sur la ruine de vous, et des vostres. Sans cest adver-
tisssement, c'estoit fait de la vie du Danoys, et des troupes
Escossoyses qui lavoient accompaigné : car le Roy Angloys

Trahison du Roy Anglois sur Amleth.

conviant son gendre, avec les caresses les plus grandes qu'un
amy sçauroit faire, à celuy qu'il cherist autant que soimesme,
avoit dressé le piege pour l'atraper, et luy fare dancer un
piteux bal, pour l'accomplissement des nopces de luy, et de
sa nouvelle Dame. Mais Amleth y alla couvert d'armes, et
ses gens aussi armez sous leurs habits qui causa que le Danoys
eschappa avec une playe bien legere de cest estour, lequel fut
la voye toute desfichee de la baitaille mentionnee cy devant,
et en laquelle le Roy Angloys perdant la vie, son pays fut
pillié et saccage, pour la troysiesme fois, par les Barbares des
isles, et du pays de Dannemarch.

Vviglere tyran occupe Dunnemarch.

Amleth victorieux, et chargé de despouilles, accompaigné
de ses deux femmes, reprenant la route de son pays, entendit

Neither is it in the power of that thiefe that hath stoln your heart, nor my fathers choller, to hinder me from seeking to preserve you from the cruelty of your dissembling friend (as heeretofore by counterfetting the madman, you prevented the practises and treasons of your uncle Fengon), the complot being determined to be executed upon you and yours. Without this advertisement, the Dane had surely been slain, and the Scots that came with him ; for the king of England, inviting his son in law to a banquet, with greatest curtesies that a friend can use to him whom he loved as himself, had the means to intrap him, and cause him dance a pittiful galliard, in that sort to celebrate the marriage betweene him and his new lady.   But Hamlet went thither with armour under his clothes, and his men in like sort ; by which means he and his escaped with little hurt, and so after that hapned the battaile before spoken of, wherein the king of England losing his life, his countrie was the third time sacked by the barbarians of the ilands and countrie of Denmark.

CHAPTER VIII

How Hamblet, being in Denmarke, was assailed by Wiglerus his Uncle, ana after betrayed by his last wife, called Hermetrude, and was slaine : after whose death she marryed his enemie, Wiglerus.

HAMLET having obtained the victory against the king of England, and slaine him, laden with great treasures and

comme Vviglere son oncle et fils de Rorique, aiant oste les
tresors Royaux à Geruthe sa sœur, et mere d'Amleth, s'estoit
aussi saisy du Royaume, disant que Horvvendille ni les siens,
ne le tenoyent que par usufruict, et que c'estoit à luy (en
estant le proprietaire) d'en donner la charge à qui bon luy
sembleroit. Amleth qui ne vouloit avoir querelle, avec
le fils de celuy, duquel les prepredecesseurs avoient pris leur
grandeur, et avancement, feit de si beaux et riches presens à
Vviglere, que se contentant, il se retira du pays, et terres du
fils de Geruthe. Mais au bout de quelque temps, Vviglere,
desireux de tenir tout le pais en sa subjection, afriandé par la

Scanie et
Sialandie
Provinres
de Septen-
trion.
Trahison
d'Herme-
trude contre
son mary.

conqueste de Scanie, et Sialandie, et que aussi Hermetrude)
que Amleth aymoit plus que soymesme) avoit intelligence avec
luy, et luy avoit promis mariage, pourveu qu'il l'ostast des
mains de celuy qui la detenoit, envoya defier Amleth, et
luy denoncer la guerre à toute outrance. Ce bon et sage
Prince aymant son peuple, eust voulu chercher les moyens
d'eviter c'este guerre, mais la refusant il voyoit une grande
tache pour son honneur, et l'acceptant sa fin luy paroissoit

Une mort
honorable
plus à choi-
sir que une
vie contemp-
tible.

certaine : le desir de conserver sa vie l'esguillonnoit d'une
part, et l'honneur le poussoit de l'autre, mais à la fin se souvenant que jamais peril quelconque ne l'avoit esbranlé de sa

accompanied with his two wives, set forward to saile into Denmarke, but by the way hee had intelligence that Wiglere, his uncle, and sonne to Rodericke, having taken the royall treasure from his sister Geruth (mother to Hamblet) had also seazed upon the kingdome, saying, that neither Horvendile nor any of his helde it but by permission, and that it was in him (to whom the property belonged) to give the charge therof to whom he would.   But Hamblet, not desirous to have any quarrell with the sonne of him from whom his predecessors had received their greatnes and advancement, gave such and so rich presents to Wiglere, that he, being contented, withdrew himselfe out of the countrey and territories of Geruths sonne.   But within certaine time after, Wiglere, desirous to keepe all the countrey in subjection, intyced by the conquest of Scanie and Sialandie, and also that Hermetrude (the wife of Hamlet, whom he loved more then himselfe) had secret intelligence with him, and had promised him marriage, so that he would take her out of the handes of him that held her, sent to defie Hamlet, and proclaimed open warre against him.   Hamlet, like a good and wise prince, loving especially the welfare of his subjects, sought by all meanes to avoyde that warre ; but againe refusing it, he perceived a great spot and blemish in his honor, and, accepting the same, he knewe it would bee the ende of his dayes.   By the desire of preserving his life on the one side, and his honor on the other side pricking him forward, but, at the last, remembering that never any danger

Hermetrude betrayeth Hamlet her husband.

vertu et constance, ayma mieux choisir la necessité de sa
ruyne, que perdre le loz immortel que acquierent les hommes
vaillans és entreprises de la guerre. Aussi il y a autant de
difference entre une vie sans honneur, et une mort honnorable,
comme la gloire a d'excelence par dessus le mespris et con-
tennement. Mais le pris qui gastoit ce vertueux Prince,
estoit le trop de fiance qu'il avoit en sa femme Hermetrude,
et l'amitié trop vehemente qui luy pourtoit, ne se repantant
du tort faict à son espouse legitime, et pour lequel (peut estre
ceste infortune lui estoit survenue : et n'eust jamais estimé,
que celle qu'il cherissoit sur toute chose chere, l'eust trahy si
laschement, et ne luy souvenoit des propos de l'Angloyse, qui
luy predit que les embrassemens de ceste autre, seroient aussi
bien cause de sa ruyne, comme ils luy avoient ravy le meilleur
de son sens, et assoupy en luy celle grande prudence, qui le
rendoit admirable, par les pays voisins de l'Ocean Septen-
trional, et en toutes les Allemaignes. Or le plus grand regret
qu'eust ce Roy affolé de sa femme, estoit la separation de
celle, qu'il idolatroit, et s'asseurant de son desastre, eust voulu,
ou que elle luy eust tenu compaignie à la mort, ou luy trouver
mary qui l'aimast, lui trepassé, à l'esgal de l'extreme amour
qu'il luy portoit : mais la desloyale avoit desja pourveu
à ses nopces, sans que son mary fallut qui se meit en
peine pour luy en pratiquer : lequel elle voyant triste pour

Dissimn-
latio de la
Royne Herme-
trude.

whatsoever had once shaken his vertues and constancy, chose rather the necessitie of his ruine, then to loose the immortal fame that valiant and honourable men obtained in the warres. And there is as much difference betweene a life without honour and an honourable death, as glory and renowne is more excellent then dishonour and evil report.

But the thing that spoyled this vertuous prince was the over great trust and confidence hee had in his wife Hermetrude, and the vehement love hee bare unto her, not once repenting the wrong in that case done to his lawfull spouse, and for the which (paradventure that misfortune had never hapned unto him, and it would never have bin thought that she, whom he loved above all things, would have so villainously betrayed him), hee not once remembring his first wives speeches, who prophesied unto him, that the pleasures hee seemed to take in his other wife would in the end be the cause of his overthrowe, as they had ravished him of the best part of his sences, and quenched in him the great prudence that made him admirable in all the countries in the ocean seas, and through all Germany. Now, the greatest grief that this king (besotted on his wife) had, was the separation of her whom he adored, and, assuring himselfe of his overthrowe, was desirous either that she might beare him company at his death, or els to find her a husband that should love her (he beeing dead) as well as ever hee did. But the disloyall queene had already provided herself of a marriage to put her husband out of trouble and care for that, who perceiving him to be sad for

l'amour d'elle, et se devant absenter de sa compaignie, elle
pour le coifer d'avantage, et l'encourager d'aller à sa deffaicte,
luy promist de le suyvre par tout, et de jouyr de mesme
fortune que luy, fust elle mauvaise, ou telle qu'il la souhai-
toit, qu'il luy feroit cognoistre de combien elle surpassoit
l'Angloyse en affection en son endroit, et que la femme estoit
malheureuse, laquelle craignoit de suivre et accompaigner son
mary à la mort : si qu'à l'ouyr parler, on eust dit que cestoit
l'espouse d'un Mitridate, ou Zenobie Royne des Palmireniens,
tant elle s'affectionnoit à la matiere, et faisoit parade de sa
constance et ferme amitié. Mais à l'effect on veit combien
vaine fut la promesse de ceste volage Princesse, et combien
mal s'esgaloit la suite de ceste Escossoise, à celle rigeur de
chasteté, qu'elle gardoit avant qu'avoir savouré les embrasse-
ments d'un mary. Car Amleth ne fut pas si tost au camp,
qu'elle trouva les moyens de voir Vviglere, et la bataille
estant donnee, et le miserable Danoys mys à mort, Hermetrude se rendit avec les despoilles de son mary mort, entre
les mains du Tyran, lequel plus que content de ses metamor-
phoses tant desirées, donna ordre que soudain fut solemnisé
le mariage acheté avec le sang, et richesses du fils de
Horvvendille. Ainsi n'est deliberation de femme, que une
bien petite incommodité de fortune ne demolisse et face
alterer et changer, et que le changement du temps ne per-
vetisse, tellement que les cas fortuits, subjet à la sagesse
d'un homme constant, esbranlent et ruent bas la loyauté

Marginal notes:

La femme de Mithridat suyvoit son mari à la guerre. Zenobie vaillante Roine Ascatique.

Desloiauté d'Hermetrude.

Inconstance des femmes.

Cas fortuits sujets à nostre constance.

her sake, when shee should have absented her selfe from him, she, to blind him the more and to incourage him to set forward to his owne destruction, promised to follow him whether soever he went, and to take the like fortune that befell to him, were it good or evil, and that so she would give him cause to know how much shee surpassed the English woman in her affection towardes him, saying, that woman is accursed that feareth to follow and accompany her husband to the death : so that, to heare her speake, men would have sayd that shee had been the wife of Mithridates, or Zenobia queene of Palmira, shee made so greate a show of love and constancy.   But by the effect it was after easily perceived howe vaine the promise of this unconstant and wavering princesse was ; and howe uncomparable the life of this Scottish queene was to the vigor of her chastitie, being a mayd before she was marryed.   For that Hamlet had no sooner entred into the field, but she found meanes to see Wiglere, and the battel begun, wherein the miserable Danish prince was slaine ; Hamlet but Hermetrude presently yeelded her self, with all her dead slaine. husbands treasons, into the hand of the tyrant, who, more then content with that metamorphosis so much desired, gave order that presently the marriage (bought with the blood and treason of the sonne of Horvendile) should bee celebrated.

Thus you see that there is no promise or determination of a woman, but that a very small discommoditie of fortune mollifieth and altereth the same, and which time doeth not pervert ; so that the misfortunes subject to a constant man

naturellement glissante de ce sexe variable, et sans nulle asseurance ne fermeté. Veu que tout ainsi que la femme est facile à promettre, aussi est elle pesante et paresseuse à tenir, et effectuer ce quelle aura promis comme celle qui est sans fin, ny limite en ses desirs, se chatouillant en la diversité de ses aises, et prenant plaisirs en choses nouvelles, desquelles tout aussi tost elle perd la souvenance : et en somme telle qu'en toutes ses actions elle est precipitee, convoiteuse, et ingrate, quelque bien ou service qu'on luy sçache faire. Je me esgare, à ce que je voy, en mes discours, vomissant choses indignes de ce sexe : mais les vices de Hermetrude, m'ont faict plus dire que je ne pensois, joint que l'autheur d'où j'ay pris ceste histoire, me forçoit presque à suivre sa trace, tant, y a de douceur et nayveté à poursuivre ce propos : et tant il me sembloit estre veritable, veu le succez miserable du pauvre roy Amleth. Telle fut la fin d'Amleth, fils d'Horvvendille. Prince de Jutie, auquel si la fortune eust esgalé ce qu'il avoit de bon en soy naturellement, je ne sçay lequel des Grecs et Romains eussent eu l'honneur de l'advantager en vertu, et excellence : mais son desastre le suyvant en toutes ses actions, et luy vainquant la malice du sort avec l'effort de sa constance, il nous laisse un exemple notable de grandeur de courage digne d'un grand

Imperfections et vices de la femme.

Saxon Grammarien escrit ce discours.

shake and overthrowe the naturall slipperie loyaltie of the
variable steppes of women, wholy without and any faithfull
assurance of love, or true unfained constancy: for as a
woman is ready to promise, so is shee heavy and slowe to
performe and effect that which she hath promised, as she
that is without end or limit in her desires, flattring her selfe
in the diversitie of her wanton delights, and taking pleasure
in diversitie and change of newe things, which as soone shee
doth forget and growe weary off: and, to conclude, such shee
is in all her actions, she is rash, covetous, and unthankefull,
whatsoever good or service can bee done unto her. But
nowe I perceive I erre in my discourse, vomitting such things
unworthy of this sects; but the vices of Hermetrude have
made mee say more then I meant to speake, as also the
authour, from whence I take this Hystorie, hath almost made
mee hold this course, I find so great a sweetnesse and live-
linesse in this kinde of argument; and the rather because it
seemeth so much the truer, considering the miserable successe
of poore king Hamlet.

Such was the ende of Hamlet, sonne to Horvendile, prince
of Jutie; to whom, if his fortune had been equall with his
inward and naturall giftes, I know not which of the auncient
Grecians and Romans had been able to have compared with
him for vertue and excellencie: but hard fortune following
him in all his actions, and yet hee vanquishing the malice of
his time with the vigour of constancy, hath left us a notable
example of haughtie courage, worthy of a great prince, arming

Prince, se fortifiant d'espoir és choses mesmes qui estoyent sans couleur d'aucune esperance, et qui en tout s'est rendu admirable, si une seule tache n'eust obscurcy une bonne partie de ses louanges. D'autant que la plus grande victoire, que l'homme peut acquerir, est celle qui le faict seigneur, et dompteur de ses affections, et laquelle chastie les efforts desreiglez du sens affolé en ses convoitises : car l'homme a beau estre fort et sage, que si les chatouillemens de la chair le surmontent, il s'avillira, et arrestera apres les beautez, et deviendra fol et insencé à la poursuite des femmes. De telle faute a esté chargé le grand Hercule des Hebrieux Sanson, et le plus sage d'entre les hommes, suivant ce train, y a faict diminution de son sens, et la pluspart des grans, sages, vaillants, et discrets par apparence, de nostre temps, dançans une pareille note, donnent de beaux indices de leur gaillardise, prudence, et saincteté, Mais vous qui lisez cecy, je vous prie ne resembler l'araigne qui se repaist de la corruption, qui est és fleurs et fruicts dans un verger, là ou la belle recueille son miel des fleurs les plus soëfves et mieux flairantes qu'elles sçait choisir : car l'homme bien né, faut qui lise la vie du paillard, yvrongne, cruel, voleur et sanguinaire, non pour l'ensuyvir, n'y souiller son ame de telles inmondices, ains pour eviter la paillardise, fuir le desbord et superfluité és banquets, et suivre

Quelle est
la plus
grande
victoire en
l'homme.

L appetit
charnel
a gasté
les plus
excellents
hommes
de la terre.

Pourquey
on lit les
histoires.

himselfe with hope in things that were wholy without any colour or shewe thereof, and in all his honorable actions made himselfe worthy of perpetuall memorie, if one onely spotte had not blemished and darkened a good part of his prayses.   For that the greatest victorie that a man can obtaine is to make himselfe victorious and lord over his owne affections, and that restraineth the unbridled desires of his concupiscence; for if a man be never so princely, valiant, and wise, if the desires and inticements of his flesh prevaile, and have the upper hand, hee will imbase his credite, and, gasing after strange beauties, become a foole, and (as it were) incensed, dote on the presence of women.   This fault was in the great Hercules, Sampson; and the wisest man that ever lived upon the earth, following this traine, therein impaired his wit; and the most noble, wise, valiant, and discreet personages of our time, following the same course, have left us many notable examples of their worthy and notable vertues.

But I beseech you that shall reade this Hystorie not to resemble the spider, that feedeth of the corruption that shee findeth in the flowers and fruites that are in the gardens, whereas the bee gathereth her hony out of the best and fayrest flower shee can finde: for a man that is well brought up should reade the lives of whoremongers, drunkards, incestuous, violent, and bloody persons, not to follow their steps, and so to defile himselfe with such uncleannesse, but to shunne paliardize, abstain the superfluities and drunkennesse

la modestie, continence, et courtoysie, qui recommande Amleth
en ce discours, lequel parmy les banquets des autres, demeu-
roit sobre, et ou chacun se penoit d'accumuler thresor, cestui
cy simplement, n'esgallant les richesses à l'honneur, il con-
sentoit de faire un amas de vertus, qui l'esglassent à ceux qu'il
estimoit Dieux, n'ayant encor receu la lumiere de l'Evangile :
afin qu'on voye et parmy les barbares et entre ceux qui
estoyent esloignez de la cognoissance d'un seul Dieu, que
nature estoit esguilonnee à suivre ce qui est bon, et poussee à
embrasser la vertu, ny aiant jamais eu nation, tant farouche
fut elle, qui n'ayt pris plaisir à faire quelque chose ressentant
le bien, pour en acquerir louange, lequel nous avons dit estre
le salaire de la vertu et bonne vie.   Je prens plaisirs à toucher
ces histoires estrangeres, et de peuple non baptisé, afin que la
vertu de ces grossiers donne plus de lustre à la nostre, qui les
voyans si accomplis, sages, prudens, et advisez a la suitte de
leurs affaires, tascherons non de les imiter, estant l'imitation
peu de chose, mais à les surmonter, ainsi que
nostre Religion surpasse leur superstition,
et nostre siecle est plus purgé, subtil
et gaillard, que la saison en
laquelle ils ont vescu.
Et fait paroistre
leur vertu.

N'y eut onc barbarre qui ne feit quelque bien pour estre loué.

FIN DE LA TROISIESME HISTOIRE

in banquets, and follow the modestie, courtesie, and con-
tinencie that recommendeth Hamlet in this discourse, who,
while other made good cheare, continued sober; and where
all men sought as much as they could to gather together
riches and treasure, hee, simply accounting riches nothing
comparable to honor, sought to gather a multitude of vertues,
that might make him equall to those that by them were
esteemed as gods; having not as then received the lighte of
the gospell, that men might see among the barbarians, and
them that were farre from the knowledge of one onelye God,
that nature was provoked to follow that which is good, and
those forward to imbrace vertue, for that there was never
any nation, how rude or barbarous soever, that tooke not
some pleasure to do that which seemed good, therby to win
praise and commendations, which wee have said to be the
reward of vertue and good life.   I delight to speak of these
strange histories, and of people that were unchristned, that
the vertue of the rude people maie give more splendor to our
nation, who seeing them so compleat, wise, prudent, and
well advised in their actions, might strive not only to follow
(imitation being a small matter), but to sur-
mount them, as our religion surpasseth
their superstition, and our age more
purged, subtill, and gallant, then
the season wherin they lived
and made their vertues
knowne.

FINIS.

NOTES

p. 1. The text of these difficult lines is normalized, and does not reproduce the form found in any of the MSS., the oldest of which is Codex Regius 2367, in the Arna-Magnæan Collection at Copenhagen, from which the frontispiece, containing the lines, has been taken, through the good offices of Professor Finnur Jónsson. The lines, according to the MS., read as follows (with the abbreviations expanded):—

> Hvat qveþa hrœra grotta
> hergrimmastan skeria
> ut firir iarþa skauti
> eyluðrs nio bruþir
> þær er lungs firir laungu
> liðmelldr skipa hliþar
> baugskerþir ristr barþi
> bol amloþa molo.

The chief textual variations in the MSS. are as follows (W. = Arna-Magnæan MS. 242; T. = the Utrecht MS.; U. = Upsala MS.):—l. 1, Hvatt (T.); kvaþum (U.); griota (U.); l. 3, fra (U.), iarðar (W., T., U.); l. 5, er *omitted in* W.; lunzs (U.); l. 6, milldr . . . hilldir (U.), *for* melldr . . . hliþar.

On the passage, cp. Finnur Jónsson: *Den Norsk-Islandske Skjaldedigtning* (Arna-Magnæan Commission, Copenhagen, 1910).

The paraphrase and interpretation of the lines vary, according to the different authorities. Professor Finnur Jónsson arranges the words thus:—

"Kveða níu brúðir skerja hrœra hvatt hergrimmastan eylúðrs Grótta út fyr jarðar skauti, þær es fyr löngu mólu Amlóða meldrlið; baugskerðir ristr lungs barði skipa hlíðar ból;" *i.e.* "they say that the nine brides of the skerries move, violently, the stormy sea, outside the edge of the land, cruelly to men,—they who long ago ground on the quern of Amlóði; the ring-breaker cuts the wavy sea with the stem of the ship" (quern = meldlið, *i.e.* meal-bin; cp. lið = ship).

313

Vigfusson and Powell (*Corpus Poeticum Boreale*, 1883, Vol. II. pp. 54–55) translate the lines—" Men say that the nine Maidens of the Island-Mill, *the ocean*, are working hard at the host-devouring Skerry-quern [the sea] beyond the skirts of the earth : yea, they have for ages past been grinding at Amlodi's meal-bin, *the sea.* Let us furrow the waves with the prow of my ship."

Dr. A. G. Brodeur, in the translation of *The Prose Edda* (New York, 1916), p. 140, gives the following rendering :—

> " They say nine brides of skerries
> Swiftly move the Sea-Churn
> Of Grótti's Island-Flour-Bin
> Beyond the Earth's last outskirt,—
> They who long the corny ale ground
> Of Amlódi; the Giver
> Of Rings now cuts with ship's beak
> The Abiding-Place of boat-sides."

p. 47, l. 23. In Professor Joseph Wright's *Dialect Dictionary*, we find duly recorded the Yorkshire phrase to *play Hamlet with*, to play " the deuce" with ; to give one a " good blowing up," *e.g.* " Mi muðə pleəd amlit wi im fə stopin āt lat ət nīt," *i.e.* " my mother played Hamlet with him for stopping out late at night" (quoted by Professor Wright, from his own personal knowledge of the idiom. In an interesting article in the *Yorkshire Weekly Post*, August 4, 1917, my lamented colleague, Professor Moorman, discussed the phrase and its usage in Yorkshire. " To play Hamlet" with a thing is to smash it in pieces. There is also " Hamlet to pay," where Hamlet is " a bogey of the popular imagination " = " there will be the devil to pay." In the West Riding the bogey is " Hamlet," but Professor Moorman discovered that a Yorkshire variant is " Avlot" or "Avleck." " Last winter," he wrote, " was a terrible one for the rabbits on the Yorkshire fells ; they descended into the valleys and endeavoured to avert starvation by gnawing the bark from the trees in woods, gardens, or hedgerows. When I pointed out to a Swaledale woman the damage they had caused, her reply was : " Eh ! rabbits has fair played *Avlot* wi' t'trees this winter," while in Upper Wharfedale the same phrase took the form " to play *Avleck.*"

Professor Moorman explains that the name Hamlet could hardly be changed in modern times to Avlot or Avleck, even with the help of such a phrase as " to play havoc" as intermediary between

NOTES

the two, and thinks we have here a memory of the terror struck in
the hearts of the Yorkshire farmers of the tenth century by the
harrying raids of Anlaf Curan. Thus we have still in local speech
some corroboration of the theory set forth in this Introduction in
respect of the Hamlet and Havelock legends. The interchange-
able Yorkshire forms " Hamlet," " Avleck," " Avlot," are indeed
most noteworthy, and deserve further investigation. Professor
Moorman and the writer were corresponding on the subject shortly
before Professor Moorman's death.

p. 51. Professor C. J. S. Marstrander, in *Bidrag til det Norske
Sprogs Historie i Irland* (Videnskapsselskapets Skrifter. II. Hist.-
Filos. Klasse, No. 5, Kristiania, 1915), holds that the equation
Amlaidhe = Amlōði cannot be justified, and postulates Haflıði as
the Northern equivalent; but this latter name is not found in any
of the Annals. It may be that according to regular phonetic law,
O.N. Amlōði would not become Irish Amlaidhe, but this refutation
seems to beg the question, and other considerations may have to be
taken into account in dealing with proper names, the origin and occurrence of which open up many difficult questions. Folk etymology
and association of ideas must often be considered. The equivalent
forms of names do not always follow normal phonetic laws, and
the fact that they do seem to be contrary to these laws often leads
to the right solution of origin and history.

No derivation of Old Norse Amlōði (= Hamlet) has yet been
accepted. In *The Literary History of Hamlet* by Dr. Kemp Malone
(Heidelberg, 1923), " Anle ōðe," *i.e.* " Mad Ole," is adduced as
the origin of the name, Anle being identified with Onela, the
Swedish king, in *Beowulf*. It is not likely that Dr. Malone's
etymology, any more than his identifications, will be accepted.
All the same, to the present writer it is of interest that Irish
transmission for the form of the name " Amlōði " is postulated
" as parallel to the Irish transmission which must be assumed
for the story,"—so writes Dr. Malone, in his article " On the
Etymology of Hamlet," in the *Philological Quarterly* (Iowa, April,
1925), where he replies to an adverse review of his book, in the
previous October number of the *Quarterly*, by Professor A. Le Roy
Andrews. Dr. Malone agrees with me that the tale " originated
and reached its final form among the Scandinavian settlers in the
British Isles," and further supports my theory referring the Middle
English " amlaȝe " to the Irish form Amlaidhe (cp. *Literary History
of Hamlet*, pp. 52–58). At the same time it should be noted that

it is not clear, as Dr. Malone states, that the Middle English "amlaʒe" can hardly be interpreted otherwise than an equivalent *in sense* to amlóði, *i.e.* "mad fool," the point emphasized in the passage in the *Wars of Alexander*, is the diminutive and mean aspect of Alexander. *Ablach* or *Aploch*, and other Gaelic derivates in the dialects, must be recalled in this connection (see further on the point, *Hamlet in Iceland*, pp. lx, lxi). Dr. Malone quotes merely ll. 3540–3545 from the *Wars of Alexander*, for "amlaʒe," but it occurs also in l. 1705, and this instance is all important for the exact force of the word.

II. SAXO'S LATIN TEXT

p. 94. The Latin text is from the *editio princeps*, 1514. The first critical edition, by Stephanius, appeared in 1644. Other editions were those by Klotz in 1771, and by P. E. Müller and Johan Velschow, 1839–1858. The great edition of Saxo, edited by Alfred Holder, published at Strasburg, 1886, is a monumental achievement, and gives all textual and bibliographical data.

There is no manuscript of Saxo's work; only small fragments have come down to modern times.

In 1894 appeared "the First Nine Books of the Danish History of Saxo Grammaticus translated by Oliver Elton . . . with some considerations on Saxo's sources, historical methods, and folk-lore, by Frederick York Powell" (London, David Nutt), published for the Folk-lore Society as an extra issue for 1893. To this scholarly work, from which, by kind permission of Professor Elton, the English rendering of the Hamlet section is here reprinted, the reader is referred for information concerning Saxo, his work, materials, methods, etc. It contains also a valuable appendix by Professor Elton on "Saxo's Hamlet."

For various reasons it has seemed advisable to print from the first edition; two or three slight changes have been made, and these are noted in the accompanying textual notes, where H. = Holder, St. = Stephanius, Gh. = Gheysmer, and E. = Elton.

In Gericke and Moltke's *Shakspeare's Hamlet Quellen*, Leipzig, 1881, the Latin text was printed from Müller and Velschow's edition, 1839–58, with German translation.

TEXTUAL NOTES

p. 96, l. 14. animo. H. animos (Stephanius).
p. 98, l. 3. vivos. H. uiuis (St.).

p. 98, l. 15. metui. H. mutui (St.).

p. 104, l. 22. cervice. (St. omits this.)

p. 106, l. 9. illo. H. illum (St.).

l. 13. iudicio. H. indicio (Madvig).

p. 110, l. 17. est. H. *omits* (St.).

l. 19. superatisque. H. superatis (St.).

p. 112, l. 8. colloquio. H. colloquii (Madvig).

l. 19. concenso. H. conscenso (St.); Gh. conscenderet.

p. 114, l. 22. supervacuum. (So St., but 1514 edn. reads superuacū).

p. 116, l. 12. fraudi. H. fraudis (St.).

p. 120, l. 2. igitur (2). H. *omits* (St.).

l. 4. humana. H. humani (Gh.).

l. 5. quadam. (So St., but 1514 edn. reads quoddam).

p. 124, l. 2. contusus. H. confusus (St.); E. abashed; Gh. erubescens;

p. 136, l. 1. artibus. H. artubus (St.).

l. 16. charitati. H. caritatis (St. charitatis).

p. 138, l. 8. proculcatis. H. proculcate (St.) (it might be taken as abl. abs.)

p. 142, l. 2. quoque sibi. H. quoque quod sibi (St.).

l. 7. Horwendilli jugulum. Horwendilli iugulum confossum (*or* abscissum; *or* Horwendillum iugulatum; *or* Horwendilli iugulationem) St. E. "Saxo seems to use *jugulum* in the sense of murder."

p. 144, l. 21. equidem. H. siquidem (Madvig) (enim, Gh.).

p. 150, l. 15. St. *omits* que.

l. 16. perlegissetque reginæ . . . erat. St. (reginæ . . . erat) perlegissetque.

l. 23. conspicuis. St. conspicuæ.

p. 154, l. 14. tuos in me. H. meos in te (St.).

p. 156, l. 21. seriatim. (So St., but 1514 text feriatim).

p. 158, l. 4. ipsa. H. ipse (St. ipsae; 1514, ip̄a).

p. 160, l. 1. Undensakre. H. Vndersakre (Petersen).

p. 102, l. 15. ligneos uncos creare, "to fashion wooden crooks"; Müller suggested that underlying this was a play upon O.N. krókr = (1) a crook, (2) trick.

p. 106, l. 19. sabulum perinde ac farra; *cp.* Snæbjörn's lines discussed in the Introductory Essay.

III. Belleforest and the Hystorie

Belleforest's *Histoires tragiques*—a collection of tragical stories in the first instance translated from Bandello—appeared in successive volumes, the first being privileged in 1565. In the fifth volume of this edition, dated 1576, but privileged 1570, we have the story of Hamlet, not found in Bandello, and clearly derived from Saxo Grammaticus. There is ample evidence that Belleforest was acquainted with Saxo's history, and had used it for his *Harengues Militaires*, (privileged Feb. 4, 1570). The title-page of the 1576 edition of Volume V. is as follows :—" Le cinqviesme livre des histoires tragiques, Le succez, & euenement desquelles est pour la plus part recueilli des choses aduenuës de nostre temps, & le reste des histoires anciennes. *Le tout faict illustré, & mis en ordre, par François de Belleforest Comingeois.*"

The collection of *Histoires tragiques* must have been very popular, and there are many editions of the volume containing the Hamlet story.

In 1881, in *Shakespeare's Hamlet Quellen*, Moltke's edition of Belleforest's *Histoire* was published, printed from a Lyons edition, 1581. Gericke, who prepared Moltke's work for publication, compared it with the 1582 Paris edition, and found important variations, indicating that this later text was altogether preferable, and accordingly he added the chief variant readings.

Capell was the first to call attention to the black-letter quarto, dated 1608, of *The Hystorie of Hamblet*—of which only one copy is known, in the Capell Collection in Trinity College, Cambridge. He referred to the *Hystorie* in this the third volume of his *Notes*, and again, more fully in the first volume of his edition of Shakespeare, where he emphasizes that it is translated from Belleforest. Collier printed it in the first volume of his *Shakespeare Library*, 1841. Moltke reprinted it in his *Hamlet Quellen*. It was Gericke who noted that the 1582 edition of Belleforest seemed to be the edition used by the English translator, and for this reason was to be preferred to the 1581 edition.

Dr. M. B. Evans, in *Der Bestrafte Brudermord* (Hamburg and Leipzig, 1910; *Theatergeschichtliche Forschungen*, hrsgg. von Berthold Litzmann), made an exhaustive examination of the five editions found in the British Museum,—Lyons 1576, Paris 1582, Lyons 1583, 1601, Rouen 1604; he printed the text of Belleforest from Lyons 1576. This edition contains all the marginal notes found in

the others, though these differ among themselves. Paris 1582 is
the only one with considerable textual variations ; its title-page
claims that it is " reveu, corrigé & augmenté." [1]   So also Lyons
1583 ; but this and the later editions do not reproduce its insertions ;
they go back to Lyons 1576.   This last-named edition and Lyons
1601 generally agree against Lyons 1583 and Rouen 1604; Paris
1582 stands alone.

The Hystorie of Hamblet (1608) contains the additions and many of
the variants of Paris 1582, but in not a few minor places it follows
readings found in some of the other editions ; the translator therefore
either consulted more than one edition, or used one not among the
five now available in the British Museum.   Still, taking the
variants comprehensively, it may safely be stated that Paris 1582,
if not actually the text used by the English translator, comes very
near to it ; the cases against Paris 1582 are of little importance.
Even in punctuation and the use of new paragraphs The Hystorie
seems to follow the 1582 edition.   The chief textual differences in
the editions are given in the accompanying notes on pp. 168–
288.   Accordingly, this text is now reprinted.

If, however, this 1582 edition is important for the English
Hystorie of Hamblet, it is noteworthy that the 1576 edition seems to
have been used for the English play from which was derived
Fratricide Punished, as preserved in its German form (cp. note on p.
210, 6).[2]

Opinion differs as to whether the 1608 quarto of The Hystorie of
Hamblet is the editio princeps or a revised and later issue of an edition
now lost.   There is no evidence in favour of an earlier publication.
The present text is obviously later than Shakespeare's Hamlet,
which has influenced the translator in two important situations.
In Belleforest (as in Saxo) the Counsellor hides under a quilt
(F. loudier, lodier ; L. stramentum): Hamlet jumps on this quilt
(sauta sur le lodier, cp. Saxo, p. 112, 19–20); in The Hystorie the
quilt becomes a curtain or tapestry—"hangings" and "arras,"

---

[1] Cp. p. 164; the device appears to be a man escaping from a
burning city, with a servant carrying his box ; vide Silvestre's
Marques typographiques (Paris, 1867), Nos. 141, 289; the latter is
the nearer to that on the title-page of the 1582 edition.

[2] See also Dr. Evans's Der Bestrafte Brudermord: sein verhältnis zu
Shakespeare's Hamlet (1902).

from Shakespeare.   And, further, the English translator adds what is not found in Belleforest or Saxo, the very words of the play, "A rat! a rat!"

It is argued, however, that these variations may have been due to later revision of an earlier text, and in support of this view it is pointed out that the two forms "Hamblet" and "Hamlet" are found in this 1608 *Hystorie*, the former being actually on the title-page.   Whence the inference is drawn that the title-page reveals the existence of an earlier edition.   It is indeed strange that, notwithstanding the popularity of *Hamlet*, we should have in 1608 the spelling *Hamblet* (recalling the late Latin *Amblethus*), and I had long been inclined to lay stress on this form, with the intrusive *b*, as perchance an earlier English form, before the play had become popular.   I now have no doubt that it is a seventeenth-century spelling, and is similar to common spellings of the period, *e.g.* "*Hamblets* of the Tower," or "Tower *Hamblets*" (1648).   It may indeed attest the popularity of the name, that we have *Hamlet* thus conforming to a common spelling of the period.   Anyhow, nothing, in my view, is to be built on the variants *Hamlet, Hamblet*, as proof of an early date for *The Hystorie*.

p. 168, l. 1.   *amis:* so the editions L. 1576, P. 1582, L. 1601; later editions "ames"; *Hystorie*, "soule."

p. 170, l. 7.   *ou:* L. 1576, & ; *Hystorie*, "or."

p. 174.   "Hist. Troisiesme": L. 1583, "Histoire Cinquieme"; R. 1604, "Histoire CVIII."

p. 176, l. 8.   *la France d'autant*, etc.: L. 1576, "la France.   Ca ie m'estime pour plusque satisfait en ce contentement & grande liberté d'esprit," *etc.*

p. 178, l. 11.   *en leurs biens:* L. 1576, "en la robe."

p. 182, l. 22.   L. 1576, "tascha avec une honesteté de se le rendre."

p. 184, l. 22.   *Ne voila . . . mort:* not in L. 1576.

p. 192, l. 3.   *et asseuré que:* L. 1576, "& que"; *Hystorie*, "assuring himself."

p. 192, l. 11.   *Et bien . . . sagesse.* This sentence, with its important reference to Brutus, is not in L. 1576.

p. 196, l. 17.   *Si cela . : . vengeance:* not in L. 1576.

p. 210, l. 6.   *le fard d'un plus dissimulé:* L. 1576, "le fard d'un pleur dissimulé; *Hystorie*, "the vail of a dissembling creature." The 1576 edition evidently gives us the source of crocodile tears in *Fratricide Punished*, as Mr. Marshall Evans has suggested.

p. 230, l. 11.   *vers . . . monde :* not in L. 1576.

p. 236, l. 7.   *comme :* L. 1576, "contre."

p. 258, l. 17.   *quelque face et forme de justice :* L. 1576, "quelque justice."

p. 260, l. 6.   *Car . . desir :* not in L. 1576.

p. 286, l. 15.   *franchement :* L. 1576, "freschement."

p. 288. l. 16.   *Et de fait elle :* L. 1576, "Et elle ; *Hystorie,* "And to conclude."

11